shell lake massacre

Books by Peter Tadman

Shell Lake Massacre
The Survivor

shell lake massacre

Peter Tadman

Detselig Enterprises Ltd.

Calgary, Alberta, Canada

Shell Lake Massacre

© 1992 and 2001 Peter Tadman

National Library of Canada Cataloguing in Publication Data

Tadman, Peter

Shell lake massacre

ISBN 1-55059-228-9

1. Hoffman, Victor Ernest, 1946- 2. Mass murder -- Saskatchewan -
- Shell Lake. 3. Mass murder investigation -- Saskatchewan. I. Title.
HV6535.C33S53   2001   364.15′23′0971242   C2001-911524-5

Detselig Enterprises Ltd.

210-1220 Kensington Rd. N.W., Calgary, AB, T2N 3P5

Phone: (403) 283-0900/Fax: (403) 283-6947

E-mail: temeron@telusplanet.net

www.temerondetselig.com

We acknowledge the financial support of the Government of
Canada through the Book Publishing Industry Development
Program (BPIDP) for our publishing activities.

ISBN 1-55059-228-9

SAN 115-0234

Printed in Canada

DEDICATION

To Phyllis and Kathy. Two exceptional
individuals who provided immense inspiration.

Acknowledgments

F IRST and foremost, I am greatly indebted to those mentioned throughout this book who recognized the merit of a journalistic record and were willing to share information in the interests of accuracy. Many contributors — especially members of the Peterson and Hoffman families — recalled sorrowful matters that were notably painful. They did so because they wanted the story told for the lessons that may result. For that, I am extremely grateful.

Recognition must go to Canadian Press (CP) — "Canada's national voice in print" — and the once widely circulated Canadian Magazine. Those who provided invaluable assistance include: Gillis Purcell and John Dauphinee who are both now deceased, Andy Garrett, Bob Colling and the late Ross Munro.

In addition, as was the case with *The Survivor*, I am appreciative yet again of the Edmonton Journal and the tremendous help given by two of its members: Steve Makris and Dave Reidie. Mr. Reidie, now an executive with the Southam Inc. newspaper, spent a harrowing five days in the Shell Lake district capturing irreplaceable images. Many of his photographs — all of them unforgettable — are being published for the first time.

Ashley Geddes of the Calgary Herald assisted in obtaining background on two cases within the section entitled "Reference: Mass Murder" and I am much obliged.

Lastly, for their unwavering faith and patience, I sincerely thank my family, friends and all of the caring individuals who have been so generous in supporting this non-fiction work.

Definitions

HEALTH experts claim that one in every 20 Canadians will suffer some form of mental illness during their lifetime.

It is estimated that two percent of the population will have an episode of schizophrenia which is a severe form of psychopathology in which the personality seems to disintegrate. As Philip G. Zimbardo wrote in 'Psychology and Life' published by Scott, Foresman and Company: "Perception is distorted, emotions are blunted, thoughts are bizarre, and language is strange ... We do not yet know what causes a person to take the wrong path in life that can lead to the cul-de-sac of schizophrenia."

From the fourth edition of 'Blakiston's Gould Medical Dictionary', published by McGraw-Hill Book Company, comes the following:

> **schizo-phre-nia** (skit'so-free'nee-uh, -fren'ee'uh, skiz"o-) *n.* [*schizo-* + *-phrenia*]. A group of psychotic disorders, often beginning after adolescence or in young adulthood, characterized by fundamental alterations in concept formations, with misinterpretation of reality, and associated affective, behavioral, and intellectual disturbances in varying degrees and mixtures. These disorders are marked by a tendency to withdraw from reality, ambivalent, constricted, and inappropriate responses and mood, unpredictable disturbances in stream of thought, regressive tendencies to the point of deterioration, and often hallucinations and delusions. Syn. *dementia praecox.* See also *acute schizophrenic episode, catatonic type of schizophrenia, childhood type of schizophrenia, hebephrenic type of schizophrenia, paranoid type of schizophrenia, residual type of schizophrenia.* **schizo-phre-nic** (-fren'ick, -free'nick) *n. & adj.*
>
> **paranoid type of schizophrenia.** A form of schizophrenia in which delusions of persecution or of grandeur or both, hallucinations, and ideas of reference predominate and sometimes are systematized. The patient is often more intact and less bizarre in other areas, but generally is hostile, grandiose, excessively religious, and sometimes hypochondriacal.

Victor Hoffman, who you will come to know throughout these pages, explained it this way: "It is like another world or better yet, another reality of war."

Tragically, as the precise origin of this mysterious curse that plagues so many remains unknown, so does the cure.

Introduction

ON August 15, 1967, in the village of Shell Lake, Saskatchewan, nine members of the Peterson family were savagely murdered. The unsuspecting victims were slaughtered with repeated blasts from a rifle to their heads. Mercifully, perhaps in a fit of erratic compassion, the killer allowed four-year-old Phyllis to live.

What happened in that tiny rural community was the bloodiest crime in the country's archives — motiveless and apparently clueless.

A massive police probe later discovered that a patient, seething within a schizophrenic darkness, had been prematurely released from an insane asylum shortly before the senseless waste of humanity.

Shell Lake Massacre is an authentic journal of the lives and deaths of the Petersons. It also penetrates the mind of Victor Ernest Hoffman who hails as a classic example of someone failed by the system.

— *PT*

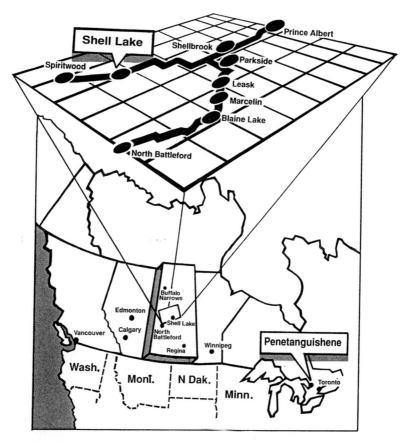

THE TERRITORY — *Shell Lake was like countless farming communities scattered throughout the wheat-golden countryside. As you will note, it is out there somewhere, marked only by an inconsequential dot on the map. Up until one horrible day, few people were aware of it and not many more cared. All of that was soon to change.*
— *Edmonton Sun map by Don Kew*

PART ONE

ROAD TO MADNESS

Contents

INTRODUCTION   11

PART ONE: Road To Madness   15

CHAPTER I: Journey To Insanity   19

CHAPTER II: Catch The Devil   37

CHAPTER III: A Noise In The Night   48

CHAPTER IV: In Cold Blood   59

CHAPTER V: Monster Search   75

CHAPTER VI: Captured   109

CHAPTER VII: Global Reaction   123

CHAPTER VIII: Limits Of Sanity   137

PART TWO: Devil's Rampage   151

JOURNEY TO INSANITY

I

T HE Battlefords, two communities divided by the fast-flowing North Saskatchewan river, echo history. A land of pioneers, the area was once the Capital of the Territories. Known as the Gateway to the Northwest, it still houses the police post that sheltered nearly 600 residents who sought refuge during the 1885 Rebellion. As a grim reminder of an era of guns, buffalo, fur-traders and explorers; visitors are invited to witness the mass grave of eight Cree warriors who were hanged — by the neck until dead — for their role in the Frog Lake Massacre. It was a time when Indian uprisings were a regular occurrence on the Great Plains of North America.

S ASKATCHEWAN, which contains the Battlefords, derived its name from the Dene word "Sisiskatchewan", meaning the river that flows swiftly. The province covers more than one-quarter million square miles — almost the size of Texas. In excess of one-million people live here, making their homes in countless villages, towns and Indian Reservations. They also inhabit a dozen cities. Bordering

Montana and North Dakota, neighbors to the east and west include Manitoba and Alberta.

The region is the world's largest exporter of uranium, claims nearly two-thirds of the globe's recoverable potash reserves and produces greater than 60 percent of the wheat grown in Canada. Its geography changes dramatically in every direction. The southern part is as flat as flat gets with endless miles of farmland. The southwest boasts mountain air while the north holds 80 million acres of forest. The terrain of the west central Battlefords has rolling hills, lush green valleys and innumerable blue lakes with sprawling, sandy shores. It also has a major mental health facility.

THE Battleford Hospital for the Insane, built following a government commissioned study in 1907, is a maze of inter-connected red brick and white mortar buildings. A giant, concrete smokestack rises in the midst of a cluster of now old and faded masonry. Situated on the eastern edge of the North Battleford city limits, the hospital for the mentally vanquished sits high atop the shore of the splitting waterway. More than 14,000 residents populate the northside city; a mere 4,000 plus four-dozen are in the historic south town, separated by the longest bridge in the territory.

Construction of the asylum began in 1912 and two years hence, February 3, 1914, it accepted its first group of patients when some 346 inmates transferred from a penitentiary to the east. It would not be until many years later, a little more than half-a-century, when the most infamous patient of all would darken the wide hallways of this treatment centre for dementia. He too arrived from where the sun rises, although the distance in miles travelled was not nearly as great.

ON Saskatchewan Highway Number 40, leading from North Battleford in an east-north-east direction to Prince Albert, a sign reads: Blaine Lake 62-P.A. 130.

It is a two lane artery leading to some of the finest land in Canada. The route, typical of many roads throughout the province, runs through miles and miles of farming country. Granaries, roadside mailboxes and dilapidated buildings are common within the austere plains and its folds of earth.

J ANUARY 12, 1968 — It was overcast with the sun trying valiantly to break out and warm the surrounding snow laden fields and the rich, arid soil below.

A weather-beaten windmill, a clump of bush and a poster exclaiming in part the qualities of a candidate in an election since past, all flashed by.

It is fair to say that most travellers would find the trip relaxing to a degree of boring. Miles and miles of sameness. A travel agent's worst nightmare. A cynic, after only a short distance, might complain that there is nothing to see. A realist could rightly respond, "Around here, that's about as interesting as the scenery gets."

The road rolls into the ditches which in turn are blended and seemingly wedded into the adjoining fields. Mile after mile or kilometre after kilometre. Acre after acre or, if you will, hectare after hectare. It may not be pretty but it's constant. Besides, if you travel through the area — or even if you don't — you will never be accused of missing any wonders of the world. For the locals, the harshness of the landscape is not an issue. They'll take its onetime reputation as 'the breadbasket of the world' over beauty any day. After all, they'll argue, you can't have everything and if there's a choice, putting food on the table beats whatever comes in second.

The majority of the farms appeared deserted. The area is subjected to severe, cruel winters and it is essential, if one remains for the duration, that windows are boarded up, equipment put in storage and fuel stockpiled. The elements can be unforgiving.

Approaching oncoming traffic was an elderly, wizened man

suitably dressed for the frigid, bleak conditions. His outer clothing consisted of a dirty brown parka, a reddish-orange toque, heavy corduroy slacks and boots of which bright red felt could be seen protruding over the top. He was accompanied by a scruffy looking mongrel, making the old adage of 'man's best friend' seem very appropriate. In fact, it may have been his only friend but most certainly was the sole companion at his side. Insofar as the true prairie dogs, none were in sight. The gophers, with their pocket-like cheek pouches, were staying off the road, lost in their worldly domain of rodent hibernation.

The communities whizzed by, many invisible from Highway 40.

A gravel pile loomed and with it a sign with a rather portentous message making it abundantly clear that unlawful removal would mean prosecution.

A school zone and then its reason.

An old shack, a tire hanging over a fence post, a cluster of mailboxes and grain elevators — Saskatchewan's answer to the Texas oil wells.

Marcelin was entered by rounding a curve and being greeted with five towering grain elevators, a service station and the revelation that the community's garage man operated the local school bus which was parked outside his place of employ.

Leaving Marcelin — if you blinked you could miss it — was a flock of starlings. It summoned thoughts of Alfred Hitchcock's "The Birds" and the accompanying feeling of unnatural and terrifying events that can happen.

A truck hauling lumber, an empty auto-carrier and the words, "Don't be a litterbug", brought back reality.

Another sign — then within what seemed a very quick mile — the unremarkable community of Leask.

The journey was near completion and after stopping at a modern Shell Oil service station, obtaining directions from a muscular, crewcut attendant with a large German Shepherd watchdog at his side, it was learned the place for which these many miles were travelled was a mere minutes away.

The farm, now so close, was home to Robert and Stella Hoffman and their 14-year-old son Allan. The parents and brother of Victor Ernest Hoffman, 21, who the day before had been found not guilty by reason of insanity on two counts of non-capital murder. The charges had been laid following the nation's most heinous crime — the brutal and senseless killing of nine members of an innocent family.

ROBERT Hoffman was born in Russia in 1911. He came to Canada the following year with his parents, Emma and Reinhold, both of German descent. The family settled at Silvergrove, Saskatchewan and began homesteading the rugged area about 16 miles from where Robert would eventually establish his own farm. The eldest of 10 children, he was obligated, after completing grade school, to help his parents support the large family. Robert, a robust man, moved south of Leask in 1927 and in 1936 started working the land on which he lived. The year previous he had married Stella Dominick. Born in Poland, she was one year his junior. The newly married couple began life together in the dirty 30's, a time of hardship spanned by the great depression. By 1953, after a period of 18 years together, they had established a farm that provided them and their brood of seven children with all the necessities of life. It had not been easy for the work-roughened couple.

Eileen was the first, born in 1936; Richard and Marion followed within the next two years; Lorraine was born four years later; Victor Ernest on January 15, 1946; Bernice a year later; and Allan in 1953.

The children were more fortunate than their parents and for the most part received a greater degree of formal education. The eldest, however, did not finish grade nine.

Her father explained, "She met her man and married."

Richard and Victor both reached the same level as Eileen; Lorraine, Marion, and Bernice received accreditation for grade 12; and Allan was still attending Junior High School.

A seemingly normal, rural family that appeared no different from any — just plain, ordinary country-folk living on the sprawling prairie.

The description applied until August 1967 when tragedy struck. The third youngest, Victor, shattered the lives of his parents, brothers, and sisters by committing a preventable act.

VICTOR was known as a good boy but extremely sensitive. Although the other children did not mind being teased, he was much different. He would pull away, run to the couch, lie down and close his eyes. As a baby, Victor would have violent tantrums. He would throw himself on the floor and bang his head. During the next few years he began pulling out his hair. The practice continued even though he was disciplined. Victor created a permanent bald spot on the side of his head. Otherwise, he appeared to most outsiders to lead an average life. Attending classes about one mile east of home, he received his grade one to eight education at the Evergreen school at Kilwinning. He attended Sunday school, had his fair share of fights, and when caught in mischief, a word from his father could bring tears.

Psychiatrists were to maintain later that Victor began seeing the devil at the age of 10. His father put little faith in this. As he said, "The doctors are basing this on information from a very sick boy. It's impossible! You think I wouldn't know it if he saw the devil when he was only 10 years old? We worked side-by-side. He would have told me or I could have seen that something was bothering him. I don't believe that Victor was so sick when he was only 10 years old. Maybe he told the doctors this but in his present state of mind how can they believe everything he tells them? Surely if he was as sick as they say I would have had some indication. Wouldn't you think so?"

At the age of nine, a year before psychiatrists claim he began seeing spirits, Victor was involved in a situation typical of the boyish, adventurous type that he was. A model jet airplane was purchased. After being used a couple of times, Victor and his brother decided it would not hold enough fuel. Together, they built an alternate gas tank. They soldered a metal stem to it and began pumping in air pressure. The plane blew up. Engulfed in flames, Victor was thrown into the snow. He was taken to the hospital in nearby Shellbrook. Following this, Victor had a fear of fire, avoiding it as much as possible. He would not light the furnace, he refused to ignite the cook stove and if forced to burn roots on the family farm the matches were carried in a glass jar.

Another incident occurred when Victor fell from a tree while playing. He cut his hip but said nothing. When his mother noticed her son limping she asked him to take down his trousers. He refused. She then told him that if he would not obey her she would cut them off with the scissors. Victor was then taken to a doctor and examined. When he was told by his mother that he could have died from the poisoning in the cut his reply stunned her.

"You wouldn't have cared," he told her.

A solitary child trying to exist in his own seclusive space. He was uncomfortable in his relationships with others. His personal attachments few. Antisocial you might say, assuredly an introvert through and through. If visitors came to the farm he would hang back although among a crowd he would always try to stand up for his rights. The shyness extended to girls. In town after school one day, Victor went into the lone drugstore to buy a book.

As his father recalled, "He was a fairly good looking guy and on this occasion was being crowded by two pretty schoolgirls who seemed to take a liking to him."[1]

---

1. Victor recalled the drugstore incident several years later. He explained, "I didn't like them — they had marriage in their eyes."

Embarrassed, Victor dropped the book and raced out of the store.

He did not feel at ease with members of his own age who were of the opposite sex. His self-confidence was low and he not only was unsure as to how to communicate with them but he also felt sexually inadequate and unfulfilled.

"He never dated any girls," according to the boy's father.

Victor was mechanically inclined. He enjoyed working on bicycles, motors and virtually any equipment that presented a challenge. He was always fixing something whether his own, his family's or his neighbors. A particular liking was correcting bent and broken wheels of bicycles. He would straighten the rim, replace the spokes and restore the item to near new condition.

Victor repeated grade three but continued classes up until grade nine at Leask. He failed his exams miserably, his lower than low disordered self-esteem plummeting. It was at this stage that the school principal told the awkward boy and his father that there was no reason in the world why he could not complete the grade and go on to receive a high school education. Accordingly, academically underachieving Victor returned to the same classroom the next year but he had lost interest. He often played hookey, preferring billiards to education.

His teachers described him as, "sensitive and shy — but not lacking intelligence."

He did not really enjoy what went with attending school. He did not like the dressing up part or the times when he would be called upon to give oral answers.

Although Victor had a distaste for his regular schooling he would reportedly always attend the Bible classes that were set up around Leask each summer. Until he was 21, at least according to his parents, Victor never once missed going to church on Sunday. Religion played a central role in the family — far too much said some.

Victor enjoyed helping his father on the farm and was

considered an outstanding worker.

Recalled Robert , "Whenever I asked him to do anything he'd be right there. He would never say no and would always do a good job."

He would think nothing of picking as much as 40 acres of roots, a back-breaking job. He worried about the future. He was petrified of what would happen when his father died. The eldest still at home, he was terrified of the responsibility of having to operate the farm. The most drastic change, according to a schoolmate, came when he left school.

"Victor just seemed to lose contact with the world."

His retreat from social life, his alienation from society, was almost complete.

V ICTOR Ernest Hoffman was 17 years of age when he finished school. He was living at home during his 20th birthday, January 15, 1966.

The husky teenager — with his medium height and strong square shoulders — lost interest in himself and the farm, withdrawing more and retreating further into his inner sanctum. Previous to this he made over $400 trapping weasels. Now he preferred to remain in the confines of home. He no longer hunted squirrels and magpies. It reached the point where time meant nothing to him. He would be asked to do a simple chore by his mother and not return home. She would find him sitting alone in the fields, gazing at the distant heavens. He would then go into the house and collapse on the couch. He would cover his face with his hands.

He was suffering excruciating headaches. He said they were caused by pressure. Victor would tie a handkerchief around his head and he would feel much better.

The tortured pattern continued throughout the winter.

The following spring he began to sit in the kitchen and laugh to himself. When asked what was so funny he would get angry. Though Victor continued to work around the farm his condition worsened. The weird events took on a life of their own.

It was Saturday, another work day for the family. Robert and his sons were contributing to the welfare of the home. They were out in the bold sun doing chores. Victor was picking roots but doing the task aimlessly. He was sitting in the family's utilitarian one-ton truck when suddenly he began to roar with laughter.

Racing over to find out the humor of the situation, Robert asked, "What's the joke?"

He received no reply.

Instead, going into a rage, Victor slammed the truck into gear, tromped the gas pedal and roared off. He narrowly missed hitting Allan who escaped within a split second of the heavy vehicle passing over the spot on which he had been standing.

This was the beginning of May 1967. It was about three and one-half months before the mind of Victor Ernest Hoffman would finally snap. His parents knew something was not right but nothing was done — they were not sure what was wrong. Even though the signs were increasingly evident, it could be explained by typical, untrained parents as, "just a change." Merely a bashful, quiet boy growing into a man and maybe — just maybe — with a temper. Perhaps it was also thought, "mental illness in our family? Absurd! Impossible!"

WEATHER-WISE, May was a good month. Work on the farm intensified. Robert, with sun-burned face and cap-paled forehead, went to town. It was May 27th. Leaving shortly after sunrise, he arrived back home at noon.

The family ate a hearty meal, relaxing afterwards with a discussion concerning the great amount of work that had been accomplished prior to noon. There was also talk of the labor yet to be done.

Victor had been seeding oats and there remained much to do. Before going back out to the fields, his father had warned him that he should take the precaution of wearing a mask as the chemical he was using was poisonous and could have serious effects if inhaled.

A short time later, Robert was jarred awake after dozing off in his favorite easy chair.

Victor had grabbed him on the leg so violently that it hurt the next day.

The troubled youth shouted, almost hysterically, "Dad, aren't you coming out?"

Startled, Robert replied "Yes" and followed his son out into the farmyard.

He questioned, "Victor, you didn't use the mask?"

His son answered, "I don't know, maybe I didn't!"

Soon, he became violently ill and began talking in circles, saying maybe he had used the mask and then again maybe he had not.

Howling with pain, Victor began rolling on the ground. He attempted to vomit but could not.

Writhing from the cramps that tore at his stomach he screamed, "Dad take me to a doctor, take me to a doctor!"

"Are you that sick?"

"I'm very sick!"

It was impossible to handle Victor and it was considered foolish to attempt taking him to a doctor in his present, uncontrollable condition. He was brought into the house where soon the spasms began to dissipate.

Robert asked, "Do you need a doctor?"

The reply was weak, "No, I'm all right."

The job of seeding continued. Victor did his work, however, the next day was unable to continue.

STELLA was in the kitchen preparing dinner. It had been a hectic time and as she prepared the meal her thoughts turned to what her other children, the five who had already left home, might be doing. She was in a happy frame of mind and thankful for the stable and good life which — for the most part — she and her family had led.

Her serenity was shattered by what sounded like an explosion.

"I looked out the kitchen window and there was Victor, he had just fired a shot from his .303 calibre rifle. As I looked out, another shot, and then another. I ran into the yard."

"Mom, I just shot the devil."

When Stella demanded the gun from Victor he went into a frenzy, dropped the weapon, jumped into his 1950 model car and spun out of the driveway.

Fourteen-year-old Allan, who had witnessed the actions of his older brother, was shaking. His mother told him to retrieve the rifle and hide it before Victor came back.

A short while later Victor did return. He demanded his weapon. Stella explained that the gun had been hidden and would not be given back to him.

Once again, in a fit of fury, Victor roared off. Once again he returned.

Livid, he ordered, "I want to talk to somebody."

His mother asked if he wanted to talk with his father.

"No."

Victor then told his mother that he wanted to see the family clergyman.

A telephone call was immediately placed to Pastor Edward Post in nearby Shellbrook.

The request was soon answered with his arrival at the Hoffman farm.

Victor was taken into the farmhouse living room and in private the two talked things out. The emotionally drained youth appeared relieved after the counselling, however, as he walked with the minister to the latter's car, he turned and stated matter of factly, "I'd like to kill Mom and Dad."

Pastor Post, in the presence of Victor, called to Mr. and Mrs.

Hoffman. He told them the boy was sick and required treatment. He must see a doctor.

I T was a Sunday when Robert and Victor arrived in the city of Prince Albert. They immediately drove to the nearest hospital. The examining physician listened as the visibly upset patient pointed to his hip.

"I have something here, it's burning a hole."

After conducting a preliminary examination it was found that Victor did indeed have something on his hip. It was a rash, irritated from the rough work clothes which he wore. The examination revealed that the rash was minor and certainly was not burning any holes into anyone's body.

A more thorough examination was conducted with Victor talking senselessly throughout.

The physician emerged to tell the boy's father, "You'll have to take him to a psychiatrist."

According to Robert, psychiatrist Dr. R.E. Jenkins who practised in Prince Albert, was unavailable. The Hoffmans returned to their farm. The journey would have to be made, once again, the following day.

After a night which passed without any major incident, father and son once more departed for Prince Albert.

Yet again, according to Robert, Dr. Jenkins was unavailable. However, a member of the same office was free to conduct the examination. While Robert waited, the long overdue probing of his son began.

Following the session, Dr. Rathana Nakintara, according to Robert, said, "This boy is very sick. He's a good boy, but very sick. I am going to have to telephone Battleford to have a place ready for him. He should leave right away."

The psychiatrist was referring to the city of North Battleford and the mental hospital located there, The Saskatchewan Hospital.

Father and son immediately began the trip toward the

government operated institution. They stopped on the way for lunch at home. Victor was extremely restless.

"He'd sleep for 20 miles, wake up and want to get in the front seat. He talked fine and then would begin to act very mixed up. He kept laying down, getting up, laying down, getting up and continued this all the way home."

The two ate very little. Robert's thoughts rambled back to the hospital in Prince Albert where the day before Victor had said, "Dad, why not go home, do your work and then come back and get me later?" At the time of the initial examination the physician had told the father that he must stay, as his son was very ill.

After lunch the two departed for North Battleford. Victor was as agitated as he had been on the way home from Prince Albert.

The Hoffmans entered the shaded, winding driveway leading from Jersey street and pulled up in front of the aged, green-covered, three storey building. Carved in stone was the year 1911 which did not make a lot of sense in that the hospital for the insane was not officially opened until the following year. It was not an issue to the father, however, as he found this entire distasteful experience beyond the realm of anything remotely sane. Gripping the black wrought iron railings, they mounted the too-short, seven steps and proceeded to the swinging wood and glass doors.

Victor was composed until reaching the front door of the institution. Upon entering and sighting a decrepit piece of furniture he became violently ill. He turned and began to leave.

"Victor you had better stay, you can't walk out," cautioned Robert.

He had always shown a great deal of respect for his father and this instance was no exception. He pivoted and moved forward. Once inside he began to feel better.

With trepidation, overwhelmed by a sick feeling at the pit of their stomachs, both warily walked the 60-foot corridor to the arrival desk. There was the lingering putrid smell of mildewed humans, sort of a mixture of urine, soiled clothes and unbathed bodies and the creamy, white grayish walls offering such a stark outline to the near-deserted nine-foot wide hallway. With a pallidness about them, they faced their greeter whose back was to the wall.

It was only a matter of moments until the matronly receptionist notified the doctor. Shortly afterwards, the boy's father left to return home.

The hospital staff by this time had Victor dressed in institutional garb and lying on his back.

He was trying to comprehend his father's departing remark that, "It won't be very long." Victor was also formulating in his unwell mind the words he had uttered in response, "I don't know if I'll come back to the farm, I think I'll try something else."

ROBERT, on the outskirts of North Battleford, entered Highway Number 40 for the journey home. Shaken, he tried to sort out the disturbing events that had appeared, magnified and finally reached a climax in the past month. He reminisced throughout every mile of the agonizing, lonely ride. Victor appeared as a nice boy, one who would never pose any serious problems. He remembered when Victor first started school and how he had taken such an interest in everything he had done. He thought of how he had grown, like a blade of grass, and how his son enjoyed life. True, Victor did not have many friends but then living on the farm, with travel at times quite difficult, this was to be expected. Jimmy Peake was his closest companion with both having much in common. He was always around the place and when he was not, Victor would be at his house. They were both good boys and enjoyed the normal things that adolescents do. Hunting was a favorite pastime and both were competent sportsmen. They pulled pranks but what child does not? Victor and Jimmy lived clean, mused Robert, and although they would take an occasional drink, it was indeed seldom. Victor would never drink to excess. Robert never saw Victor drunk.

The thoughts were not all pleasant. Victor had just been committed to a mental hospital. What had gone wrong? How had he, as a father, failed? Thoughts drifted and with them a reminder of the night Victor went over to Jimmy's house, banged frantically on the door—and when the household had been aroused — commenced to tell Jimmy's father that he wanted to kill himself.

Robert was jarred back to the present. He had overshot the roadway leading to the farmhouse. He immediately threw the gearshift of his late model Pontiac sedan into reverse, backed a few yards and entered the long driveway which would take him home.

Stella had prepared a light supper for herself and her husband. Neither was hungry. It was a time when both barely picked at the food before them. It was a hard thing to face, Victor's illness. Heartbreaking to have this happen to your own family. Robert tried to tell his wife what had been said at the hospital about Victor's condition but could not. He maintained that he was told absolutely nothing.

T HE first time they visited at The Saskatchewan Hospital, the parents requested to see the psychiatrist in charge of their son's case. They wanted to find out how serious Victor's condition was. A feminine voice informed the bewildered couple that the doctor was unavailable. Besides, she instructed them, "It would be necessary to make an appointment."

Dejected and unsure as to what to do, the Hoffmans finished the visit and left for home. They knew nothing more than they had when Victor was first admitted.

PAINFULLY SHY— *Victor, at the age of six, with his sister Bernice. Both were quiet. His shyness was excruciating.*

SCHOOL DAYS — A memento from the 50th anniversary of formal education in Leask. The 1963 school yearbook, with Victor in grade nine, described him this way: "His pastime is throwing chalk and then declaring his innocence." The Principal's message in Revue '63 called upon all students to, "carry on with the duty of doing good."

CATCH THE DEVIL

II

IT was a bright, sunny morning. The kind which would have an uplifting influence on most people. It bypassed Robert and Stella Hoffman. They were worried sick about their son.

The couple owned two farms, the one the family lived on, a half-section, and the other about a mile distant which contained three quarter-sections. With five quarters of land farmed to wheat, rape, oats and barley; and with about 50 head of livestock, including nine pigs, there were constant chores to be done. It was a typical day but somewhat slower and less enthusiastic with the worry about Victor. Robert took twice the time, nearly five hours, to complete the job. When finished, he placed a telephone call to Dr. Stanislaw Jedlicki in North Battleford and succeeded this time in making contact. The father made an appointment for that very day to find out the seriousness of his son's illness.

According to Robert, the meeting with Dr. Jedlicki almost brought tears to his eyes. He said the doctor told him that, "Victor would be a long time, maybe even one year." He recalled the psychiatrist telling him, "Victor is a sick boy. He is still seeing the devil."

Dr. Jedlicki differed with this account. He contended, "I only mentioned it because they wanted to take him in one week's time. They wanted to take him home because he improved and to serve this point I told them that he would be a long time, maybe even one year."

Asked whether he ever explained the nature of Victor's illness to the Hoffmans, Dr. Jedlicki replied, "You know they are very simple minded people and I explained to them quite clearly about everything and they didn't want to accept it."

Robert and Stella finished their anguished stay with Victor.

The trip home was fast, both parents trying to understand the meaning of the words they had heard from their son's doctor. A man with 16 years experience in psychiatry.

It was the type of thing that one never thought could happen to one's own. Victor, blessed with many qualities, including developing physical strength, suffering from a diseased mind. But both parents felt he was in good hands. They thought he would respond to treatment and in time come home.

While in The Saskatchewan Hospital, Victor remained the patient of Dr. Jedlicki. The doctor was told by Victor of many events that had occurred during his turbulent 21 years. Among them, that he had been seeing devils and angels since a child. Victor said that he had seen the devil at least once a year and as often as twice a month. The devil, he believed, had often asked about his soul.

"Sell your soul to me or you will suffer a million times."

Victor told the doctor that he had attempted to catch the devil but every time he got close he was driven back by the smell. He had also seen God and angels. God had told him he would go to heaven in October. Victor also related how the brain of a girl named Denise had been put in his head. His brain, he claimed, had been put in Denise's head. (According to his father, the more logical name would be Bernice, Victor's sister.)

L IFE on the farm was strained. The days dragged on. It seemed impossible to understand or accept Victor's illness which the doctor had said was so serious. Yet they tried to comprehend. Robert and Stella recalled to mind many incidents of Victor's past and could now see their significance.

A few short weeks later, along with the regular mail, came correspondence postmarked North Battleford. It was from Victor. In it was news that would eventually complete his travels on the road to madness. The letter was ripped open.

"Stella, it's from Victor! He says he can come home!"

Robert stopped.

"Unbelievable! It just couldn't be true?"

Dr. Jedlicki had said, "He will be a long time, maybe even one year."

Here was word from Victor, received a little more than five weeks since he was admitted, saying he could come home. It was fantastic! Why would the doctor say Victor was still seeing the devil and so sick it could take a year and then without any explanation allow him to go home? It was beyond belief.

Victor was given ground privileges at the hospital on July 13th. He was no longer under guard. He had not had a shock treatment since June 26th.

On July 26th, Robert once again travelled to North Battleford and to The Saskatchewan Hospital. He went into the imposing structure through the same doors that he had taken his son less than two months before.

As he remembered it, he pondered, "What miracle has happened? What fantastic wonderment has sent a cure to my boy in so short a time?"

As he approached the information desk the receptionist glanced up.

"Can I help?"

He asked if he could speak with Dr. Jedlicki.

The woman responded, "I'll see if I can get him for you."
Within moments she had an answer.

"The doctor is too busy to see you."

"Is it all right for Victor to go home?"

"Yes, he (the doctor) has confirmed that your son can go home."

When questioned as to why Victor could be released, the receptionist confidently answered, "When one comes in by himself he can go out by himself."

Robert thought, "It's true, when I brought Victor to the hospital we both signed the papers we were asked to sign. We came because our pastor, a physician in Prince Albert and a psychiatrist warned of the seriousness of Victor's illness. It was Pastor Post in Shellbrook and the physician in Prince Albert who had both recommended that Victor see a psychiatrist. And then the psychiatrist told me Victor must go to the mental hospital immediately, with no delay whatsoever. But it was also true that Dr. Jedlicki, the man too busy to see me, had said less than two months ago that Victor was still seeing the devil and would require treatment much longer than this."

Here was an individual, the father of a young man committed to a mental institution, a man with a limited education, and a man who in his entire life had only been to one major city outside his home territory, being given one of the biggest wonderments of his life.

"I couldn't believe it. I was very surprised. Very, very, surprised. Not unhappy but just unbelieving."

While the thoughts were racing through his mind, attendants were getting his son ready to leave.

Victor's illness, diagnosed as chronic schizophrenia, had been treated with a series of electric shocks and a tranquillizer. The tranquillizer, called Haldol, was used to stifle his hallucinations.

"A short fellow brought me some pills and said Victor

would be ready in five minutes. He said Victor was to take three of these twice a day and when they were gone I would have to go to our local doctor and have them renewed."

That was the extent of the conversation. According to Robert, at no time did anyone stress the importance of taking the pills or the dire consequences of failure to do so.

To Robert they were merely pills. "I had no idea of their importance."

Dr. Jedlicki said that everybody is informed of this. But the doctor was not there when his patient was released.

Dr. Jedlicki also claimed that the Hoffmans were told they should see him but it was noontime and they left without doing so.

Victor came into the waiting room with an attendant. His father knew something was wrong.

"He wasn't the way he should be. We went to the fair[1] from the hospital. I thought Victor might enjoy the change. Everytime I tried to talk to him, instead of turning his head, he turned his whole body. He was drugged. He had to be because it took three days to wear off."

Dr. Jedlicki denied the boy was doped.

"This is not true. This was the reaction because he was released," argued the doctor who was not present when the patient left his charge.

Robert stated that he had not been informed that his son was under sedation. More importantly, that he had not been informed of the symptoms of his son's recurring illness.

Dr. Jedlicki disagreed.

"No, no, everybody's informed. They would be told."

Dr. Jedlicki, who had authorized the boy's release, did not himself tell Robert of these important facts. The doctor can only presume that the father was told. Dr. Jedlicki did not inform Robert why his son was released. He did not alert him that the criteria used for releasing patients was whether or not

---

1. Robert Hoffman is referring to the annual exhibition held in North Battleford.

their symptoms were controlled.

Robert Hoffman's reaction was typical, "I'm not a doctor and know nothing about an illness of the mind. I trusted the hospital and believed it when I was told that Victor was all right and could go home."

July 26th. In less than three weeks the nation would be shocked.

FATHER, mother and highly disturbed son arrived back at the family home and attended to the routine. After completing the daily chores late in the afternoon, supper was served, the table cleared and the dishes washed, dried and put away.

Victor complained of fatigue and left the table early. The Hoffmans thought he was still experiencing the results of the shock treatments or the medication administered him prior to his release as he was groggy and unduly tired. He went to bed. Allan went outside immediately after supper to enjoy the midsummer evening. Robert and Stella retired to the living room and discussed how nice it was to have Victor home. Even though he was not well, they thought he would come around after the drugs had worn off.

The following day, Victor showed a slight improvement. He awoke at the same time as the rest of the family, observed while the chores were being done and then sat down to a hearty breakfast. After eating, Victor felt like working. He went out to the barn and helped his dad milk a cow.

"He was very slow. He wanted to work but just couldn't. The effects of the drugs still hadn't worn off."

His second day home he did not do any work whatsoever.

At the beginning of the third day it looked as though the medication was beginning to wear off. Victor obviously felt better. He bounded down the stairs to the kitchen looking forward to the day ahead.

"I'm ready to work. What can I do?"

His father replied, "You don't have to work if you don't feel up to it."

Victor retorted, "I just can't sit."

That day Victor went out on the sun-drenched land and began working summerfallow. He labored as he wanted — at his own speed — and paced himself. He was in high spirits and definitely seemed to be feeling better.

The days passed. Both parents viewed with keen interest the continuous changes in their son. His improvement was sporadic. One day he appeared fine, the next not as well. As far as Robert knew, his son was taking the pills given him upon his release. Sometimes, they were sure he had definitely taken his medicine — yet he would seem worse. There was no consistent pattern. As the days changed, so did Victor. He told his mother that he did not like the shock treatments that had been given to him at the hospital. He also made a strange request.

"Mom, I'll do anything you want but I won't cut the heads off the chickens. Please don't make me do that."

Robert thought back to a discussion he had with his wife prior to their son's return. They had talked about hiding all the guns that they had on the farm, however, it was the father who thought it best not to do so.

"If Victor came home and saw the guns were hidden he'd think we didn't trust him. He'd think we still considered him mentally ill."

The question concerning usage of firearms — standard fare on a farm — should not have been a matter left in the hands of the parents. Yet, according to Robert it was.

"I was never told nor was I given a list of instructions about what to do."

Dr. Jedlicki differed.

"No, no everybody's informed because we have clinics and there was one in his vicinity, that means Prince Albert. All papers are sent to clinics for follow-up."

Dr. Jedlicki, questioned in a telephone interview, was asked if the parents would be given verbal or written instructions.

"They would be just told and Prince Albert Mental Health Clinic is informed if such a patient is released."

Robert said that no one was ever in contact with him.

SEVENTEEN days after his release from the hospital, Victor's fragile condition seemed to be deteriorating. It was a Saturday, August 12th, and Robert had gone into town for supplies. When he left, Victor was working in the farmyard and seemed normal. But the father had second thoughts when he returned home around 11 o'clock that night. The lights of his 1963, maroon Pontiac, silhouetted a figure in one of the farm buildings. The patriarch climbed out of his car and walked to the garage. He pushed open the door and there was Victor. Still working, he became upset at the sight of his father.

Robert said sternly, "Victor what are you doing? You're acting the same way you did when you got sick."

Victor shouted, "I don't want to go back."

"Are you taking the pills?"

"No. I've had awful headaches and cut down."

Robert told his son of the importance of the pills. The importance of which he himself had never been told and the significance of which he was just guessing.

Father and son went into the house. Victor took his pills and went to bed.

THE next day, Sunday, Victor was unsteady. The family, good churchgoers of the Lutheran faith, very seldom missed the services. Victor was upstairs in his cramped, narrow room containing a roll-a-way bed, a dresser, and a bookcase, made by his sister from two apple boxes. He was readying himself for church. He was very seldom tardy because church was an occasion he always enjoyed, so claimed his parents. The family was ready to leave and Victor was expected downstairs momentarily. Robert, never one to be late, shouted up the stairs for Victor to hurry. His son emerged at the head of the staircase undressed and unshaven.

"I'm not feeling good."

"I guess you're not going to church then?"

The reply was emphatic, "No!"

The family, less one, departed for the place of worship and arrived only moments before the service began. A worried threesome, they prayed harder that day than perhaps ever before. They prayed for Victor and the day he would regain his mental health.

Following the services, the Hoffmans lingered outside and chatted. They were farm people, good people and the weekly religious visit meant not only a time for prayer and thanksgiving but also a chance to discuss the past week's happenings with friends and neighbors.

Returning home they found Victor still sequestered in his room.

The family spent a restful Sunday for it was the one day of the week set aside for relaxation. A day in which the regular chores were easily disposed of with the family spending the majority of time together. What folks called, a pure day.

This was Sunday, August 13th. This was the last night the Hoffmans would retire and awake with all being relatively well. In a little more than 24 hours, tragedy would strike.

The family awoke, the chores were done and breakfast was served. There was no indication of what would transpire.

Victor helped his father and brother with the summerfallowing. He worked hard. Big and powerful, he was capable of doing much more strenuous work than his father. He enjoyed the labor and at last it seemed as if everything was going to be all right. The family stopped for lunch and with the strain of Victor being sick beginning to fade it was a jovial occasion.

There was more work and then another meal.

The family settled in various places of the house to relax. Robert, Stella and Victor moved from the kitchen into the living room where they turned on the television set just in time to watch the last few minutes of the regular sportscast on CKBI Prince Albert. It was Nick Roche, a sportscaster well known in the area, and a favorite of the Hoffmans. They did not watch the weather report but there was no sign that any drastic change was in store. While the three remained viewing television, Allan had wandered upstairs to finish an article in a hunting magazine. Victor, on the couch in the living room, dozed off. He awoke and took his pills. Then — he went upstairs to bed.

Robert and Stella did not go directly to sleep. They stayed awake and talked. Victor seemed to be improving. They were happy and somewhat relieved.

Allan was sleeping. He also was comforted because it looked as though his older brother, with his disquieting, bizarre behavior, was going to be fine. So much had been unpredictable.

A few hours later, early the next morning, Robert awoke. It was the noise from the engine of a car fading down the road.

FAMILY PRIDE — The Hoffman family went into the city to have this portrait taken. Teen-aged Victor, wearing a bow-tie and worrying that his hair was too long, watched over his beaming mother. Years later he recalled that day: "My hair was a mess. Father always gave me the haircut and he didn't know how to cut hair. Boy I hated my hair!"

A NOISE IN
THE NIGHT

III

T HE village of Shell Lake is
accessible by more than
one route. From Leask
there are four choices. A driver familiar with the area would
perhaps take a municipal road from Leask to Highway 3,
make a left turn, and continue for the remaining distance.
Another alternative is driving about six miles down Highway
40 to Kilwinning, and then beginning a series of northwesterly
turns which eventually lead to Highway 3. A third option is to
continue along Highway 40 as far as Highway 3, turn west,
and keep on travelling in a northwesterly direction. The fourth
route is a short drive west of Leask, north to Highway 3, and
then northwest to Mont Nebo and on to Shell Lake.

Highway 3 passes near the settled farming communities of
Ordale, Mont Nebo, Hawkeye and finally Shell Lake. The road
is flanked on the north by a Canadian National Railway line
which winds and dips with the artery. It is a ride not much
different from travel over Highway 40 from North Battleford
to Leask. The main difference is the lack of cars, all too obvious,
and the fact that the road possesses numerous curves and hills
which makes even the most unwary of drivers knowledgeable

of the concentration required. At Mont Nebo a sign boldly proclaims — Shell Lake 12 miles. The scenery changes and the surrounding bush becomes much more dense. The rolling hills stir in a manner that gives the impression that some ulterior, mysterious form of life is propelling them.

A bridge and then a sign with an arrow pointing in a northerly direction. It indicates with suddenness the closeness of a community that would soon become splashed across newspaper headlines and read as the lead story for days on end via news agencies within and beyond the nation.

What kind of place is Shell Lake?

It appears much as many other undistinctive villages across the region — drab and uninteresting. A one street sleepy spot disturbed only by a group of children running on the road or a local farmer crossing over to the post office where perhaps all he would receive were more pamphlets outlining the advantages of a new fertilizer or seed. The community can be assessed within seconds. A house, a telephone office and a building bearing the weather-beaten sign; Lunches-Soft Drinks, with the hyphen missing and the bleached lettering not as clear as in print. There was the Sunlight cafe, a popular spot with its jukebox playing to only a limited number of booths and a bit of a deserted lunchcounter; an old dilapidated building, unused and musty; and then two stores. The other side of the village's main street lacked in the activity all too noticeable on its opposite. A service station, the post office, a combined barber shop and pool hall and then a number of buildings not exceeding in quantity those already mentioned.

Foresaking the turnoff from Highway 3 into Shell Lake, one could continue in a westerly direction for limitless miles. The opportunities are numerous, though, if the preference is to stop before going any great distance. An old building used as a schoolhouse would provide shelter, although with numerous junk cars surrounding it and with its windows boarded up, it did not seem like the kind of place where one would feel secure. Six isolated farmhouses and then another. None appeared different but one was. It was occupied by the Peterson family. Father, mother, and eight children. The home was a two bedroom bungalow, modest and much too small, but adequate for the family's needs.

J AMES Peterson, of Norwegian descent, was born within a very near distance of where he lived. The year was 1920. Married 25 years later to the former Evelyn May Finlayson, five years his junior, the two settled down to raising a family on the nearly 500 acres of marginal flatland that had only a few years before, seen to all their needs.

Evelyn, with a kindly face and gentle manner, was born of Scottish parents at Borden, Saskatchewan. She and her family moved to Shell Lake a short time later. She was described as having the patience of a saint and as a woman who would not hurt a fly. A soft-hearted lady who would wince at the sight of blood or the thought of a loved one being injured.

Churchgoers, Evelyn and Jim were in no way people who purposely kept to themselves although they did not make it into town that often.

Jim would travel into Shell Lake as regularly as possible to visit his parents and his mother-in-law — but it was difficult to leave the children. Besides, there was not that much money. Jim did not have a lot to spare and what he had was the family's.

Entertainment was what they made at home. Friends would drop by for the occasional card game or a glass of beer. There was the television and of course the children were always playing hide-and-seek, baseball or the sorts of games that keep kids busy. Generally, times were not prosperous but it seemed that everyone was in the same boat.

The children were many. Kathleen was born in 1947, Jean three years later and Mary within four years. The fourth and fifth were also girls. Dorothy in 1956 and Pearl in 1957. Four years later, William appeared on the scene, to be followed a year later by Phyllis May. Then another year and the second boy, Colin. The ninth Peterson child, Larry, was born a year and a-half later.

A large family but this was the norm. There were many such families in the district.

The Petersons were very close. God-fearing and hardworking, they formed a combination resulting in a happy, fruitful life.

The family as a unit was defined as being self-sufficient. The family head was described as a virtual non-drinker, a good man and one who never harmed anyone. A calm man but no coward.

As one area resident put it, "Jim Peterson didn't have an enemy in the world."

Certainly, things were not always as they could have been. Like the time dad's car was ransacked and stripped of its tires. Hard to take, but these things happen, don't they? Actually it was just the work of some local youngsters who probably had nothing better to do. They were apprehended, the tires returned and for their foolishness the culprits received a suspended sentence.

A happy family, with the parents loving and caring for the children as only parents can and with the offspring responding as only children are capable. As they grew, their character was evident. It shone. They went to school and they helped on the farm. They swam with friends in Shell Lake and they shared games with these same playmates at home. Normal, fun-loving children.

Kathy, the eldest, received her education — as did the others old enough to attend — at the Shell Lake School. She had no trouble attaining her grade 12 diploma. Quiet and refined, she was a girl who stayed close to home. When there was a dance she attended with her parents. It was a family occasion. Kathy met and fell in love with a boy who lived no more than five miles from her home. Lee Hill's parents farmed the land near the spot where James Peterson decided to stake his future. Lee attended school at Spiritwood, a neighboring community to Shell Lake.

A beautiful couple, Kathy and Lee were married July 7, 1967. It was a windy, gritty day on the wheat plains, the kind when the earth moves, with soil swirling for miles. The ceremony was conducted in the same church that years before had witnessed the marriage of Kathy's parents. A small reception followed the marriage of Jim and Evelyn's eldest. It was held at the Legion Hall and saw the catering bill come to just over $66. Seventeen-year-old Jean was there. She had been a bridesmaid at a time which meant both joy and sadness. The joy was for her sister experiencing one of the happiest moments of her life. The sadness was for herself because her older sister, who had been out living on her own for about a year, was now married and about to depart the area.

"It would seem so different."

The young newlyweds moved to Chetwynd, British Columbia where they would make their home.

It seemed strange and lonely around the Peterson farm with Kathy gone. It would take quite a bit of getting used to.

Jim realized that soon his second eldest, Jean, would probably be leaving. He decided to give her a treat. He knew how much she enjoyed running and how well she had done in local competition. He was proud, as was the entire family. He decided to give Jean a week at the Legion track and field camp at Dundurn, Saskatchewan.

"She deserved it and it would be fun for the whole family to go and watch her race," he reasoned.

The summer days and nights continued. Jim had the chores to do and with all the children now at home for the holidays he had lots of help. An abundance of assistance and an equal amount of distraction. With eight still at home there was never a dull moment. A month had passed since Kathy's wedding and the family was beginning to accept the fact that she was now gone.

Little Phyllis, a cute, chubby darling who tagged behind her father almost everywhere, would now ask only once a week, "Where's Kathy, huh?"

This was the Peterson family. Big, not only in number but in the way they lived. Loving, innocent and well respected. They were known as generous, kind, fine people. Salt of the earth.

AUGUST 14th was just another day in the family's life. It was perhaps a little more exciting for the children because they had visitors. Jim's sister Eveline (Evie), 38, and the wife of Helmer Helgeton, had brought two of their children over to visit their cousins. She fondly recalled: "It was a lovely day and the kids had a ball. They rode horseback and giggled so much you'd think this had to be the best day of their little lives."

Jim was busy haying and with the children occupied he accomplished a full day's work including some at the nearby Lang farm. The hours rolled by and soon the time had come for the Helgeton family to leave for home. It had been a wonderful time. As the children traipsed off to bed they were still giggling and jostling each other.

WILDREW Lang, a close friend, was in the house having coffee and cookies with Jim and Evelyn. Wildrew, who was 15 years old when he first met Jim, 12 years his senior, is a gentleman farmer in the truest sense. He is reserved, soft-spoken and extremely polite. They fast became friends, sharing equipment and the never ending work that comes with life on the farm. Earlier that evening, they had gone into town to look at a combine that they were thinking of buying. Mary was going to go, to spend the night at her grandparents. At the last moment, for some unexplained reason, it was decided that she should stay at home.

When the partners returned, Evelyn was working in the garden and the dogs, just ordinary farm dogs including Skippy, were putting up a fuss. Evelyn thought they were barking at one of the horses. It could have been the bay mare, Old June, Jim's since 1941, or perhaps the ponies, Babe or Peggy, that had the dogs upset. Maybe it was one of the cows. Whatever it was, they soon settled down.

Now, the two men were making plans for the next day. Tomorrow there would be lots of work. Jim and Wildrew, a bachelor, would clean out feed bins and move the 50 bushels to a grain elevator. Jim would make about $70 for the grain. He planned to use it for Jean's holiday and the family trip to Dundurn. The Ladies Auxiliary had earlier recognized Jean's efforts with a $30 award.

Wildrew, who reckoned he used to smoke a pack of tobacco a day — roll-your-owns which amounted to nearly three packages of regulars — decided it was time to head home so he could get a good start the next morning. Jim walked him out to the driveway. The night was clear with a full, bright moon. A touch on the cool side and both felt that there could be frost before daybreak.

THE last light in the Peterson house was dimmed around 11 o'clock. The precious moments before dropping off to sleep are a good time to reflect. Jim could look back with satisfaction on what the family had accomplished in an era of rural pilgrim's progress.

First of all, the farm had been purchased from his parents. What problems there had been. The first house with no water. The roads impossible. Sure, it was a larger house — a two storey structure with a big kitchen — but they pretty well had to move, with the roads and such. Now they would have to expand this one and move the other one in. Assuredly, lots of work but for a family like theirs it would be worth it.

Jim Peterson, unaware that death stalked and that his family would soon be in mortal danger, dropped off to sleep. Encroaching terror was the furthest thing from his mind.

A N older gray Plymouth bearing Saskatchewan licence plates roared past the turnoff into Shell Lake. It continued west along Highway 3. The driver and lone occupant was agitated. He had been home in bed but had become restless and departed early that morning to go for a drive.

An old schoolhouse, a hawk on a telephone pole, a farm and then another. Suddenly the car began to skid. A foot slammed against the brake pedal. The rapidly moving vehicle shot beyond a roadway on the right. Its momentum carried it past what could have been its murderous destination, the Alvin Simonar farm. Inside the house the five members of the family slept soundly, unaware of impending doom.

The car came to a halt a few feet beyond the entrance which it had passed. The driver glanced around. He would enter the laneway on his left.

White in color, with green trim, it was a small frame house. The four room structure included one bedroom off the living room and another off the kitchen. The distance that remained was about 200 yards.

It was now daylight and the sun was beginning to creep up into the sky. Perhaps this woke Jim or perhaps he heard the noise in the night.

Almost dozing off, he sat on the edge of the mattress with his feet dangling above the cold, linoleum covered floor. From the sound of it, the car was still a couple of minutes away. When it arrived, he would see what the driver wanted. The rest of his family was sleeping peacefully.

PETERSON FAMILY — *The last group photo. It was captured at the baby's spring christening — a few scant months before mid-August. (Left to right) Mary, 13; Dorothy, 11; Jean, 17; Pearl, 9; Phyllis, 4; Kathy, 19; Colin, 2; Evelyn, 42; William, 6; Jim's mother, Martha, 71 and Jim, 47, holding Larry, 1 1/2. Martha, who lived with her husband nearby, was not in the ill-fated house when the lights dimmed on August 14, 1967. Neither was Kathy who was married and living in B.C.*

COUNTRYLIFE—The property had lots of space for the large family to enjoy.
— *Journal Photo by Dave Reidie*

WINTER FUN — *Four-year-old Phyllis was the biggest rider. All were enjoying the snowy weather.*

IN COLD
BLOOD

IV

THE sedan slowed, finally coming to a complete stop. The ignition was turned off and its lone occupant stepped out into the moon illuminated landscape.

His distorted mind was reeling. Hunting and then the beauty of spruce bushes — then the desire to kill.

"Just bang, just like that, my mind went on to kill people."

Violently the door of the lonesome, shadow-filled house was pushed open.

"Who is it?"

There was no answer.

Jim fearfully asked again, "Who is it?"

Once again there was no response.

"Who is it? Who's there?"

The intruder was now in sight. Jim would have seen his weapon. Like a cornered animal he backed up and jumped onto the bed.

A shot rang out and Jim reacted. Jumping at his assailant he kept moving in. Closer and closer, all the time taking bullets to his body. Grabbing his attacker by the neck he tried to choke him but could not. He was nearly dead. Jim continued to stumble forward but as the last shell was fired he slumped to the floor.

The father of nine children was within moments of death. The cold blooded act had taken place before the eyes of his wife and within earshot of eight of his children. They were shrieking and crying, in a state of terror, with the shaking and trembling uncontrollable.

The baby, Larry, awoke and began sobbing. At one and one-half years he was too young to understand the horror of the madness but could not escape the foreign, piercing sounds.

Five-year-old William burst into tears and as he did, so did little Colin. It was a madhouse. Screaming, screaming, and screaming — it would not stop.

Calmly, the intruder walked outside. He systematically reloaded his rifle and returned. His mission was not finished.

Breathing heavily, Jim was sprawled on the floor. A shot, another and then a third. The protector, the guardian, was dead.

The girls were next. They were awake and they knew.

"Don't shoot me, don't shoot me, please don't shoot me."

Jean cried, "I don't want to die, I don't want to die."

They ducked beneath the bed covers hopelessly attempting to avoid this ungodly thing that was happening. They were desperately wanting to thwart this maniac who had just murdered their father and was attempting to do the same to them.

The rifle rang out repeatedly. Jean and Mary, nearing death, in the same cramped room as their nine-year-old sister Pearl, their four-year-old sister Phyllis and their two brothers, William and Colin, were shivering in fear.

The killer's head was now spinning. A feeling of immense power swept his body. He looked down at the faces of the trembling, innocent children and there was no compassion. No mercy.

The gun discharged again, and again.

Colin was huddled in a corner at the head of the bed.

"Mommy, Mommy."

A shot. The three-year-old was dead.

Four-year-old Phyllis had crawled under the bed-covers and was left alone.

"She can't see me. She can't identify me."

Methodically, the killer jumped out the lone window in the death room. He had heard a noise and knew that someone was trying to escape. Silently moving around the house, he spotted a figure. It was the mother of all these children, trying to flee with her baby. At about the same time, she sighted the killer.

She pathetically pleaded, "Don't murder me!"

The words had barely been uttered when the first shot ripped into her back. Collapsing, she fell to the ground. She was shot again, and again, and again. Nearby was the baby. Whimpering, he was uninjured.

The killer returned inside.

Jean and Mary, the two eldest, were shrieking.

Eleven year old Dorothy was also still alive and also hysterical.

"They don't want to die, the bullet in the head just doesn't want to kill them. I can't shoot them anywhere else, I must shoot them in the head because then no evidence. I can cut the heads off and take them with me, then I'll have the bullets."

The cries were becoming more faint. The family was slowly dying. Then the gun fired again, and again. They were dead. Murdered in cold blood. In their own home. The shrill screams had stopped.

The Peterson slayer was not finished.[1] He returned outside

---

1. The killer later related that he went back outside and shot the baby. A police officer at the scene said in his opinion the baby was shot at about the same time as the mother. He said at that point the gunman lost his urge to kill and Phyllis was spared. The policeman stressed, however, that the view was solely his own and the only person who really knows is the one who pulled the trigger.

where the Peterson baby lay near his now lifeless mother. A shot was fired and then a second. The infant was dead. Shot through the head.

JIM Peterson had stopped seven slugs while attempting to ward off his attacker. His wife, offering no resistance whatsoever, was shot four times. The seven children had been punctured with a total of 16 bullets. A father, mother and seven of their children slaughtered. Killed like wild dogs.

Jim had three weapons in the house. An automatic pistol and two rifles. Investigating officers would later find the guns in a dresser drawer and closet. They had not been used.

The killer, in his frenzied state, tried to gather as many spent shell casings as he could. He then left, the same way he came.

ONE of the last individuals to see the Petersons alive before the carnage was Wildrew Lang. He was up bright and early on the unclouded morning of August 15th and went to the Peterson farm by way of an adjoining rutted back road. Jim was not around but Wildrew, in shirt-sleeve weather, began working without him. He started loading the wheat. By 8:30 a.m. two bins were emptied and still, Wildrew was alone.

"Jim must have overslept."

About a half-hour later, Wildrew, lean and wearing his favorite straw hat to ward off the hot sun, decided to find out why Jim had been delayed. Walking up the lane into the yard he noticed the cows had not been milked. The door of the house was ajar.

Skippy, who traditionally had a special bark for his friend, was hushed, almost unmoving. Wildrew, who had a gut feeling that something was dreadfully wrong, later recalled, "He came and met me and never made a sound, he stayed on the inside of my leg."

Sensing something was terribly amiss, he called Jim's name.

There was no response.

"I walked up to the house and knocked on the door. There was no answer. I then opened the porch door and stepped inside. The kitchen door was already open and there was Jim, lying just inside the kitchen on his stomach. He was dressed only in his underwear shorts and there was a lot of blood around. He wasn't moving. I figured he was dead."

Wildrew could not believe his eyes. It was a house of horror — beyond imagination. How did it happen? Who could have done this, and in such a manner?

The Peterson's 10-year-old station wagon was parked outside. Wildrew frantically ran to it, turned the ignition key and roared off. He travelled the four miles to Shell Lake and telephoned the Royal Canadian Mounted Police (RCMP) detachment at Spiritwood, 16 miles west of the murder scene. He then returned to the highway at the farm entrance and frantically awaited the arrival of police.

Corporal Barry Richards entered the blood-drenched home. He first noticed the body of Jim lying face down on the floor. In the living room he saw the body of 11-year-old Dorothy. In the bedroom, off the living room, were the bodies of five more children. Jean, 17, Mary, 13, nine-year-old Pearl, five-year-old William, and two-year-old Colin. All were motionless. The policeman recoiled in horror and stepped out to the porch. Returning inside within moments, he once again entered the bedroom.

He saw something moving, "the only sign of life."

He went over to the bed, moved the red splattered blankets, and uncovered the sole survivor. Four-year-old Phyllis was huddled between the bodies of her dead sisters. She had been partially covered by a blanket. Her head was positioned near her deceased sisters, Pearl and Jean. Her eyes were darkened with fear and appeared twice their normal size. She was shaking. Nearly exhausted, the little girl had remained awake while nine members of her family were wasted. She huddled in the same room of terror where three of her sisters and two brothers were now devoid of life. Corporal Richards tapped the delicate child on the shoulder. Propping herself up with her elbows, she looked into his eyes and in a soft voice weakly asked, "Where are you going to take me now?" The officer gently gathered her into his arms and carried her outside. She was placed in the care of the Alvin and Marjorie Simonar family who lived across the highway — the family whose house the killer had bypassed.

The Simonars had a feeling something was wrong when they awoke earlier that morning. "Their dog was acting queer and the horses running loose in Jim's field did not seem right," reflected Marjorie.

They saw Wildrew rush off in Jim's station wagon and when he returned with a policeman it was the beginning of the unimaginable. Marjorie recalled: "Phyllis was covered in blood, she wanted her pyjamas washed and I did that and put them back on her. She knew what had been going on, there had been lots of noise. I asked her what happened and she told me she had crawled into bed and snuggled down real close to Jean. She had the covers pulled up and saw a man looking in the dresser drawer. She said, 'my daddy was laying on the floor' and that was about all."

The Simonars, who live in a home that often has the sweet scent of fresh baked buns, had their door locked that night. Had anyone knocked, they would have opened it. That was the type of response when strangers in the night came calling around Shell Lake. The people were trusting and liked to assist. It also helped that they knew that their living area was not murder prone.

The policeman got into his patrol car and raced the four miles to Shell Lake. He contacted the RCMP sub-division headquarters at North Battleford and Dr. J.R. Michaud of Spiritwood. Then — he returned to the crime scene. Arriving back at the Peterson farm, the Corporal waited for Dr. Michaud to arrive. The two shaken men then began walking to the now eerily quiet dwelling that had been turned into a morgue.

Nearing the only entrance, the front door, they spotted something on the ground at the northwest corner of the building. It was Evelyn. The 42-year-old mother of nine, the woman described as having the patience of a saint, was breathless. Four bullets had riddled her body. She was slumped behind a rain barrel. Her infant son was nearby. The diaper clad baby was also a casualty of the intruder's private war.

Less than one hour after the horrific discovery, the relatives and friends of the victims were beginning to learn the magnitude of the senseless massacre.

Roy Lang, a brother to Wildrew, operated a road patrol on Highway 3. Flagged down by Wildrew, he was told some of the grim detail of what had been discovered. Speeding into Shell Lake, Roy informed, within 15 minutes, Helmer Helgeton and his wife and a neighbor. Helmer and Evie were fearful. Disbelieving, they drove to the home of Jim's other sister, Elsie Mayo. From this point, the relatives journeyed to the scene of the wanton attack. They were apprehensive at what would be learned. They were then advised that all but one member of the family was dead. They were also told how violently their loved ones had perished.

Dazed, Helmer drove into Shell Lake. He had to advise Jim's parents that their son, daughter-in-law and seven grandchildren had been slaughtered.

Fred Peterson was a man of 86 years. His wife Martha was 71. Both had lived very satisfying lives but on the morning of August 15, 1967 both wished they too were dead. When informed of the violence and the ferocious, unrelenting manner in which their son and family had been killed, the elderly Petersons immediately went into shock. They were admitted to hospital along with Mrs. Martha Finlayson, 70, the mother of Evelyn.

All three suffered from the effects long after their release.

It was of such magnitude! So sudden! So horrible! Beyond all reason! Why? Why? Why?

Why to Jim and Evelyn?

How could anyone butcher those helpless little children?

It was unthinkable, unspeakable. The cold, callous crime was the bloodiest in the country's annals, bestial in nature.

AMONG those at the scene was Village Constable Clifford Johnstone. The first thing he saw was Evelyn's body lying behind the house. Ed Simonar — Alvin's brother who operated the local garage and would serve as foreman of a quickly assembled coroner's jury — was quoted as saying, "Powder burns indicated the victims had been shot at close range."

REINFORCEMENTS were beginning to arrive. The Royal Canadian Mounted Police would begin the job of investigating what was the worst random mass murder committed in Canada — a country that was celebrating its 100th birthday. The chilling evil was motiveless and apparently clueless.

EMERGENCY — One man calls for assistance. The others, all in a state of disbelief, try to collect their thoughts.
— Journal Photo by Dave Reidie

LIVING ROOM — Corporal Barry Richards, as he entered the eerily quiet house, knew that the father was dead. He then spotted the body of Dorothy on this cot. Corporal Richards continued on to the next room.

— *Journal Photo by Dave Reidie*

*CHILDREN'S BED-
ROOM — The bodies of
Pearl and Jean were dis-
covered in one bed. In
another, were the corpses
of Mary, William and
Colin. Phyllis, who had
huddled between Pearl
and Jean, was miracu-
lously — alive.*
— Journal Photo by Dave Reidie

PARENTS' BEDROOM — The family was looking ahead to the next month. Evelyn, with baby bottle nearby, escaped through this window with Larry in her arms.

— *Journal Photo by Dave Reidie*

WAR HERO — *Jim fought for his country. He died hopelessly trying to defend his family.*
— Journal Photo by Dave Reidie

HOBBY HORSE — As a shocked policeman walked through the living room to get outside for fresh air, he idly rocked the children's plaything.
— *Journal Photo by Dave Reidie*

MOTHER & CHILD —
The bodies of Evelyn and the baby were discovered near the rain barrel.
—*Journal Photo by Dave Reidie*

SILENT WITNESS — *The haunting look of a bedraggled childhood companion. What happened before Teddy's feeble eyes was unspeakable.*

— *Journal Photo by Dave Reidie*

MONSTER SEARCH

V

INSPECTOR Brian Sawyer, the officer in charge of the RCMP's North Battleford Subdivision, learned of the macabre shooting while driving to the force's detachment at Wilkie. Following initial word over his mobile radio, the Inspector raced to the rural office and telephoned his second-in-command in North Battleford. Staff-Sergeant Ken MacLeod, Sergeant Gerald Fraser who was in charge of the General Investigation Section, and Constable Michael O'Donnell, an identification expert, were dispatched to Shell Lake. All the other 'ident personnel' were away and had to be contacted.

Staff-Sergeant Ken Ferguson was the north section NCO and it was in this area where the shootings had occurred. He also departed for Shell Lake and upon arrival was the officer-in-charge. It was his responsibility to determine the type of crime. He had responsibility for the operational procedure. The south section NCO, Staff-Sergeant Ronald Sondergaard, was in charge of co-ordinating policemen to the scene. It was also his job to assign the searchers to the areas for which they would be concerned.

The Inspector returned to his headquarters and waited. It seemed like forever.

The 37-year-old Commerce graduate from Sir George Williams University in Montreal had been taught to dispose of matters in an orderly process. He was tempted to disregard his training. Finally, the Inspector learned what had been keeping his investigators. They had received a tip that a man was seen going into the bush near the death scene and they had checked it out.

As the initial investigation began, word was not long in getting to the news media and in turn to the public. It was divulged that nine persons — a mother, father and seven of their nine children — were found shot to death in their farm home. The names were withheld.

A follow-up story carried the pertinent information (the names) along with the fact that the bodies were discovered by a neighbor who went to the farm to help Jim Peterson. Another fact contained in the story was very important: a weapon had not been found. It also stated that a doctor "doubts it is a case of murder-suicide." The first reaction by many was that it must have involved a despondent member of the family who decided to end it all. This was not the case. It was not murder-suicide but rather the work of a lunatic. A monster, running loose like a rabid animal. A raving homicidal maniac.

Stories continued to spew from Canadian Press teletypes in newsrooms across the country.

"There is no apparent motive for the death of nine members of a family described by neighbors as well liked."

"Police described the murder weapon only as a firearm. They say it has not been found."

One report stated, "the body of Mrs. Peterson was found in the yard, Mr. Peterson's body on the porch and the children in bed."

There were numerous stories, many accurate, and others that were not, primarily because of the lack of official information available. It was difficult to describe something as horrendous as this. It was beyond the limits of sanity.

Police photographers had taken pictures and a sketch was made of the interior of the house. Dusting for fingerprints was also carried out. The entire inner part of the home was powdered twice for fingerprints. None were found. The killer had worn gloves. Investigators also removed blood stained linoleum that contained boot prints with a diagonal diamond pattern on the sole and a 'V' on the heel.

The bodies were taken to Prince Albert for autopsies. An RCMP officer was present to take possession of the slugs found in the victims as well as other items that could be used for courtroom exhibits.

The Royal Canadian Mounted Police, lauded as one of the world's most efficient crime fighting organizations, was in command.

Inspector Sawyer announced, "Dogs are being used in the search of bush country. A search party of up to 250 persons is ready to go."

Roadblocks were being set up throughout the northern part of Saskatchewan and the manhunt was underway. At seven o'clock that night, some 10 hours or so after the grisly discovery, a local radio station reported the first break.

"One spent cartridge is the only clue reported so far in the slaying."

Granted, it was something new, but it seemed so small and the area so large to be probed.

Although the radio report mentioned only the one piece of evidence, police had compiled more. Three slugs had been found, along with five, .22-calibre cartridge cases. Smooth tire tracks on the driveway leading to the Peterson farm had also been noted and the necessary impressions were taken. The hunt continued for the murder weapon.

Some 40 police officers began the search of all farms in the Shell Lake district. Four teams of men, about 10 to a team, were involved. The prime area, known as the envelope of probability, was a strip of land some 50 miles long and 20 miles wide. Roadblocks were lifted to put additional manpower into the search. Tracking dogs were being utilized.

Reports of unfamiliar vehicles seen in the area were prevalent. Countless interviews would have to be conducted. There was the job of checking out motor vehicle registrations. Three women had noticed "a strange car" in the vicinity of the Peterson home prior to midnight on August 15th. They were on their way to play bingo and had remembered the last three digits of the vehicle's licence plate number. A farm-to-farm search was being conducted in the hope that hundreds of inquiries would provide some lead. The big stumbling blocks remained: A lack of enough meaningful evidence, no motive, and no witness. No witness, that is, except for Phyllis. A petrified youngster found physically unharmed with the bodies of her dead brothers, sisters and parents nearby.

Tension was mounting. The villagers and the residents of the sparsely populated farming region were afraid. There was fear the killer or killers would return. A loaded gun was ready in almost every home. Lights burned all night long. This was country that was wide open. Doors and windows were usually never locked.

"Nobody would ever break in around here."

They were wrong and they knew it. As they tried to grasp the meaning of what had happened they prepared for the unknown. Doors were bolted, windows fastened and fathers remained awake 24 hours to guard their families. Sleep did not come easily.

AUGUST 16th, the day after the gruesome discovery, the painstaking farm-to-farm search continued. The officers and their dogs were attempting to turn up articles that might have been thrown away by the killer or killers. Still no motive and still the weapon had not been found.

According to news reports, "The weapon is believed to have been a .22-calibre firearm and at least in some cases had been fired at short range."

The reports were correct on both counts. The RCMP crime detection laboratory in Regina — home to the force's training academy — had determined that probably one of three makes of a .22-calibre rifle killed the family. A ballistics expert established this following a meticulous examination of spent casings and shells recovered from the spartan murder house.

The work of a fiend, a diabolical madman. He had fired, and fired, and fired — and at such close range. So close that he could see the tears streaming down the faces of the children as he took their lives — one by one.

One of the first reported developments looked hopeful. Police confirmed that a check was being conducted on a tip that a light blue car had been seen in the village the night before the murders. The police also knew at this time what the single survivor had told her uncle Helmer. He had picked Phyllis up from the Simonar home and was taking her to his farmhouse when she started talking. Here is how her uncle related the conversation.

"She said, 'Mommy ran away with the car last night.' I asked her where her daddy was and she said, 'He was on the floor.' I asked her what her daddy was doing on the floor and she replied, 'That was where the man put him.' I then asked her if someone had come to the house last night and she said, 'Yes.' I asked her if she knew who it was and she said 'No,' but added that he was going through Jean's drawer. She told me she saw her mother run out to the car with the baby in her arms."

According to Helmer, Phyllis was not told the fate of her family.

He believed, "she seemed to know what happened although she did not seem to understand the meaning of it. Phyllis also seemed to think her mother would be coming back."

The next day, while playing, Phyllis "out of the blue" stunned her uncle. She told him, "My daddy and I should be going out berrypicking now."

I
T was discovered that the killer had also robbed the family. The amount was less than $10.

While the police searched for traces to the mass slaying, the lone eyewitness remained under guard at her uncle's home. She was only three and one-half miles from where only a few hours before hideousness had struck. There remained a remote possibility that the killer or killers might return to stifle the only one who miraculously escaped the rage of the night.

F
EW substantial clues were reported. Investigating officers were patient. The search required meticulous police work. Sifting around the property, overturning rocks and checking buildings on surrounding farms. Hundreds of inquiries were being put together in an attempt to come up with a lead. A lead that, hopefully, would piece this unconscionable tragedy together.

Investigators bought a pair of high rubber boots in Shell Lake. The pattern was the same as prints found in blood near the body of Jim Peterson. The boots, black with red sole and trim, had been manufactured in Taiwan. It meant checking every such shipment of Formosan product from wholesaler-to-retailer-to-customer. Prince Albert was the main distribution point and therefore it was imperative to examine waybills originating from the northern Saskatchewan city. A wholesaler had distributed about 1,800 pairs of the type of footwear in question.

GROUND SEARCH —
Police tracking dogs were brought in the morning after the horrible discovery. Fields, ditches, cow paths and grazing pasture all had to be covered.
—Journal Photo by Dave Reidie

HANDS & KNEES—It was painstaking work. Any square inch of ground could provide a vital clue.

— *Journal Photo by Dave Reidie*

THE SCANNER — A
metal detector probes for
foreign fragments close to
home.
— Journal Photo by Dave Reidie

FURTHER AFIELD —

The tracking intensified. One constable said: "We woke up yesterday with nine bodies. Today we still have nine bodies and that's all."

—*Journal Photo by Dave Reidie*

NEWS gathering operations from afar were beginning to prod police for information as to a possible local angle. The *Vancouver Sun*, a widely read British Columbia newspaper, reported an intriguing story. It said that details of a 1958 triple murder in Vancouver had been rushed to Saskatchewan because the unsolved case bore similarities to the slaying of the Petersons. The Vancouver killings happened June 10, 1958. An unknown person or persons shot and clubbed to death Mr. and Mrs. David Pauls and their 11-year-old daughter, Dorothy. The killings occurred in the Pauls' home. The family had moved to British Columbia in 1940 after farming in the Waldheim area of Saskatchewan, not too many miles southeast of where the bodies of Mr. and Mrs. Peterson and seven of their children were discovered. The newspaper also reported that a .22-calibre weapon was used in both multiple slayings, both were without apparent motive, and police had not yet found the weapons in both cases. According to the report, details of the Vancouver case were being sent to Inspector Sawyer in North Battleford.

A new perspective to the Peterson murders had come to light. The fact that three persons brutally silenced had lived in such close proximity to Shell Lake; the fact that a .22-calibre weapon was used in both cases; the fact that both were without apparent motive; and the fact that police had not found the weapons indicated more than just a remote possibility that the crimes could be connected.

The Vancouver story was quashed less than two hours after it gained national prominence. The press liaison officer in the Peterson case, Staff-Sergeant Sondergaard, told reporters there was no connection.

"There is absolutely no substance to the report."

He did not elaborate but it was not necessary. His answer was emphatic.

Issuing a general comment on the carnage, the Staff-Sergeant said, "It is hard to fathom a stranger coming into an area, picking a farm and wiping out a family. We have not ruled out the possibility that it was someone in the area."

Stories persisted that the Peterson killing was the work of a person who had murdered before. The largest newspaper in Saskatchewan's capital city, The *Regina Leader Post*, reported that the RCMP were working with police in California on a possible link between the Shell Lake murders and the shooting of four members of a family in the southern state. The killing of a mother, father and their two sons, had taken place near San Bernadino on August 15th, 1965. Two years to the day that the Petersons were exterminated. A .22-calibre weapon had been used and the act was conducted in a manner that was not dissimilar to the Shell Lake tragedy.

The RCMP issued a terse 'No comment'.

Another report from the west coast sparked new life into the case. The story said that Vancouver police had been asked to watch for a man wanted in connection with the mass murder. The suspect was identified as being of Indian extraction; 24 to 25 years of age; six feet to six foot-six inches in height; 170 pounds; and wearing dark pants, black shoes and a purple colored jacket or sweater. According to the dispatch, the police were quoted as saying, "The man hitchhiked west from Prince Albert on Tuesday, the day of the murders."

Reports continued to come from far and wide.

CFCN Radio and Television News in neighboring Alberta, learned from "a usually reliable source", that a farm laborer was being sought. The suspect, whose name was withheld, was reported to be travelling by car bearing Saskatchewan licence plates. The man was said to have numerous stolen weapons in his possession. Among the weapons was a .22-calibre firearm. The RCMP in North Battleford, in a telephone conversation with me, declined to either confirm or deny the report. Inspector Sawyer said he did not care to comment either way.

As the search intensified, plans were underway for the funeral of the nine Petersons. The family members would be buried Saturday, four days after their lives were stolen from them.

MASS GRAVE — It entered our vocabulary with the Shell Lake killings. Before then, Canada had not known mass murder. Members of the sombre crew quietly went about their repugnant work.

— Journal Photo by Dave Reidie

INCONCEIVABLE — Speechless, two of the grave diggers stare at the cavernous pit. The names of the victims were written in chalk on the ends of rough wooden boxes that would hold the caskets. The baby would be buried with his mother.

— *Journal Photo by Dave Reidie*

THE Reverend Gerald Spence of the Anglican parish of Leask, which takes in the surrounding area of Shell Lake, was in charge of arrangements. He had known the Peterson family since 1966. At that time he prepared Kathy, Jean and Mary for confirmation. He later performed the ceremony in March 1966. The Reverend Spence had also given marriage instruction to Kathy, beginning near the end of May, 1967 and lasting over a period of about three weeks. On the last Sunday of June 1967 — the 25th — he baptized Colin, Larry and Phyllis; and on July 7th, he married Kathy and Lee Hill. It was this man who was now charged with the last rites for the Peterson family — a clan very close to his heart.

He first became aware of the deaths when he arrived home from Marcelin around 10:00 a.m., August 15th. Reverend Spence, who was completing last minute preparations prior to leaving for a holiday, received a message that had been telephoned to his home from Mrs. Mervin Madsen. The details were sketchy, however, it told that Jim and some of his children were dead and others in the family were missing. The pastor drove to Shell Lake, obtained further information from Mrs. Madsen, and then drove to the Peterson farm.

"I met a policeman and asked him how many were dead. He said nine. He walked one way and I walked the other — until we could face each other."

According to the minister, he was then taken around the house. Following this he viewed the body of Jim on the floor. He noticed the bullet holes in the screen. Then, as Reverend Spence recalled, he was brought around to the back of the house where he observed the mother.

"She was lying on her side in a running stride. Her head was toward the house and the baby had crawled around behind her. I say this because the infant's toes were still digging into the grass. The baby was lying near the mother's back."

Reverend Spence said he then went around the house and saw some men sitting by a hedge. They were Wildrew, and

Helmer and Cyril Mayo who, like Helmer, married one of Jim Peterson's two sisters.

"Then two men drove into the yard. They worked for a firm involved in carrying out the work of artificial insemination. The men apparently had been at the Peterson farm the night before the murders and when they left about 10 p.m. had closed the gate. They related this to the police. Boots worn by one of the men fitted footprints found in the vicinity."

Following this, according to Reverend Spence, the men did the necessary farm chores while the police continued to take photographs in and around the house. At around 2 p.m., the police were ready to have the victims identified. Reverend Spence was one of those who was faced with the horrible task.

"I went in the house with an RCMP Staff-Sergeant and Alvin. All the children had a calm and peaceful look as if there was [1]no struggle whatsoever. Jim was on the floor and it appeared as though he had been sleeping on the [2]chesterfield across from Dorothy, when he had gone to the door to see who

---

1. There are only two people who could know exactly what happened in the Peterson home during the early morning hours of August 15th. Phyllis related very little of any consequence. The killer told police a story of piercing screams, strange noises, and gurgling sounds. Questioned on this, an investigating officer at the scene said he was satisfied that the version told by the murderer was the correct one.

"There is nothing to indicate otherwise. The original noise (the uproar created while seven shots were pumped into the father) and size of the house would indicate that the members of the family would be awake. We're satisfied that this is the way it happened. Whether he ordered them to stay in the beds or whether they were afraid to move is another matter."

2. Concerning Jim sleeping on a chesterfield in the living room, the killer would later tell police. "I walked in the house and I see a guy, he was just sitting there on the bed then he said, "Who is it?" He kept on saying that and when he saw the gun, he jumped up on the bed and I shot him. He jumped off the bed and kept coming at me."

An RCMP officer, questioned on this, said he was satisfied with the version given by the killer.

"Jim's clothes were draped over a chair in the bedroom. I'm satisfied that he was sleeping in the bedroom prior to the killings."

Another point raised by Reverend Spence was his feeling that Evelyn attempted her escape with the baby by going through the door.

He said, "If she had gone out the window she would have been lying in a different position."

The RCMP differed.

"The bedroom window was pushed open to the top. If she had gone out the door she would have had to go past the killer. There's no question that she made her escape attempt through the window."

was there.

All of the other children were in bed in their room. Jean had her hands under her cheek and it appeared as if she hadn't moved. They were all sleeping when they were shot. All were in normal sleeping positions. Half-a-bottle of milk was in the baby's crib. Outside, the window screens were propped up against the window. Mrs. Peterson lay there in a dress. It appeared as if she had been feeding the baby not long before the shootings."

NEITHER brother-in-law went inside the house that reeked with the stench of death. According to Reverend Spence, they asked if they could be excused. They came close to retching.

"When we came out of the house, the Staff-Sergeant and myself went for a walk. About all we said was, 'How could anyone do this?' His concern was that people were already saying, 'Why haven't you done something?' I asked him where he was going to start and he replied, 'My training says right here.'

"Soon afterwards the coroner, Dr. Calvin S. Lambert of Leoville, arrived." Reverend Spence said there was a problem getting one because it had to be someone who had not had any medical connection with the family for the previous four months.

"Once the coroner finished his work I met with him and when he asked who would take the funeral I told him I assumed I would. Helmer Helgeton overheard this and asked if I would stay with the relatives until, 'this is all finished.' I agreed to."

The minister then returned to Leask to try and obtain the birth, baptismal, confirmation and marriage records of the victims.

"One of the church wardens, Ernie Frank, offered to drive me back to Shell Lake on the night of August 15th. I had some of the records and knew where the rest would be so I decided to go back to the Peterson farm and give what information I had to the police. There was no roadblock when I left Shell Lake earlier but there was one when I returned. We were stopped and while a constable with a high-powered rifle held a gun on us, his finger was on the trigger, the other policeman did the talking. They let us proceed. I turned the records over to a policeman at the home and we returned to Leask. By this time the bodies had been moved and the house sealed off."

PLANS for the burial service were well underway by the next day. Reverend Spence travelled to the home of Helmer where he met Kathy and Lee. According to the minister, the young couple broke down and wept. He then discussed the solemnities with Helmer and it was decided that both would travel to Prince Albert to finalize arrangements. Reverend Spence, Mr. and Mrs. Helgeton and Mr. and Mrs. Mayo, set out for Prince Albert. The two women were left at Shellbrook where they would visit their parents. The men continued on to Prince Albert. Once there, they travelled to the funeral parlor where they picked out the caskets. At the suggestion of Reverend Spence, eight caskets were chosen rather than nine.

"I suggested the baby be buried with his mother. I thought it was fitting."

On the return trip to Shell Lake, the men stopped at Shellbrook where they visited the elderly Petersons. According to Reverend Spence, it was a good visit.

"They too had no bitterness. They had no idea who the killer was. They were sure he was mentally ill."

REPRESENTATIVES of news gathering agencies remained at the search headquarters. It had been moved from Spiritwood to Shell Lake. Still concentrating around the murder scene; the checking of firearms, interviewing neighbors and tracing 'strange vehicles' con-

HEADQUARTERS — The central gathering point for investigators. Reporters were given limited information during scheduled briefings.
— *Journal Photo by Dave Reidie*

tinued. Staff-Sergeant Sondergaard, who was to have retired but was pressed into service upon discovery of the crime, was questioned on the possibility of FBI involvement in the manhunt.

"It's unlikely that FBI facilities will be requested," he replied. Elaborating, he offered: "It's hard to fathom a stranger coming into an area like this, picking a farm and wiping out a family. We have not ruled out the possibility it was someone in the area although there is nothing definite on this. We are not holding anyone for questioning."

The Staff-Sergeant added, "Police departments have been alerted for several suspects."

Investigators from the plain-clothes section were reconstructing every stage in the life of the Peterson family. Details were uncovered that were unknown by even the closest relatives — like the dispute Jim and another man had in a hayloft. The argument had taken place in 1938.

The police were unable to turn up anything against the family.

As a spokesman said, "There was no scandal, dissension, or anything."

Extensive interviews were conducted with Kathy. As far as she was concerned, the family had no enemies. Both Kathy and Phyllis were transported to Saskatoon where Phyllis was taken to a psychologist. It was hoped she would divulge something that might help in the investigation. She did not.

The search continued. There was hope the consciousless crime would soon be solved. There was also despair that perhaps it would not. The reasoning behind this was that the warped thinking of such an insensible intruder, or however many people were involved, would be so inextricably distorted that police, with no normal pattern to follow, would be stumped.

Radio reports that an all points bulletin had been issued for a male suspect were quickly denied. Inspector Sawyer, in refuting the story, did confirm, however, that a communique had been issued once and "possibly twice" in connection with "a man" — not necessarily a suspect.

The Inspector added, "In such a matter the RCMP like to disseminate the information as widely as possible." The specific details were not given to reporters.

There was relatively nothing new reported. Patrol cars with officers and dogs were dispatched from point to point. Information was still being sought about persons who were known to have travelled from northern Saskatchewan around the time of the slayings. As police requests reached various cities, the speculation mounted that a definite suspect was being sought. Each was categorically denied.

As one investigating officer said, "The search is still wide open."

INSPECTOR Sawyer informed his now 75 member troop that the same ground would again have to be examined. Each of the four teams would take a different section in the hope that something would be uncovered. The investigators were also informed that it would be necessary to have all owners of .22-calibre rifles, fire two shots. The spent casings would be forwarded to the crime laboratory in Regina, the queen city, where investigators were skilled in scientific crime detection.

The nearby Sandy Lake Indian Reserve was checked out.

There were no leads reported. The RCMP were continuing to co-ordinate their efforts with police departments throughout North America. Despite widespread inquiries, there was no official indication that the intense activity would be abandoned in the immediate vicinity. Questioning in the village — population 250 — intensified.

A police spokesman said, "The questioning and minute search of territory within 20 miles of the Peterson house has revealed no clues."

Service stations were also part of the probe. Policemen were interested in gas purchases made during the early morning hours of August 15th. There was nothing learned that would aid in solving the multiple homicide without calculated motive.

Inspector Sawyer knew what would happen if the efforts failed to produce results. More officers would be called in. As well, the focused area would be enlarged.

THREE days after the dawn of terror, it appeared as if no headway was being made. The scene shifted to the village of Shell Lake where funeral arrangements were being made by the residents of the small farming community. A trust fund was also well underway. Its purpose was to defray the expense of the burial and also take care of the material needs of the survivor.

It was also 72 hours after the victims had been discovered that Phyllis talked of the chilling violence that took place. The police had never attempted to talk to Phyllis because of the strain it would have placed on her. Kathy gently tried to get her to relate anything that might help in the apprehension of the person or persons responsible. On the third night — it was just before bedtime that Phyllis was the most vulnerable — she talked to her sister.[3] She did not say much and could not describe nor relate anything that was of any help. Outside, two RCMP officers remained on guard. They were posted to the Hill farm home where Kathy and Phyllis were staying following the older sister's arrival back in the region with her husband Lee. The sentry was assigned one of the most nerve-wracking tasks. It meant waiting throughout the night, having to check every sound. The movement of livestock, snapping twigs, and

---

3.The police could have released fictitious data to the public, leaving the false impression that more information had been obtained from Phyllis than was the case. This could have been done, in an attempt to entice the murderer or murderers out into the open. It could also have resulted in the guilty leaving the area. It was something that was deemed, "too risky."

other noises in the bush — all had to be investigated. It was pitch black, lonely shadowed country, and each rustle could have been someone attempting to finish off the two remaining members of the Peterson family. Fear filled the stock-still air.

A report was circulating that the search had been narrowed to one suspect. Officials would neither confirm nor deny the story.

"We are checking every possible lead."

Optimism was evident, if only because of the sheer indefatigable determination being shown by investigators. The stark reality that 27 of 28 bullets had riddled the victims, that most had been fired from short range, and the depraved manner in which the family had been annihilated, spurred the manhunt on to enormous heights. Members of the force were in a state of enervation. They were also obsessed in their relentless quest for potent evidence.

Operating from relocated headquarters in Shell Lake's municipal hall, a statement was issued that was meaningless.

"We have no suspects in mind."

The announcement was made on the eve of the interment of the Peterson family.

That night, as well as all others during the investigation, the police officers met at 10 o'clock at their headquarters. Behind closed doors, all the information garnered to that time was reviewed. Every aspect of the investigation, even items which seemed to have little importance, were completely analyzed. The investigation was thorough. No shred of information, no matter how trivial, was overlooked. While the investigating officers met in private, the news media were not forgotten. Briefings were held three times daily. At 10 a.m., 2 p.m. and again at 8 p.m.

Inspector Sawyer had a theory that the murderer was psychotic. All persons with such a history would have to be checked out. This included not only former mental patients, but penitentiary releases as well.

CORPORAL Charles Nolan was located outside the prime area but the distance was not that great. In charge of the Shellbrook detachment, about 35 miles east of Shell Lake, he received information, by way of a casual conversation, that a boy who lived near Leask had been recently discharged from a mental hospital. Corporal Nolan, who received the tip from a farmer who lived in the Leask district, would check it out.

SOME 1,500 people were in attendance for the outdoor service conducted by the Reverend Gerald Spence of Leask. He had received several telephone calls after the killings and had been offered help from numerous clergy. According to Reverend Spence, it was decided two days before the funeral that Canon Douglas Gregory of Meadow Lake, Saskatchewan would assist. The day before the funeral, Reverend Spence met with members of the RCMP to finalize plans for an orderly procedure.

"I was concerned about the possibility of photographers getting between myself and the family. It had also been decided that the entire funeral service would be held at the cemetery. Numerous factors were taken into consideration: the stress on the family, the police using the hall in Shell Lake and the traffic problems that would be encountered driving from Shell Lake to the graveyard. I suggested that the whole service be conducted at the graveside. The relatives were agreeable and so it was suggested that there be one big grave with timbers used to lower the coffins into place. The grave was dug on Friday, the day before the funeral."

The Royal Canadian Legion provided a guard of honor. It was for the head of this victimized family who had served overseas for his country during the Second World War. Jim Peterson had joined the Canadian Army as soon as he was of age. He remained in the service for three years before being honorably discharged with the rank of Lance Corporal in

1946. He had never been injured but had come close. Jokingly, while talking about his service, he would always recall the story of how he just about did not make it. His shaving kit would be produced, and with it, the all too noticeable bullet hole that had ripped through its casing. Following his discharge, Jim had been active in the Legion for a number of years. Later, he let his membership lapse. He had rejoined about a year and a half before the tragedy and had attended the majority of the organization's meetings. The Royal Canadian Legion was represented for this man. A man who died, not fighting for his country, but valiantly trying to protect his family from an apparently cunning intruder who had gone berserk. He had arrived and departed without detection and robbery seemed a highly unlikely motive.

The grave was 16 feet long, 10 feet wide, and six feet deep. It was standing open, ready to receive the bodies of the ill-fated family. Eight caskets were needed. The body of one-year-old Larry would be with the remains of his mother.

Reverend Spence arrived at the cemetery at about 1 p.m. to prepare for the funeral. The service began at 2 o'clock. A quiet, sombre ceremony conducted in the normal church service. It was an attempt to be a comfort to all. As those observing the last rites listened, some only heard a few of the words delivered by the preacher. Many were distracted by the improbable sight before them, others were lost in private moments of meditation.

"Ever since the moment last Tuesday when word of this tragedy reached out into the community; every one of us has wished and hoped and prayed that we would wake up tomorrow morning to find that this is not so. Much as we all would wish this had not happened — it has!

"We are all struggling with our feelings and our fears and it would be so easy to become very bitter in

*our thoughts and within ourselves; even though we
know that this would not change the situation nor
bring the family back to us.*

*"I would like to share with you a small part of the
experience of this past week which I have had and
which has been a great help in keeping bitter thoughts
from crowding into my mind and beating me down
into the depth of despair.*

*"Some of you may know that I went into the home
with the police and identified the members of the family
for them. I saw each one lying where they had been
shot; I saw something else too, something I cannot
explain, a mystery, but a mystery which has taken the
bitterness out of this terrible tragedy for me and I
would share it with you now. There was no look of pain
on the face of any one of them, we cannot imagine the
horror and terror that must have existed for a time, no
one will ever know. But in the midst of all that terror
and pain and fear, an unseen hand stretched out, and
a power that is greater than any we can imagine
touched each one; and in the place of fear and pain,
came calm and peace.*

*"On each face was a look of calm and peaceful quiet,
in the midst of all that horror, God came and touched
each one and gave them release from all the pain and
fear. They were at peace. That sight has kept me going
this past few days, I share it with you now that it may
support both you and I in the days to come.*

*"They rest in peace, I am sure of that, but as time
goes on we will all need reassurance of this. I ask your
prayers for the members of the family who are left and
for myself as I minister to them in the days ahead."*

Jim's coffin was draped with a Canadian flag. The Royal
Canadian Legion conducted a service. Members saluted the

coffin as a bugler sounded The Last Post.

Schoolmates, family, friends and the curious were all in attendance. The list was numberless — estimated conservatively at 1,500 people, six times the population of the community.

A bouquet of roses was on the coffin of Evelyn and the baby. The coffins of the other children bore single red roses.

Tears streamed down ashen, grief-stricken faces as the nine family members were lowered into the enormous, empty grave. The eight caskets were covered with dirt. The common tomb, located at the base of a large Spruce tree, had no headstones. Small back markers with white lettering spelled out the names of the victims. An incredible sight.

Mary J. 1954-1967

Dorothy E. 1956-1967

Pearl E. 1957-1967

William J. 1961-1967.

Located behind the first four victims were more.

Jean M. 1950-1967

Colin A. 1964-1967

Larry F. 1966-1967

Evelyn M. 1925-1967

James F.H., with no birthdate evident.

It seemed beyond the realm of the possible. A sight never to be forgotten, witnessed in the tiny farming community by locals and outsiders who never would have imagined in their worst nightmares that such a ghastly and horrid scene would ever present itself — yet it was unfolding before their very eyes.

THE 17-minute Anglican service was over. The cemetery began returning to the quiet and serenity that was there before and would once again prevail.

During the funeral, investigators were at work. A police guard hovered near Phyllis, posted at the home of her aunt and uncle, Helmer and Evie, while they paid their last respects. Meantime, police photographers from Saskatoon were at God's Acre taking pictures of the crowd. Inspector Sawyer had also instructed his members to record the licence numbers of the parked vehicles. Certainly, it was a longshot but it was necessary. Every possibility had to be scrutinized. None could be discounted.

NEWS outlets continued to report the number of people who had attended the burial, along with the chilling background leading up to it. CFCN Calgary had learned that a man was in custody and was being questioned in connection with the case. It appeared as if the vital break had come. Investigators were flown to the southern Alberta city to interrogate the suspect.

Within hours, RCMP Staff-Sergeant E.R. Blatta, issued a statement saying that questioning of the suspect had concluded. The Staff-Sergeant said that reports pertaining to the interrogation were being sent to Shell Lake. He declined comment as to whether or not the man had been released. In Shell Lake, Staff-Sergeant Sondergaard also reacted.

"I have not read the reports as yet and do not care to comment until such time as I do."

Shortly afterwards the police officer issued a statement that concluded the issue.

"To our satisfaction he was nowhere in the vicinity of Shell Lake at the time of the murders."

He went on to say that the person picked up in Calgary was of no more interest to police.

The man had not been charged by Calgary police but had only been taken into custody for questioning. It seemed futile, as though the detached slayer had disappeared into thin air when he escaped into the dark.

The public was beginning to wonder whether the reprehensible crime would ever be solved. Detectives were very clear, however, in saying that a break could come within the next day or so. When that statement was issued a prime suspect had already been arrested. He was taken into custody three hours after the funeral and would soon be charged with the blood-curdling atrocity that had rocked the nation.

THE PROCESSION — No church in the area had room for such a service. Canon Douglas Gregory and Reverend Gerald Spence begin the solemn ceremony as they move toward the graveside.

— Journal Photo by Dave Reidie

FINAL CASKET — Legion members lift the eighth coffin onto its resting place of timbers. Larry was laid to rest with his mother who died holding him.

— *Journal Photo by Dave Reidie*

STILLNESS OF DEATH — *Comfort without words.* — Journal Photo by Dave Reidie

UNTOLD MOURN-
ING — Six times the 250
population of Shell Lake
paid their respects. All
stores and businesses in
the village were closed.
— Journal Photo by Dave Reidie

LAST POST — The sound of a lone bugler while Legion members saluted the flag-draped coffin of the slain husband and father.

— Journal Photo by Dave Reidie

GRIEF STRICKEN —
*The needless waste of so
very many innocent lives
broke the hearts of many.*
— *Journal Photo by Dave Reidie*

CAPTURED

VI

R OBERT Hoffman knew something was wrong. He awakened August 15th to discover that his son Victor was gone. It played on his mind that he had heard the engine of a car, fading down the road, early that morning. At the time he did not want to believe that it was Victor but now he was unsure. He began to worry at the thought of his son's actions since his release from The Saskatchewan Hospital.

Yet, "last night it seemed as if everything was finally going to be all right."

He started doing the daily chores. The job began at 6:30 and entailed milking the cows and feeding the pigs. Victor was not around to help.

According to Robert, the dust-covered sedan pulled into the yard around eight o'clock. Victor, who was driving, would later relate that it was shortly after 7:30. Showing no sign of having been in trouble, he stepped out of the car and began walking over to the garage. He stood there for some time before his father noticed he had returned.

"Where have you been," Robert demanded.

"Oh! I went to the other farm to see if there was any deer."

Victor's father did not detect anything that indicated his son had done anything untoward. The two proceeded to finish the chores. Robert, carrying a pail towards the pasture, was startled when Victor's voice boomed.

"What are we going to do?"

The question was uncalled for. It was as obvious as the cows themselves what was going to be done.

Taken aback, Robert asked, "Are you through with the summerfallow?"

"No, I'm not," Victor answered, slowly.

He then picked up a bucket and began milking the cows. It was time for breakfast. As father and son entered the house, the younger Hoffman seemed to be in a dream world, as if in a descent from the land of the living. Almost as though he had plunged into an emotional abyss.

Ironically, as the family tuned in for the local news, the only radio in the house began acting up. Emitting a few words, it would then static, finally going mute. The two men had not heard any of the report, however Stella had. She managed to hear portions of the top story.

She announced, "There's been an awful accident at Shell Lake."

The only other words she had heard were "kill" or perhaps it was "killed".

Her husband replied, "We can't help it if people kill themselves."

Remaining silent, Victor did not react. With his head bowed, his blurry blue eyes downcast, he continued gulping his meal.

Following breakfast, the mother remained in the kitchen tidying up. Her husband and son went outside to begin haying. The job was strenuous. Victor, tiring, his energy wasted, wanted to go into the house and sleep.

"The pills from the hospital are making me feel drowsy."

As his son went in to rest, Robert wondered. He thought of

numerous things: the hospital, the pills and how his son was acting. Continuing his work, the musings gradually disappeared.

It was foolish. The hospital must be right. They must know that Victor is normal or they would not have released him.

As Stella was to say later: "If the psychiatrists said Victor was all right, how were we to know any different."

THERE was little change within the next two days. The work, the meals and the rest periods all combined to fill the time and make it pass quickly.

Friday, August 18th. Robert went into town. The family needed groceries but primarily the trip was made because of a lack of fuel for the farm equipment. Robert stopped at a neighbor's along the way and was immediately asked if he had heard the details of the terrible tragedy at Shell Lake. He had not and related how the family radio had broken down before all of the news item had come across. The story was then read to him because his glasses had been forgotten at home.

"I couldn't believe it. It just didn't seem possible."

Robert returned home. Following lunch, he began unloading bales of hay from a rack located near the main area of the farmyard. Victor was not wholeheartedly contributing to the work. He was exhausted. He seemed laggardly, his movements sluggish, his mind numb.

CORPORAL Charles Nolan along with five other policemen arrived at the Hoffman farm and entered the yard.

"That's quite a load you've got there," one of the officers shouted.

There was no reply.

"How many guns do you have?", a policeman inquired.

Visibly shaken, Robert replied, "I'll go and have a look."

He was not accustomed to dealing with the law. Upset, he

went to Victor's car where he thought the .303-calibre rifle would be located. Victor said he had been out looking for deer on the other farm and his father had not seen him remove the gun since his return.

Opening the door to show the police the .303-calibre rifle, Robert was stunned. Lying across the back seat was a .22-calibre weapon. It was a discovery he had never expected.

"It wasn't used that often. Only to scare off rustlers and bears, and none had been around for so long I can't remember when. I certainly never expected to find it in the car. It was usually left hanging in the garage."

Spotting the weapon at the same time as Robert, Corporal Nolan grabbed it. Appraising the .22-calibre Belgium Browning pump-action repeater, the officer requested the youth's father to unload it. Five or six shells were removed.

Examining his find, Corporal Nolan happened to glance over to the front porch of the home. He became alarmed — spotting two pairs of rubber boots. One pair looked familiar. The gun, as well as the boots, were taken and the police departed. Before they did, Victor worried that he might need the boots the next day because his feet could get wet. His father assured him that he would get them back.

A quiet, affable man, Corporal Nolan felt confident he had seized the right weapon. He persisted in his belief even though the gun had not been made by one of the three companies listed by the lab. What they did not know at the time was that the company that made the con-fiscated rifle, for a brief period, used barrels manufactured by one of the firms cited. Corporal Nolan was undeterred and later would be commended by Crown prosecutor Serge Kujawa. His diligence was "key" said the lawman, "When the evidence was rejected he would not allow them to let go."

ARRIVING at command headquarters, Corporal Nolan handed his exhibits over to his commanding officer. Inspector Sawyer in turn passed them to an identification expert. Several rounds were fired and the spent casings studied. Then — it was decided to forward the exhibits, by plane, to the crime lab.

Inspector Sawyer dispatched a patrol car to the Hoffman property to keep it under surveillance. The next morning, when the Inspector received word that the weapon had not been ruled out, a second unit was sent to the farm.

Police would also talk with residents of the Leask district to try and determine whether Victor knew the Peterson family. Their queries failed to disclose any association.

Although the Hoffman residence was under surveillance, the RCMP continued to check other leads. A clairvoyant had approached authorities in Winnipeg, Manitoba and provided information which he claimed would result in the apprehension of the killer. The data was relayed to the search headquarters, considered and subsequently written off.

VICTOR was out in the fields haying with Allan. It was now another day but still the episode with the police played on their minds. Robert was the first to notice. The police were back.

Inspector Sawyer had received a telephone call from a ballistics expert in Regina.

"Is it the gun?" the Inspector asked.

The answer was definite: "In my opinion it is."

It was later revealed that the unusual impression left by the firing pin was the deciding factor. More than 50 firearms had been examined before the Hoffman rifle was identified as the murder weapon. It had been fitted with a home-made firing pin and it was this mark that distinguished it from the other guns that had been seized.

Sergeant Fraser, Corporal Arnold (Gus) Gawthrop and

several other members of the force were advised of the findings. They were ordered to obtain a search warrant and did so
by driving to Shellbrook. It would have been faster to get one
in Shell Lake but there was fear that word would get to the
news reporters attending the Peterson funeral. Police cruisers
were driving up and down, bordering the farm. The patrol
cars repeated the process again and again. One of the cruisers
moved into the centre of the farmyard. At that precise moment, one of the dogs, Rex, a Labrador Cocker Spaniel mix,
reared. Hair standing on end, and baring its teeth, the mostly
black animal, Victor's favorite, began emitting a series of
penetrating barks. At that exact second, Robert wondered,
"Did Victor do that? Could he be responsible for what had
happened at Shell Lake?"

By this time, her hands trembling, Stella was out in the yard.
She heard the police radio blare.

The order was, "Move in!"

A policeman asked her where Victor was.

"He's in the fields with Allan."

A second squad car was positioning itself to ward off any
trouble from Victor's father. It was impossible to predict how
he would react.

"If they're going to take him they'll take him," was what
went through Robert's mind.

Allan stopped the tractor. Sergeant Fraser told Victor, who
was riding in a mower behind the unit, that he wanted to talk
with him about the Peterson murders. The arrest was made.
Victor, sensitized by his surroundings, was not visually surprised. He surrendered willingly and without protest. He
acted as if nothing out of the ordinary was taking place. Before
departing for North Battleford, the hard-driven 1950 Chrysler
product, Victor's, was removed from the farm.

C ONVERSATION during the 80-mile ride to North
Battleford was stilted. Sergeant Fraser asked Victor
if he had been away from home recently.

"I went to Leask on Tuesday and bought some .22-calibre shells and a pocketknife."

"Why the knife?"

"I wanted to cut string."

The suspect then asked where they were going. When informed they were travelling to North Battleford it was a jolt to his sensibilities.

"You mean to the hospital?"

"No, to police headquarters."

Victor remained outwardly calm, almost nonchalent. His voice affectless.

Sergeant Fraser questioned, "Have you heard about the killings?"

"Yes, dad told me after coming back from town. Our radio didn't work and I didn't watch the television news," replied Victor.

Corporal Gawthrop asked, "Victor, do you have a .22-calibre rifle?"

"Yes, the cops took it."

There was utter stillness. Then, Victor, throwing caution to the wind, blurted out what he had been struggling to hold inside.

"If my gun killed those people, does that make me a murderer?"

Neither officer replied.

Sergeant Fraser asked, "What kind of a person would kill the Petersons?"

Victor responded, "They'd have to be crazy."

The tension-filled journey continued.

Corporal Gawthrop remarked, "It was lucky two of the Peterson children survived."

There was no comment. Victor stiffened. The police car passed a cemetery.

"There are a lot of dead people in there," Victor said.

The interior of the squad car was stilled.

T HE trio arrived at police headquarters shortly after 6:30 that evening. The formal questioning began. Asked to outline his activities around the time of the murders, Victor said that on Monday night he went to Jimmy Peake's house to see a new shotgun. His friend was not home but his sister was. After talking with her for a while, Victor said he went home and fell asleep on the couch.

"Dad got me up about two hours later (11:30) and I went up to bed."

Victor continued to tell the officers that he could not sleep and finally at about 4 o'clock the next morning, went outside to work in the garage. He said that about an hour later he went to the family's other nearby farm to see if there were any deer. The officers were told that he was back home shortly after 7:30, had breakfast and went back to work.

"What about the rubber boots, Victor?"

"Someone took them."

"How did they get back?"

There was no answer.

Sergeant Fraser asked, "Did you know the Petersons?"

"No."

Victor was left alone with Corporal Edgar Kuhn. There were no more questions. Shortly afterwards, Corporal Gawthrop and Sergeant Fraser returned.

The Sergeant was blunt, "We don't believe your story about the boots."

There was no reply.

Corporal Gawthrop said firmly, "You might as well get it off your mind."

Subdued, Victor lowered his head. The room went deathly silent.

"Okay I killed them, I tried to change the rifling on it. I should have burned that house, then you would not have found those cartridges. I thought I picked them all up. I stopped at the gate. I don't know what made me do it. I collected 17 cartridges. If that dog had been there I never would have gone in. I didn't want to shoot anymore, the one left didn't see me."

The two policemen brought out the tape recorder. The play and record buttons were punched simultaneously but the device failed. Corporal Gawthrop left the building. He ran a few hundred yards to his home where he would get his own machine.

The interrogation room was like a mortuary. It was soundless. Then, Victor began wondering aloud as to his future. He paced the floor.

"Do you think I'll get the chair?"

He was told that the electric chair was not used in Canada. Victor was again without sound. He then spoke.

"Oh, yeah. They hang 'em. I'll bet you I get at least 50 years."

Again, no one said a word. The prisoner then glanced around the room and spotted two gun holsters hanging on a coat rack. The guns had been removed.

"I could grab one of those guns and kill you all, but I can't kill anymore."

Victor was placed in a cell. His clothing would be sent to the RCMP laboratory where particles of blood would be found on his previously seized boots, baggy blue jeans, red and white polka dot handkerchief, and brown leather gloves.

A few hours after the arrest and the grim services at Shell Lake, The Royal Canadian Mounted Police issued a statement. CP bulletined the long awaited information. The country's largest news gathering agency reported,

> "A man has been arrested in Saskatchewan's Peterson family murder case. He has not been identified. And police have given limited details of the arrest. It was made late in the afternoon, about two hours after the

funeral of Mr. and Mrs. James Peterson and seven of
their children who were buried in a common grave at
Shell Lake, 50 miles from Prince Albert. The Petersons
were found shot to death Tuesday. The arrest followed
a routine investigation, and the man taken into custody
put up no resistance. He'll appear in court either
tomorrow (Sunday) or Monday. Police also said a .22-
calibre rifle they found has been identified as the murder
weapon."

I immediately telephoned the RCMP at Shell Lake. Less than an hour before, a statement had been issued from the same office saying that there were no new developments to report.

A police spokesman said the arrested man would probably be arraigned in North Battleford magistrates court the following day.

According to the officer, "It's expected he will be formally charged with capital murder."

The name, age and place of residence of the suspect was withheld. It was not revealed where the man was apprehended.

Staff-Sergeant Sondergaard said, "Evidence in the case is substantial and a gun that was seized has been identified as the murder weapon. The accused was apprehended by one or two members of the force."

Another spokesman told me, "The big question now is whether he'll ever stand trial. He'll probably be given a psychiatric examination in North Battleford."

CORPORAL Gawthrop and Sergeant Fraser left police headquarters. It was now after midnight. They travelled to the home of Inspector Sawyer to inform him of their revealing conversation with the accused. Over a meal, the two policemen outlined the facts to their commanding officer.

The manhunt was over. Exhaustive police work, conducted 24 hours a day, had produced results. The arrest came only four days after the horrid discovery in the little farmhouse at Shell Lake.

Inspector Sawyer praised the work of his men who had a fixation with solving the repulsive, savage encounter.

He said the result was indicative of what can happen with "long, hard, plodding investigative work."

ALTHOUGH some believed there was a truly unshakeable case, others knew differently. It was not clear-cut. There was no lawyer present during Victor's interview. The statements, said one top legal mind, "were probably not admissable." It would be necessary to place the accused at the scene and that could only be done by gathering additional evidence. Pictures, money, a wallet or anything else that would link the slayer. As the legal expert told me, "Until Victor got into a car and went to the pasture to get that stuff — we had nothing."

THE announced arrest brought sighs of relief. The murderer, apparently, had been caught. It was safe to go outside after dark. One could stop worrying that the killer would return. This was the response, even though the suspect had not been formally charged in a court of law. People jumped to conclusions. It had been a tragedy that caused them to shed tears openly. It had resulted in them shuddering at the sound of anything strange. It had been nerve-shattering. They were glad it was over. The residents of Shell Lake and area slept better that night than they had since learning of the brutal slayings. They slept, however, in all-embracing anticipation. Who was this despicable human being? What connection did he have with the Petersons? Why did he kill the children? Is he someone we know? Perhaps when his name was released, the secret of the massacre would no longer remain a mystery. Perhaps then a motive for such a distorted, contemptible act would come to light. The night passed — much more peacefully than those preceding it.

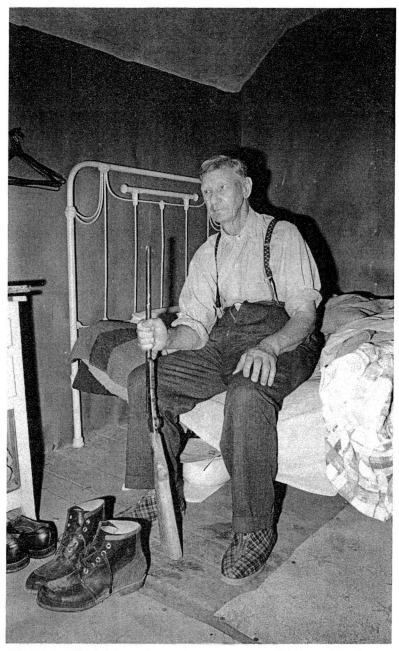

SYMBOL OF FEAR   *Armed with an ancient .22 calibre rifle as he sat on his bed, 80-year-old Nelson Moore represented the fear that gripped residents of the area. Mr. Moore, a friend of the family, lived in a tiny log cabin just down the road from the Peterson farm.*   — *Journal Photo by Dave Reidie*

122

TERROR-STRICKEN COMMUNITY—There are no guns sighted in this village hall meeting but farmers had been carrying them everywhere. Now that an arrest had been made such gatherings could cease.

— *Journal Photo by Dave Reidie*

GLOBAL
REACTION

VII

R OBERT and Stella knew that their son had been taken to North Battleford. They also knew he would be questioned in connection with the slayings. What they did not know, maintained the father, was that he would be charged.

The day following Victor's capture, Robert was visiting a nearby farm occupied by very good friends. He listened as the radio blared.

> *"The RCMP in North Battleford have released the name of the man they are holding in connection with the slaying of the James Peterson family at Shell Lake last Tuesday. Police today identified the man as 21-year-old Victor Ernest Hoffman of the Leask District."*

Robert broke down and wept.

"I never cried so much in my life. It pretty near killed me."

The broadcast continued. More details, including a statement by Inspector Sawyer.

"All necessary security precautions have been taken to

safeguard the suspect. The evidence to support the charge is substantial."

News reports said the police advised the Hoffman family to retain a lawyer. Robert said that someone, he was not sure who, suggested he get counsel but it was not the RCMP.

The evidence was indeed massive. The crime laboratory had not only found traces of human blood on articles taken from Victor at the time of his arrest. The technicians would also examine two wallets, with identification in the name of Jean Peterson and her mother. The billfolds, which according to Victor contained seven dollars, were located in the crevice of a large rock on the Hoffman farm. He had taken police there and also shown them where he had thrown the cartridges in tall, thick grass. What some call, "prairie wool."

Robert was astonished.

"Did my boy really kill those people? It just couldn't be?"

The news was out.

Stella took it as one might expect — total denial.

"Victor couldn't have done it."

The suspect's younger sister, Bernice, telephoned her parents. She had heard the story the same way as her father, via a radio newscast. She was attending school away from home and was shocked to hear about her brother. Weeping, she told her father she would be unable to complete her examinations. Bernice wanted to come home.

Robert told her, "Work and pass for my sake."

She succeeded with her tests.

I T was Sunday, August 20th, and the reign of terror had ended. With the release of the suspect's name, relief swept the area. Still, there was no indication of a motive. There were no details as to the background of this man accused of systematically slaughtering nine people.

I placed a long distance call moments after the suspect's name had been released. It was to the Hoffman residence.

Stella answered. After identifying myself, the questioning began.

PT — Was your son ever in a mental hospital?

Stella — Yes. He came home near the end of July.

PT — How long had he been there?

Stella — Since the end of May.

PT — Did you know the Petersons?

Stella — No! No!

PT — To your knowledge, did Victor?

Stella — No! No! It's out of line. We're in a different district.

PT — Where is your farm in relation to the Petersons?

Stella — Oh gosh! I don't know.

PT — Did Victor talk about the killings?

Stella — No! No!

PT — No mention at all?

Stella — No! No!

PT — Had he ever been in trouble with the police?

Stella — I can't tell you nothing about that.

PT — You have five children?

Stella — Oh gosh! I have seven.

PT — How old is the youngest?

Stella — Fourteen. That's all the information I'll give you.

PT — Fine, what you've said helps very much. Why did Victor go to North Battleford?

Stella — Seeding grain. He was poisoned.

At this point the conversation concluded. Stella terminated it by slamming down the telephone receiver. She was sick.

This day, she was the country's most important woman. Her son had been arrested in connection with the senseless loss of so many lives. The information garnered from her would afford some insight into what possibly triggered the dementia on the early morning of August 15th.

News gathering sources from near and far were clamoring

for more details. The content of Stella's interview was widely distributed to numerous sources.

Associated Press, Canadian Press, Broadcast News, the *Vancouver Sun, Standard Radio News,* and the country's privately owned television network, *CTV,* were among those provided the story.

The most important piece of information obtained from Mrs. Hoffman was that her son had been a patient at a mental hospital and had been released such a short time before the killings. It not only rendered background on the accused but it also raised questions concerning his capture. During the search, Inspector Sawyer had a theory that the murderer was psychotic, a psycopath on the loose. As a result, all persons with such a history had to be checked out within the search area. It was because of this that I later questioned the Inspector concerning the investigation of released mental patients and penitentiary inmates. The RCMP has access to the files of released prison inmates so the questioning revolved around The Saskatchewan Hospital in North Battleford.

PT — Did the RCMP approach the mental institution for the names of patients who had been recently released?

Inspector Sawyer — I really don't think I should comment on that.

PT — Was a list of names supplied by the mental institution?

Inspector Sawyer — The development of a list from a jail or mental institution is not something that I would acknowledge. We checked every name introduced to us that was worthy of being checked. We were flooded with information. Every name received was checked out.

PT — Was the RCMP given any names from the hospital?

Inspector Sawyer — I don't think I should comment on that.

PT — Prior to receiving the tip from a nearby resident of the Hoffman farm, was the RCMP aware of the name Victor Ernest Hoffman?

Inspector Sawyer — Until the tip was received from the person who lived nearby, the RCMP had no particular interest in anyone by the name of Victor Ernest Hoffman.

IT was presumed that an automatic reaction of the RCMP would have been to approach The Saskatchewan Hospital for the names of recently released patients. If the request was made, then the name of Victor Ernest Hoffman should have been supplied to the police in the early stages of their investigation. It could have resulted in an arrest long before the eventual apprehension. The RCMP, like most police agencies, are usually extremely cautious in releasing information to the public via the news media.

Inspector Sawyer did divulge, however, that "Until the tip was received from the person who lived nearby, the RCMP had no particular interest in anyone by the name of Victor Ernest Hoffman." He also stated, "Every name received was checked out."

If a request was made for the identity of recently released patients — it should be emphasized that there is no reason to suggest it was not — then it seems clear that the asylum failed to provide Victor's name to the RCMP. He was released from the hospital less than three weeks prior to the murder of nine people and he lived approximately 45 miles from the scene of the crime. If the name had been supplied to the police it is reasonable to assume that an arrest would have been made much sooner than it was.

It was much later when a retired RCMP officer would confirm that the hospital had indeed refused to make available a list of names to police. It meant a time-consuming delay of having to appeal to the Minister of Justice and then to the Minister of Health. It was ludicrous but when the record was finally produced it only contained information about patients in the immediate vicinity of the crime. Missing was the name of the most important ex-patient who lived not more than one hour away.

In less than 24 hours, the suspect would be appearing in court. Attention was focused in North Battleford where he would be arraigned before a packed courtroom on the second floor of the City Police Station. It was a short drive from his RCMP cell.

REVEREND Spence, who departed on a vacation following the funeral, became aware of the arrest, Sunday, August 20th. Sadly, he discovered he knew both the victims and the family of the man arrested.

"In 1962, Victor Dominick and his wife came for confirmation instruction while I was stationed in Paddockwood, Saskatchewan. In 1964, the couple came to Leask to meet Stella Hoffman who was attending a church service. Following the service, I learned that Stella was the former Stella Dominick, a sister to Victor Dominick."

SOME 200 people waited. It was Monday, August 21st. Soon the alleged gunman could be viewed. In addition to the large crowd outside, another 50 crowded the courtroom[1] to see the suspect whisked in a side door. Handcuffed and under heavy guard while being transported from an RCMP cell, Victor was escorted by two police officers into the prisoner's box. The law would now begin dealing with him.

When his name was called he rose immediately and answered, "Yes."

A charge of capital murder in the death of James Peterson was then read to the 5'8", 165-pound spiritless accused. He was expressionless. Judge J.M. Policha of the Provincial Magistrate's court did not ask for a plea. He did, however, ask the accused if he had defence counsel.

"No. But the cops said I'd get one."

1.Among the 50 spectators inside the courtroom were: Kathy Hill; her husband, Lee; her father-in-law, and a brother-in-law. Robert and Stella did not attend. Neither did any of Victor's brothers or sisters.

Victor, who said he did not think he could get a lawyer himself, agreed to allow the court to appoint one for him.

The shy, tranquil prisoner; wearing a soiled white and blue striped shirt, was remanded 30 days for psychiatric examination to The Saskatchewan Hospital in North Battleford.

The crew-cut young man worried about his future.

"Does this mean I'll get shock treatment?"

Judge Policha replied, "I do not really know, but I believe there will be a preliminary examination by doctors."

Victor, who stroked a bandage on his right thumb throughout portions of his 10-minute arraignment, was again handcuffed to an RCMP officer. He was escorted from the courtroom. His picture, a pathetic sight snapped by a photographer from the *Saskatoon StarPhoenix* newspaper, was given front-page treatment everywhere, it seemed.

Judge Policha went out of town on business. He returned later that evening and at approximately 11 p.m. approached North Battleford lawyer George E. (Ted) Noble to determine if he would consider handling the case for the defence.

"I agreed to, providing he was examined by an outside psychiatrist. I also wanted permission to have him examined by two other outside psychiatrists. Because this is rather an expensive business, I wanted to get as many opinions as I thought were reasonable under the circumstances."

As far as most people were concerned, the mental state of the accused was not expected to be revealed for 30 days.

Public reaction mounted. It was two weeks to the day that the Petersons had been decimated. Many newspapers carried a picture of the lone survivor, four-year-old Phyllis — a seemingly very tiny child, wide-eyed with fear. The abandoned victim whose family had been murdered while she was awake, and within earshot. It moved even the hardest of hearts to sorrow and compassion.

THE relatives were to receive hundreds of letters from people who were horrified at what had taken place. The correspondence came from around the globe, the bulk from Canada, the United States and England. They conveyed different messages. Some were sympathetic. Others made suggestions and requests. Many contained donations. Two weeks to the day that the family had been attacked, the trust fund had reached almost $3,000.

A postcard dated August 18th, three days after the morbid discovery, arrived from Rockville, Maryland. The sender addressed the card to — The Eleven Petersons.

> *"It is time there is an end to the kind of insanity that caused your tragedy. It looks to me as if there was method in it, like Richard Speck."*[2]
>
> *Margaret Butcher*

From San Francisco, California came an altogether different type of letter.

> *Mr. Helmer Helgeton and Phillis (Sic) Peterson and family:*
>
> *Blessed be God, even the father of our Lord Jesus Christ, the father of mercies and the God of all comfort; who comforteth us in all our tribulation, comfort your hearts in a very special way at this time.*
>
> *Peace I leave with you, my peace I give unto you; not as the world giveth, give I unto you. Let not your heart be troubled, neither let it be afraid.*
>
> *The last enemy that shall be destroyed is death. One thief cometh not, but for to steal and to kill and to destroy: I am come that they might have life and that*

---

2. Richard Speck, 26, was convicted April 15, 1967 of killing eight young women. They were murdered July 14, 1966 in a south Chicago nurses residence.

they might have it more abundantly.

I am the resurrection and the life and that he died for all that they which live should not henceforth live unto themselves, but unto him which died for them and rose again.

Love
Esther

Printed on the outside of the fold-over type paper was the full name of the sender. Esther M. Sanders, 7 Harbor Road, Bldg. 37, San Francisco, California 94124.

There was a note dated August 27th with the postmark, Manchester, N.H. Enclosed was 10 dollars.

Mr. and Mrs. Helmer Helgeton
Please accept our deepest sympathy on the loss of your loved ones. We hope this small donation will be of some help to little Phylis (Sic).

The brief message was from Mr. and Mrs. H. Pion of 311 Reed Street, Manchester N.H. 03102 U.S.A.

People were responding en masse. The photograph of Phyllis, splashed across newspapers around the world, drew widespread sympathy. The story with the accompanying forlorn picture struck people where it hurt most — in the heart. The horror that this little girl had gone through dwelled on the minds of many. A deeply felt missive was received from London, England. It was from a mother with a child who would be just like Phyllis.

Dear Mrs. Helme (Sic) Hegleton (Sic),
This is very little doubt that my feelings towards little Phyllis are shared by millions of people throughout the world when I read of the terrible tragedy that has occurred to the rest of her family.

They have gone but poor little Phyllis is left to relive those terrible moments, and I can only imagine what her little mind must be like. I am sure that the whole world's sympathy is with her, and only time will heal her memories of those awful moments.

I have a little girl of 4, her fourth birthday is next Sunday the 20th Aug, and naturally my thoughts are always for her. She has everything bestowed upon her that can possibly be given to her, except a sister, whom she very badly wants to share her life.

Time is very young at the moment, but if in the interest of little Phyllis it is decided to give her a new outlook for life away from the surroundings of this shocking affair, I would be delighted to have Phyllis to try and replace her mother's love, and to share my little girl's life as a sister. Money cannot replace what this dear girl has lost only love to some extent to replace the family love.

If you ever consider that a change of surroundings is needed for Phyllis, whether it be for a holiday, a prolonged stay or to find a new life, I will be only too pleased to have her. References can be supplied by the Church, Doctors and Legal Professions if necessary, but my only thought is for Phyllis.

My Very Warmest and Heartfelt
Feelings K.N. Snasdell

There were writings from closer to home. From the neighboring province of Manitoba came one that was Registered. Postmarked Gladstone, Man. on August 23rd, it reads:

Dear Mr. Helgeton
Enclosed is $50.00 for Phyllis Peterson. So please give it to her.

Thank you
Walter Kreutzer

Among the correspondence were a few lines from Hudson Bay, Saskatchewan, a community north of Shell Lake.

> *Mrs. Eva (Sic) Helgeton,*
> *I guess it's useless to tell you how shocked we were to here (Sic) of the terrible tragity (Sic) in your community. One can not help but think of Kathy and her little sister Phillis (Sic) and feel sorry for them both.*
> *I hear the Legion there is starting a Phillis (Sic) Peterson Trust Fund. However right now I feel there must be something Phillis (Sic) would like or need so am sending her a dollar. It will never replace her family but maybe she'll understand other people are thinking of her even if I don't know her or any of you personally.*
> *My deepest sympathy is with you all in your very, very great loss. May the guilty party be apprehenned (Sic) very soon and brought to justice I hope.*
> *Sincerely*
> *Mrs. Rita Whalen*
> *P.S. We have one son Terry who will be 9 years old this fall, so you see how I feel about Phillis (Sic). God Bless you all.*

There was also a letter from Alberta. From grief stricken parents who a short two weeks before had lost their baby.

> *Dear Mr. and Mrs. Helmer Helgeton,*
> *Firstly, we would like to express our deepest sympathy to you and to dear Phyllis, in the great loss and sorrow you are bearing. Only God alone knows why this tragedy had to occur to innocent members of this family. On Aug 12, we lost our third beloved child, Roxanna-aged 26 mos.—whose picture I am enclosing, so we have been sorrow-stricken and understand all you dear folks are trying to bear up and still keep on*

living. We have applied to the Welfare Dept. of Vermilion for adoption, as we love children very dearly and
want to give and share all this with a child who is in
great need of a mother and fatherly love. If this child,
whom you are sheltering would be given for adoption or
placed in a foster home, we would desperately do all to
take her in. Your help in writing us would be so greatly
appreciated as this would give her a wonderful home
and all her little heart may desire to help blot out that
terrible scene of the tragic night. I shall try to describe
us as closely to your imagination as I can.

—I am 42 yrs. old, 5'2" tall, weigh 105 lbs., brunette
and have completed Grade XII standing in school. We
have been married 16 yrs. and have no family which we
would love to have so much.

Peter (my husband) is 52 yrs old, 5'10" tall, weighs
155 lbs, of fair complexion, blue eyes and brown hair. He
is a carpenter (contracting building homes) loves
children very, very dearly. We are of Catholic faith but
our minds are open to all church denominations as there
is only <u>one God</u>, so we attend and contribute to all
church organizations. We do not indulge in drinks, we
stay home and never party so all our attention would
centre on the child. We also have a well-trained police-
dog which we had got to protect our little girl should she
wander out of the yard too far. Peter's earnings are well
in the $4,000.00 yearly. We have a lovely spare room for
a little girl to enjoy, including toys from a cuddly teddy-
bear to a tricycle.

We sincerely hope this letter will lighten your burden
and we shall be anxiously waiting for a reply from you.
This way, we believe, will put much less strain on you
kind people, and on little Phyllis when you know where
the child is going, and this as well, would greatly fill the
gap in our lives which has been so hard to take. Please

give this your consideration — we greatly feel for this childs safety and will do all in our power to keep her happy and healthy. You are free to phone us <u>collect</u> (the number is 853-3979, Vermilion Alberta) or to visit us (Vermilion is 38 miles west of Lloydminster) and we live on the south side — most anybody will be able to direct you to us.

In closing then, may you be strengthened and <u>protected</u> from God above, and our love and hugs to dear little Phyllis.

Very sincerely yours,
Phyllis & Peter Skish,
Vermilion, Alberta.

The reaction from around the world was phenomenal. The Peterson relatives received more than 1,000 letters from people trying, in different words, to partially compensate for the terrible, terrible loss.

UNFORGETTABLE — *This exclusive picture of Kathy holding Phyllis was flashed around the world. It was followed by an outpouring of global sympathy.*
— *Journal Photo by Dave Reidie*

LIMITS OF
SANITY

VIII

ON August 21st, Victor Ernest Hoffman was formally charged with capital murder in the death of James Peterson. He was remanded 30 days for psychiatric examination. There was no indication that he would appear again before the one-month period had elapsed. This, however, was not the case. There were two court appearances on August 21st. Very few people were aware of the second one. It came about, according to lawyer Noble, when he agreed to take the case late into the evening of that day.

"The Crown changed its mind and said it would be stupid to send Victor back to the hospital in North Battleford because he was just released. I agreed, court reconvened, and he was remanded into the custody of the RCMP to be taken to Saskatoon where he would be given a psychiatric examination by Dr. Donald McKerracher. At that time it was indicated the independent examination would only take a few days."

Dr. McKerracher was a respected professor of psychiatry and head of the psychiatric department at the University Hospital.

MOST news sources were unaware of the second court appearance, late on the night of August 21st. The information, however, was obtained by a few reporters who learned that the accused would be back before a magistrate on the morning of August 25th; four days after the initial public display.

CFCN which had gathered the information, immediately released it to news agencies across the land. A call was placed to the newsroom of CFQC Saskatoon. The newsman answering the telephone was asked whether a reporter would be attending the unscheduled appearance.

"If Hoffman appears," was the doubting reply.

The party was then told there was no doubt of the upcoming court date. He was once again asked if a reporter would be attending.

"If he appears we'll have a man there," was the retort that lacked conviction.

A similar response was received from the newsroom of CKBI Prince Albert. The news department was surprised to learn that the Leask, Saskatchewan farmer's son would be appearing so soon after the 30-day remand. There was good cause for this because without the knowledge of the second court appearance, August 21st, the next date was not expected until late September. An RCMP spokesman in North Battleford declined comment as to what the nature of the hearing would be. He did confirm that Victor would be there.

THE findings of Dr. McKerracher were submitted. Four days from the time of Victor's first court appearance—a decision had been made concerning the state of his mental health.

On the morning of August 25, 1967, he was deemed fit to stand trial as charged. The decision was announced by Judge Policha after he received the report of Dr. McKerracher. The psychiatrist, according to defence lawyer Noble, was appointed by the court. Mr. Noble said of Dr. McKerracher, "He was almost a Crown psychiatrist, of course the point which I made some play on at the trial."

L ATER, the question "Did you expect Victor Hoffman to be found insane therefore eliminating a trial?" was randomly asked of observers.

"No, I didn't think they'd say he was insane. That would be admitting they shouldn't have let him out, wouldn't it?"

"After he was only in the hospital such a short time before, the government might as well admit they killed the family if they found him insane."

"I'm sure the government would never say he was insane. People would expect an inquiry, or do you think so? I know they made a mistake, but I know damn well they wouldn't ever admit it. Can you imagine what the people would think?"

O CTOBER 24th was the date set for the preliminary hearing. Victor was remanded to the Provincial Correctional Institute in Prince Albert. Once a suspect is arrested and charged, and kept in custody without bail, the law could only hold him for an eight-day-period without a further public remand. Because of this, Victor made numerous brief court appearances. During one quick visit, September 22nd, there was only a single spectator on hand. The routine continued until he would be returned to Battleford for the preliminary hearing.

R OBERT Hoffman was a broken, worn man — his spirit crushed. He could not fathom what had happened to his son.

"He was always such a good boy. The hospital must have known he was all right or they wouldn't have released him."

This was a man who claimed that he initially heard that his son had been criminally charged by way of a radio broadcast.

A man who admitted that he never cried so hard in all his life.

"It pretty near killed me."

Aging with mental fatigue, he travelled to see his son.

"I wanted to hear it from his own lips. I wanted to hear that my son killed these innocent people."

He received the answer.

"Yes, but I wasn't myself."

Father — How did you get out of the house without mother or I hearing you?

Son — I just did.

Father — I heard the car start about 5 a.m. Which did you take?

Son — The old one.

Father — You were back by eight, working on the motor?

Son — You should have chased after me, then this wouldn't have happened. I couldn't stop myself. It just hit me all of a sudden.

Father — Well good-bye ... Robert extended his hand through the bars ... I was proud of you when you were at home. You worked well on the machinery. I was proud of my son but my son died when that family was buried. You couldn't even kill cats at home. I would have to do it myself. Then you go and slaughter those people. How could you pump so much lead into that man?

Son — You can't hate me anymore than I hate myself ... Tears were streaming down Victor's face ... I didn't know what I was doing.

Father — Well, it is best this way. Good-bye.

Son — You mean I won't see you again?

Father — Maybe it will be easier on us both if I never see you again.

Son — Well, if I could just see you one more time. And I want to see my brother, and ask the minister to please come and see me. Oh, I wish I had committed suicide. Do they still hang people?

Father — They haven't hung anyone for a long time.

Son — I wish they would hang me. Will I ever see the outside of the world again?

Father — I can't say because you haven't been sentenced yet.

Son — Oh, I just hate myself.

Father — How soon after you did this, did you realize it?

Son — When I heard the gossip I knew what a horrible thing I'd done. I knew I did it all the time but it seemed like a nightmare. I should have used an axe.

Father — Why?

Son — Then they wouldn't have caught me. They had ballistics with the gun.

Father — Anyone who commits a crime like this gets caught eventually.

Son — Yes, I suppose so.

Father — What minister do you want to see? The one who buried the Peterson family?

Son — Yes, will he see me?

Father — He probably will.

REVEREND Post visited Victor that same day. He heard him express remorse and question whether it was still possible to "go to heaven now." He listened incredulously as Victor told him that people die differently than animals. "He fights it," stated Victor. "A funny noise comes out of his mouth and blood gurgles." The unnerved preacher, who learned that some nights earlier two cold hands had gripped Victor's throat and then floated away through the walls, noted that Victor was upset because his father's good-bye had seemed so final. He asked if his mother would come and visit but was told it would be difficult for her to get away.

FOURTEEN days after Victor had been found fit to stand trial, he sent a revealing letter to his parents. It appears exactly as written.

P.O. Box 580,
Prince Albert, Sask.
Sept. 8 [1]Sat., 1967

Dear Dad & Family

I am very sorry for what I have done to myself & the Peterson family and all the grief that I caused to you & family. Believe me I did not know what I was really going to do that morning. When I was working on that engine I suddenly got discussed and was unable to work on that engine anymore. I can recall looking at my watch and it was five o'clock then I did not know what to do and I began pacing trying think of something else to do until choretime and when I reach the door a swelling type of feeling began to grow on my right side of my head and then it went down my right side to the toes and it made me feel light, free, brave and the desire to kill. I even had the desire to kill you & whole family. Anyway I had the feeling that I should drive for an hour.

On Saturday the day you went to the fair while I was working on the engine. I was all ready to put the engine back together and I took the crankcase and I went to take it outside to wash it with casoline just before I touched the door knob the door began to shake and somebody was working the doorknob, it very violently. I open the door as quick as I could and step outside but no one was there. Later as I was putting the engine together I was aware that somebody was watching me but anyway I just keep on working on the engine.

I hope the kids at school aren't bugging Allan. Dad don't work too hard on those bales your not young

---

1. September 8, 1967 was a Friday.

anymore, you just might kill yourself. Mom you could
order a pair of sunday coveralls for the trial something
more descend, there is plenty of money of mine which
you are keeping. I would like to have my brother
Richards address.

                                    Victor Ernest Hoffman.

A letter from a son to his parents. Admitting the terrible crime, an attempt made to explain how it came about. Concern was expressed for a younger brother and worry for a parent.

"Dad don't work too hard on those bales your (sic) not young anymore, you just might kill yourself."

Normalcy in the letter? There should have been — the writer, who admitted having intercourse with animals on the farm, was judged sane only 14 days before.

The portion expressing hope that Allan was not being bothered at school was very realistic. He could well have been subjected to much abuse — but was not, his parents said. Instead, the boy's father received three threatening letters. They made him fear for his life and that of his family. The first correspondence was received August 31st, six days after Victor had been found fit to stand trial. Postmarked Craven, Sask., it was scrawled in pencil. Robert said the letter was unsigned. He remembered that it told him and his family to get out of the community. According to Robert it said in effect, "I'll take Victor and nail him to the wall and shoot him inch by inch. Why would God permit for people like you to exist?"

The Hoffmans were already overwhelmed — now this. Robert turned the hate note over to the police.

Five days later, another threatening letter was written to the family. Robert kept a copy. It is printed as received.

Sept. 5th/67
Moose Jaw Sask.

Hoffman & wife

You two dirty rats and that son of yours should all be shot. I knew those people who that son of yours shot, so that son of yours should be shot and his rotten hide burned in the incinderator, get rid of people like that. When you took him out of the mental, why did'nt watch him and see to it that he did'nt take the car and rifle and go out on a murder spree.

We should the good Canadian citizens take you all out and burn your rotten hides. I think the people should club to-gether and throw a few gallons of gasolune on top of you all and burn you. Get out of the country as you are not wanted. Those poor innocent people all murdered, I say give that son of yours the rope and burn his dirty hide in the incinter. You people should get out of the country as you are not wanted here. If you stay you might get more than you bargain for. God damn yours souls and that of your no good bastard of a son.

This letter was also turned over to the authorities.
"If you receive anymore we'll take action."
There was one more; very similar to the first two.
It was postmarked North Battleford and in essence, according to Robert, said, "We have no business living in this part of the country. We should get out."

THE Hoffman family contemplated moving from their house. The retreat, if it came about, would have meant a major upheaval but if an attempt was to be made on their lives it would have forced the assassin to first re-discover the family's whereabouts.

A family living in relentless fear because of a series of mistakes that sent their son, diagnosed as being, "very, very sick," back to his home before he was truly well again.

"You read about these things," Robert told me. "I've read about lots of tragedy but I never thought it could happen to us. I always thought it could happen to those other people. Now it's happened in my family."

T HE Canadian Mental Health Association (CMHA), Saskatchewan Division, was working on a more advanced and optimistic concept of treatment for the mentally ill. This was outlined in its report to the Saskatchewan Government in 1966 — prior to the Shell Lake tragedy.

The brief, which boasted that a great deal of progress had been made in the mental health field, referred to four stages in the evolution of the treatment of mental disorders.

"The first stage could be considered as a period of persecution when the mentally ill were punished and persecuted. The second stage could be considered as the period of segregation, when the mentally ill were 'put away' out of sight and separated from their families and communities. The third stage which could be called the humanitarian stage, included a much more optimistic approach to mental illness and a more accepting attitude towards the mentally ill.

"The humanitarian stage led to the present concepts of the Saskatchewan plan and community psychiatry. These concepts include the realization that institutionalization is harmful and that the best interests of the patient are served when they are not divorced from their work, home and community."

Stated the 1966 report, The Canadian Mental Health Association is working towards the next step which is more advanced.

"This stage demands that the mentally ill be treated so effectively that the vast majority will be cured with accurate diagnostic tests and short-term treatment methods. The recovered patients can make their way back to society without costly after-care and rehabilitative procedures."

The CMHA had recommended in its findings that expansion of research was needed.

Concern was expressed in the 1966 report "that further help for the productive Saskatchewan research is not forthcoming. We are especially concerned because of the reduction in grants available from the Federal Government."

The report also recommended that the provincial government try and persuade its Federal counterpart to increase grants because of the great importance to the welfare of Canadian society. The request was not without merit. In one major city in the province, four and one-half per cent of the children in schools were described as emotionally disturbed.

Concern was also expressed regarding after-care and re-habilitative services.

"Some of the patients appear to be ill on their release from hospital."

The report continued, "Adequate staffing and facilities for these programs are essential and should include rehabilitation measures such as provision for retraining and education, sheltered work together with community, social and recreational facilities." The point that staff morale was low was also made. It was speculated that a reason for this could be lower wage schedules for psychiatric nurses in comparison with those elsewhere.

The quality of treatment was another matter that received attention.

"The re-admission rate for all units is very high and many patients are released from hospital who appear to be quite ill."

The submission by the Canadian Mental Health Association had asked the government to implement the recommendations of the Royal Commission on Government administration which called for "a continuing departmental program planning or program evaluation group."

The study continued, "While the government established the Ad Hoc Committee on the Resettlement of Mental Hospital Patients, it did not, in our opinion, approach the program of planning and continuous evaluation on a comprehensive and permanent basis. The Ad Hoc Committee gave a good report but their work was limited by the frame of reference and the deadline which they were obliged to meet. The report made some very good recommendations, but only indicated that some of the homes investigated were found to be beneficial and others were not beneficial.

"A permanent, independent assessment committee could give us facts about the number or proportion of homes that were beneficial and not beneficial and also in what respect these homes were found to be inadequate. This information would give the Government and the public useful information which could be used to improve existing programs. We would recommend that the Government give careful consideration to the implementation of the Ad Hoc Committee's recommendations."

Discharge and re-admission policies were outlined as being inconsistent throughout the province.

"We would therefore again recommend that a careful study be made of discharge and re-admission policies and specific standards and policies be established."

There was a reference under the heading, Public Information and Involvement, that in some areas former patients were not readily accepted by society.

"In some cases the rejection of former patients is due to the fact that many people who are released from mental hospitals are still very ill. In some cases, we believe it is due to general prejudice or preconceived concepts of mental illness which are not factual in modern psychiatry."

True, there was general prejudice. And under the circumstances why not?

"We are especially concerned because of the reduction in grants from the Federal Government."

"Some of the patients appear to be ill on their release from hospital."

"The re-admission rate for all units is very high and many patients are released from hospital who appear to be quite ill."

"We would therefore again recommend that a careful study be made of discharge and re-admission policies and specific standards and policies be established."

Of course, there was prejudice. Inefficiency was so unmistakably apparent that it was impossible to have trust, belief, or faith in a government agency that would operate in such a haphazard manner.

Less than one year after this disturbing report, nine lives were needlessly terminated. They were lost because of a succession of mistakes that could have been prevented. If the recommendations of the Canadian Mental Health Association had been adhered to and the concerns acted upon the murdered members of the James Peterson family in all probability would still be alive.

THE two-day preliminary hearing before Judge Policha was underway. It was held October 24 and 25, 1967 to determine, not the guilt nor innocence of the accused — but whether there was sufficient evidence to warrant a trial.

At the beginning of the preliminary hearing, Crown prosecutor Serge Kujawa, stoical and deliberate, asked that the original information against Victor Hoffman, a single charge of capital murder in the death of James Peterson, be withdrawn. In its place, a new information was submitted which included two counts of capital murder — the first against James Peterson and the second against Evelyn Peterson.

Testimony revealed that Victor claimed to have seen angels and the devil. In one instance, the hearing was told, the accused had even described the devil. Corporal Gawthrop said Victor claimed to have fought with the devil and referred to his tormentor as being tall, black, and having no genitals. According to Corporal Gawthrop — genitals was the word used.

Judge Policha asked the accused if he had anything to say. Defence lawyer Noble informed the court that his client had nothing to say and the defence would not submit any evidence.

Victor Ernest Hoffman was committed for trial. It would begin January 8, 1968.

Clearly, he would have to be classed as one of the "many patients released from hospital who appear to be quite ill."

PART TWO

DEVIL'S RAMPAGE

Contents

CHAPTER IX: A World Of Pity 155

CHAPTER X: Terms Of Justice 163

CHAPTER XI: The Aftermath 196

CHAPTER XII: The Survivors 214

CHAPTER XIII: Condemned 236

CHAPTER XIV: The Eye Of The Storm 284

EPILOGUE: 303

CHRONOLOGY: Victor Ernest Hoffman 313

AUTHOR'S NOTE: 315

REFERENCE: Mass Murder 316

PUBLISHER'S MESSAGE: 323

NAMES: 324

A WORLD
OF PITY

IX

THE relatives of the victims received countless letters. The Hoffman family did not receive nearly as many but the number they did totalled in the several hundreds. The ones chosen for publication are printed as authored.

One of the most interesting was from Shell Lake.

> *Dear Mr. and Mrs. Hoffman and*
> *your immediate family,*
> *I hope this letter will not be*
> *too late to be, maybe a little encour-*
> *agement to you. I wanted to write*
> *right after the Peterson funeral here*
> *to let you know that you have our*
> *sympathy, also from many others.*
>
> *Often our children prove to be such a*
> *disapointment to us. This is a work*
> *of the devil, through our children and*
> *we don't know what we can say to*
> *comfort you. Except that we know*

God can and will help you if you
pray and trust Him.
    I did feel I should write and let you
know there are friends who are concerned
about how you must feel.

The letter was signed by someone with the same surname as a man once identified as a suspect wanted in connection with the murders. He was described as a Saskatchewan farm laborer who was travelling by car. The man was reported to have had in his possession, several weapons that had been stolen. They were said to have totalled three in number. A .22-calibre firearm, the same calibre as the murder weapon, was among them.

There was a letter from Hudson Bay, Saskatchewan. The woman who wrote it had, 21 days before, written to the relatives of the Peterson family.

Dear Mrs. Hoffman,

I want you to know you have my deepest sympathy and I don't hold you or any of your family responsible for your son's actions. I'm not saying Victor did right, that is for others to decide. But may God have mercy on him.

About two months ago my older sister died a horrible death of cancer, leaving 4 small children. We wonder why God let it happen? There is no answer for that but if we trust in Him I'm sure we'll understand why some day. So trust in God. It is a very sad and trying time for you and yours, but keep faith in Him. Behind every black cloud there's a silver lining.

I supose now you wonder if I knew the Peterson family? No I didn't but I sent a donation to the Phyllis Peterson Trust Fund. We must always remember there's two sides to every coin. It was tragic for the James Peterson family but it is equallay sad and tragic for your family. So please have faith in our Lord.

Our own son is only nine years old but I come from a large family and can well imagine how I'd feel if one of them were in Victors shoes. It wouldn't be good. Yet none of us knows what the future holds for us. Do we?

In closing I'd like to say once again you and your family have my deepest sympathy.

Sincerely
Rita Whalen

Following this, began the long series of letters with a religious bent.

"You'd think we never knew God and never ever went to church," lamented Robert.

The Hoffman family was a strict church going unit. Yet, from the great amount of religious propaganda sent their way, many people thought the killings occurred because of a lack of faith. Ironically, Victor thought he got far too much of it. Others thought his parents were eccentric.

An envelope from Everson, Washington contained six enclosures. They were entitled:

Failure or success: something to think about

What then?

Leaving God out

Ye must be born again

Four things that God wants you to know!

Bread of life

The latter was a small booklet containing some 64 pages. It dealt with the Gospel according to St. John.

From Dalmeny, Saskatchewan came more of the same. Among the titles were: Hid With Christ, In God, and Faith.

From Shell Lake, the scene of the horrendous crime, came the message, "Awake from Sleep!"

From Saskatoon, Saskatchewan came three pamphlets, two were identical. They were entitled, "Where the most Important issue in life is concerned — Let's Be Sure!" Also "Four Things that God wants you to know." These were among innumerable postcards, pamphlets, and letters received by the Hoffmans. The majority were unsigned.

Dear Mrs. Hoffman,

Being a mother myself I find my heart goes out to you in this time of shock & grief.

There are no words to convey my sympathy, but maybe it will help to know that it is there. I do hope that time will soften the shock & life become normal again.

I meant to write earlier but I caught my hand in a grain auger & am just getting to write legiblly again.

Yours sincerely
Mrs. L. Schoonover
Ridgedale

A card, "The Secret of Living", included a brief note.

My prayer is that God will give you folks the strength and courage you need at this time. Only God will care and understand so turn to him for the strength you need.

Sincerely yours
Jean Weberg (Mattock)
909 Esq Rd. Victoria B.C.

Only three letters to the family issued threats. Most of the others, mainly those pertaining to religion, disturbed them. They were offensive, simply because of the persistent idea that the family had to be atheists in order to have one of its members commit such a dastardly deed. If anything, quite the reverse was true.

Dear Mr. & Mrs. Hoffman & Family:

I'm awfully sorry for you, and my heart goes out to you dear parents and family. Amidst a world full of churches today, you'd think crime would be on the decrease, instead it's on the increase. Evidently the churches are not preaching God's sincere truth as found in the bible.

The letter, which filled three pages, said in part, "In Exodus 6;3 God says 'His name is <u>Jehovah</u>!' Mathew 24;9 reads 'Ye shall be hated of all nations for my name's sake.' Mathew 24;14 reads 'And this gospel of the <u>Kingdom</u> shall be preached in all the world for a <u>witness</u> unto all nations and then shall the end come."

It concluded, "I do hope that I can bring you some comfort with my letter."

The anguish that it caused was nearly unbearable. Unfortunately, it was only the first of many. Whether they wished to or not the Hoffmans learned a great deal about Jehovah. There was no choice. It finally reached a point where the letters from those they termed fanatics could be sensed within moments of being opened. They were filed in the nearest garbage can.

Robert and Stella were also recipients of free legal advice. People wanting to do the work of the court-appointed lawyer. The exhortations were discarded. The majority of mail delivered to the Hoffmans only added to the sorrow and despair.

EVERYTHING was happening so fast. Tomorrow, January 8, 1968, their son would be appearing in court. There was one bright spot amidst the gloom. Victor would not stand trial as originally indicted. He was initially charged August 21, 1967 with capital murder in the death of James Peterson and the information was withdrawn at the preliminary hearing to be replaced with two counts of capital murder — the first against James Peterson and the second against Evelyn Peterson.

Now — he would be arraigned before the Court of Queen's Bench facing new indictments. Two counts of non-capital murder; one against James Peterson and the other against Evelyn Peterson, would be read to him. The change to non-capital murder followed an amendment by Parliament to the definition of capital murder. The amendment was given Royal Assent December 21, 1967; 19 days before the date that Victor would face his accusers.

According to defence lawyer Noble "The Crown could have elected to proceed with the capital murder charges but chose otherwise."

Eight days before the trial, Prosecutor Kujawa was quoted as saying the Crown had intended to proceed with the capital murder charges, however, the new definition of capital murder changed the category. "We have no alternative but to proceed on the lesser charge," the stone-faced prosecuting attorney announced.

Capital murder now pertained to the slaying of an on-duty policeman or prison guard. Conviction resulted in mandatory capital punishment — death. Non-capital murder now meant the slaying of any other person, other than an on-duty policeman or prison guard. Conviction was punishable by life imprisonment with the possibility of parole.

It was some 22 years previous that the province had a lynching. Jack Loran, 20, who shared his father's passion for homebrew, swung from the gallows in Regina on February 20,

1946. Loran, with a history of sexual frustration and unexplained voices in his head, had killed a farmer during a robbery. Shorty, as he was called, was the last human hanged in Saskatchewan.[1]

Victor Ernest Hoffman would not face a similar fate. It was little consolation for his parents, a small mercy, but then again, they had such a minimal amount to be thankful for since their son had become ill.

---

1. The condemned man's defence team, Murdoch Alexander MacPherson and his son Sandy, believed their client was insane. It was a time, however, when the profession of psychiatry was given little credence. Years later, as he presided over the Hoffman case, the hanging still bothered the younger MacPherson.

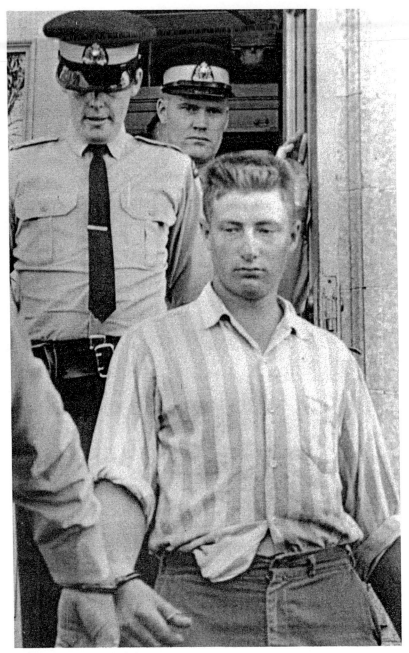

SUSPECT CHARGED — *RCMP officers escort Victor from court after he was formally charged with capital murder in the death of Jim Peterson. Unsteady and unkempt, he was whisked away for a psychiatric examination.*

— *Canapress Photo*

TERMS OF JUSTICE

J ANUARY 8, 1968. In a few hours Victor would face two charges of non-capital murder. The trial would take place in the same 60-year-old Battleford courthouse where he had been committed following the two-day preliminary hearing. It was just across the river from where he had been treated for his mental disorder.

The trial was to begin at 10 o'clock. It was hoped that a motive would be revealed. A reason — no matter how demented — for the sadistic killings. There were so many questions unanswered. How could anyone butcher the family in the manner in which it had been done? Could it be that Victor had known the Petersons? Did he have an interest in one of the girls? Was it a grudge killing? Perhaps a disgruntled ex-boyfriend? As people began to congregate outside the venerable building everyone had the answers. The air was thick with rumors and pervasive, malicious gossip.

"He knew the older girl and when she rejected him and married a short time later he went berserk."

Standing nearby, a whiskered farmer disputed the theory.

"Jim Peterson had employed this mad dog and when he

fired him he took revenge."

There were others who just did not know.

"Sure, he had robbed the family. For less than $10 why kill nine people? At least the mother and children?"

As the time drew near for the court proceedings to begin, the talk persisted. Somebody said Merv had told him the trust fund for Phyllis stood at more than $18,000. Mervin Madsen was the secretary for the endowment set up by the Royal Canadian Legion's Shell Lake Branch. Less than a month after the killings, the contributions totalled approximately $4,000 and at that time an official felt the donations had probably reached an end. Another $14,000, however, was donated within the following four-month period.

A member of the Saskatchewan Legislature, approaching the steps of the courthouse, stopped to talk with a reporter. The newsman dashed directly to the nearest telephone. It was not really anything new.[1] Yet for some, any angle meant a story.

"Little Phyllis will definitely be considered by a board administering a provincial Act under which innocent victims of crimes and violence may be compensated," pontificated the elected official.

This had been said before but on this day, for some, it was again news. Today, the curious were remembering all the abject details and any bit of information would do.

A blizzard was raging, plummeting temperatures to the 10-below-zero fahrenheit mark. The people waiting outside, clinging together in bunches for warmth, and those on coffee row, began to ruminate about what had happened. One of the most intriguing tidbits was told by an elderly farmer from the Kilwinning district. He lived only a few miles from the Hoffmans.

He related, "Victor was a good boy and wouldn't do anything like this without reason. I heard Mr. Peterson had seen

---

1. The Saskatchewan Crimes Compensation Board had announced in October that the official guardian of infants, on behalf of Phyllis, made application for compensation.

that a boy from Shell Lake was committed to the North Battleford hospital and this guy put Victor up to the killings. I heard that this guy knew Hoffman was going to be released and made a deal whoever gets out first would wipe out the Peterson family. Sure it was this way! How else would he know where they lived and everything."[2]

One man claimed that Victor had been in trouble before.[3] "In 1964 he stole some guns from the hardware store in Leask. He caused lots of damage but his dad returned the guns and paid for what was wrecked."

Another bystander, a burly man, said Victor went over to his friend's house, Jimmy Peake's, during the early morning hours of August 15th.[4] "He went over to the house and talked through the screen door with Jimmy. Victor said he was going to shoot someone. Jimmy felt he had talked Victor into going home but it looks like instead he went straight to Shell Lake."

Someone said the police arrested Victor after the accused purchased 15 boxes of .22-calibre shells on the afternoon of August 15th.

A police spokesman, questioned about this later, said, "there is no truth to it. Certainly, he purchased shells prior to the killings but there is no evidence that he bought any after the deaths."

---

2. Robert Hoffman says Victor confided in him, following the trial, that a patient at the mental hospital in North Battleford told him of the Peterson farm. According to Robert, Victor maintained that the patient outlined the location of the farm and also described the house. Robert stated that Victor had given him a name, which according to Victor, was that of the patient who passed on the information. The RCMP, after examining the claim, discarded the story. They called it, "Unsupported word."

3. Robert confirmed that in 1964, Victor admitted taking some guns from the hardware store in Leask. According to the father, there was also damage done which amounted to around $300 to $400. He said restitution was made and no criminal charges were laid. Charges in fact were laid, followed by a conviction.

4. Jimmy Peake said Victor did not come to the Peake house during the early morning hours of August 15th. He stated there was no truth to the story. It was erroneous.

S PECTATORS began filing into the courthouse. It was packed — many had to stand in the narrow hallway leading to it. Mr. Justice M.A. (Sandy) MacPherson, an incisive adjudicator, was presiding.

The 21-year-old prisoner, who stared broodingly, was led into the tight quarters, handcuffed and under heavy guard. Previous to this, he had been examined by Dr. McKerracher at the request of defence counsel Noble.

"I asked Dr. McKerracher to examine him to see whether or not he was still fit. Fitness to stand trial can vary. In fact it can vary from day to day. It's all a question of whether he understands what's going on — the charge he faces, who is on the jury, what's going on in court. The position I intended to take was that if he (Dr. McKerracher) said Victor was unfit then I would raise the issue. I would then put McKerracher in the box, he would testify Victor was unfit and the jury would have to try that issue whether he was fit to stand trial or unfit to stand trial. The thing is that you have a decision to make. If you raise the question of his fitness to stand trial and put somebody in the box who says he's unfit, the jury could, when they come to reach a verdict, confuse the issue with sanity. If they find him fit to stand trial and three or four days later I'm asking them to find him insane at the time of the act, there's a bit of a problem. In view of the fact of McKerracher's opinion, that he was fit, I didn't raise it because I felt it would confuse the issues of the jury."

The matter of Victor's soundness of mind was not raised at the beginning of the trial. It was therefore presumed that he was mentally competent. The onus would be on the defence to prove that he was insane at the time of the act.

A plea of not guilty was entered and the court proceeded to select a jury. There were 50 names on the list. Defence counsel Noble challenged seven, including three women. Crown prosecutor Kujawa challenged five. Within 20 minutes the tribunal had been chosen. The job was complete. The non-capital murder case of Victor Ernest Hoffman was underway in Court of Queens Bench. A 12-member all-male jury would determine his innocence or guilt. It did not appear as if the trial would be too lengthy. Statements by lawyer Noble indicated that the defence would call perhaps only four witnesses. He thought the proceedings would not last any longer than four or five days. With a total of about 18 or 19 witnesses expected to testify it was not anticipated that the legalities would last any longer than a maximum five days.

Wildrew Lang, who farmed about three miles southwest of the Peterson property, was the first to discover the grisly scene. He related to the court that he had gone to the Peterson farm on the morning of August 15th to help clean out some grain bins.

"I walked over to the house and knocked on the door."

There was no answer. The porch door was open and Wildrew went inside. Through the kitchen, he sighted the lifeless body of Jim Peterson. He was on his stomach. A pool of blood stained the linoleum.

"He was dressed only in his underwear shorts and there was a lot of blood around. He wasn't moving and I figured he was dead."

The court was then told by the witness that he ran to the Peterson station wagon and drove the four miles to Shell Lake. He telephoned the police at Spiritwood, then returned to await the arrival of investigating officers. The first policeman on the scene was Corporal Barry Richards a non-commissioned officer in charge of the RCMP detachment at Spiritwood. The two men travelled the 200 yards to the farmhouse. The policeman entered the ominous dwelling.

The second witness called by the Crown was Robert Hoffman. The ruddy-faced, broad-shouldered farmer was visibly shaken. He was a defeated man. As he took the stand and as the questioning began, the now soft spoken father described his son. Shy, retiring, a boy who didn't drink, smoke, or date girls. He never drank to excess and would only very seldom take a cigarette. He loved hunting and was normal until early in May.

Robert continued, "About the first of May I noticed he used to talk to himself and laugh out loud to himself."

Victor had never done this before. It was the turning point — the time of no return. The court would now hear the background of the events that led to the macabre night at the Peterson farm. The father continued to relate that on another day in May, Victor was sitting in a truck at noon. He was laughing to himself out loud.

"I asked him to tell me the joke. He slammed the truck into gear and took off."

Court was told that Allan, Victor's younger brother, just got out of the way in time. It was at this stage, the father told the hushed audience, that it was decided Victor needed help. He was admitted at the end of May, the 29th, to The Saskatchewan Hospital in North Battleford. Details of the admittance and conversation between hospital personnel and the parents were lacking. The court was told that Victor was released July 26th.

Frantically, reporters were taking down notes as fast as the evidence was being given.

Robert testified that on Friday, August 11th, his son began acting very odd. He was restless and numerous times would drive off in his car. He would not tell anyone where he was going. When he returned, he refused to explain where he had been. On the night of August 14th, only a few hours before the mass killing, Victor had taken a nap before going upstairs to bed. It was early the next morning, the father told the court, that he awakened to hear a car engine fading in the distance. Robert added that he had a habit of waking at that hour. He said that on the night of August 14th, as on the others, he went back to sleep. The next morning he went out between 6:30 and 7 o'clock and began doing the chores. Victor did not appear until about an hour or so after.

"He drove into the farmyard," the witness said, "I asked him where he'd been."

Victor replied that he was down at the other farm, the family's second expanse of land north of where they lived, to see if he could spot any deer. The court was told that following the arrival of the accused back home he appeared normal and began to go about his work. Robert said that until the time his son began to talk and laugh to himself he would never say much. He would seldom communicate.

"He was the kind of boy who would answer your questions but that's about all."

The court was told that when the father went to the mental hospital to pick up Victor, it was evident that he was not well. He did not look well. He was rigid. His whole body was stiff. He was quiet, very quiet, and he did not say much.

As the witness concluded, it was learned that jury members would be allowed to go about their daily business when not at the trial. The jury was cautioned, however, not to discuss the proceedings with anyone. Mr. Justice MacPherson warned the 12 members that if they were asked about it they were to say nothing.

He explained, "Even if it's to the point of being rude."

As a snowstorm continued to rage, RCMP Corporal Richards was called to testify. Richards, the first policeman to arrive at the scene of the crime, related that when he first entered the house he noticed the body of Jim Peterson. On a foldaway cot in the living room was the body of 11-year-old Dorothy. The corpses of five other children were found in two double beds in a room off the living room. The Corporal then told how he stepped out on the porch but re-entered the house within a few moments. He went back into the bedroom.

"There was something moving between the bodies of two girls that were sprawled across the bed."

As the Corporal stated, "It was the only sign of life I saw."

The only signal of survival that the policeman discerned was Phyllis with her still, staring eyes. Lying between the bodies of her dead sisters, her face was pressed tightly against the mattress. She was in that room with the dead members of her family for such a long time. This was the diminutive, dainty child who investigators were convinced had shivered in fear during all that noise. She had listened to the screaming, the crying and the strange gurgling sounds — until all was quiet. She was shaking as the policeman lifted her into his arms. He was a stranger and the terrified girl, quivering with fright, wanted to know where he was taking her. The Corporal's eyes brimmed with tears as he told that Phyllis was carried outside, placed in the custody of Alvin Simonar, and then taken across the highway to the safety of the Simonar home.

"Wildrew Lang remained at the crime scene," testified the unnerved officer.

Corporal Richards then affirmed how he raced to Shell Lake to telephone for reinforcements. His call to subdivision head-quarters in North Battleford was brief. A man and six children dead. A woman and child missing. The murder weapon was also missing.

Corporal Richards also called a doctor. He then began his return to the murder-site to await reinforcements and Dr. Michaud.

Walking toward the door of the dwarfish, chalky-looking dwelling, he noticed something on the ground. The body of Evelyn Peterson was slumped near the northwest corner of the building. Nearby, was a tiny baby, Larry. There was no gun to be found. Murder-suicide was ruled out.

FOLLOWING the testimony of Corporal Richards, RCMP Sergeant Fraser was called on a voir dire. It concerned the admissibility of a taped and written statement taken from the accused.

Corporal Gawthrop was also called on the voir dire (a trial

within a trial) to determine the allowability of the statements.

T HE sixth witness to take the stand was pathologist Dr. Oliver G. Lane. He told the court in clinical, dispassionate detail that the seven children suffered a total of 16 bullet wounds. The father had been shot seven times and the mother four times. Dr. Lane also testified that all of the wounds suffered by the children were to the head. He said none of the victims had been sexually assaulted.

It was not given in evidence that many of the lacerations were "contact wounds." Also, the court was not told by Dr. Lane that the mother had been shot in the back and had suffered one "exit wound." Nor was the court told that the father had three "exit wounds," and one of the children two such gashes.

According to Dr. Lane, "The reason why my evidence was short, factual and limited to absolute essentials; was that the defence was not denying the facts but relying on a plea of insanity."

I T was Tuesday, January 9th, and the start of the second day of the trial. Jurors would hear evidence that included a signed statement and an audio recording of the voice of the accused. Corporal Gawthrop, who told the court that the recorded voice was that of Victor, added that the taping was done shortly after the apprehension. The tape contained the voices of three persons: Corporal Gawthrop and Sergeant Fraser and the accused. Victor's voice was monotone and unemotional. There was not a flicker of feeling. His answers are given tonelessly, as if the cold blooded killing of nine people was an everyday occurrence. The inflectionless pace is unchanged for 22 minutes.

Sergeant Fraser — (Spells last name) HOFFMAN. Now maybe Victor, we'll start Monday night, hey? You went to bed?

Hoffman — Yes

Sergeant Fraser — Weren't you feeling very well?

Hoffman — Feeling real good.

Sergeant Fraser — Feeling real good, what time did you wake up?

Hoffman — I don't know for sure if that is the same day dad told me to wake up. He woke me up there on the sofa, and then he told me to go to bed and I woke up at about three o'clock. I think that was the same day.

Sergeant Fraser — Go ahead tell us.

Hoffman — I woke up about three o'clock. I went outside and urinated, came back inside, and laid down on the sofa. Tried to sleep there for a while, couldn't sleep. I was thinking about the motorcycle I was going to put it together. Thought about that for an hour or so and then I went outside. I went to the garage to work on the motor. I worked on that motor for a whole hour. Then, I just got tired of it. I got sick of it. I'd do something else. What was I going to do with all that time I had? I couldn't sleep, so I just jumped in the car to go for a drive.

Sergeant Fraser — Is that the gray car?

Hoffman — Yeah, of course ... I had to fill it with gas. I drove down to the bush, out to the barrel. Filled it full, emptied the barrel, all the gas that was in the barrel.

Sergeant Fraser — And then where did you go after you filled it with gas?

Hoffman — I drove down the road out to the new highway, down to the number 40 highway,[5] the black top. Up to Kilwinning and straight on up north and I kept following that road. I wanted to see how much Spruce there was on it. I was going to hunt squirrels this winter. I kept driving until I hit the black top again. Then I just followed that black top, just kept driving. And then, then after it got just about daylight, the sun was just starting to come up, I saw this house on the left-hand side of the road. There was a gate there and I

---

5. Victor told his lawyer that he had an urge to stop at the community of Parkside and that he almost braked and pulled into the Simonar property across the highway from what became his deadly destination.

drove down to it. I just drove in there and started shooting.

Sergeant Fraser — Now, tell us what happened inside the house.
Like from the time you went up to it.

Hoffman — Well, I went up to it. Before I went up to it, my mind
was absolutely away from hunting. I was thinking about Spruce
bushes, to see if there was any and there was none. Just bang, just like
that, my mind went on to kill people. So, I drove to the gate, opened
the gate, and drove in. Went to the house, I walked and no dog
bothered me at all. I walked in the house and I see a guy, he was just
sitting there on the bed then and he said, "who is it?" He kept on
saying that and, when he saw the gun, he jumped up on the bed and
I shot him. He jumped off the bed and kept coming at me. He grabbed
me right by the neck, here. He was trying to get me, but he was shot
and I kept on shooting at him with the gun until the gun was empty,
and I shot the last shell into him. He fell down. He finally hit the floor.

Sergeant Fraser — Where was he lying when you left him?

Hoffman — Right beside the door. He was on his fours, he wasn't
on the floor completely.

Sergeant Fraser — How was he dressed?

Hoffman — He only had his shorts on.

Sergeant Fraser — Then, what next?

Hoffman — Then I walked outside and I filled the gun right full.

Sergeant Fraser — And then?

Hoffman — I went back in. I finished him off. Then I started
slaughtering the girls.

Sergeant Fraser — Was anyone awake?

Hoffman — Yes, they were awake. Those two girls were awake.
They screamed at me, "don't shoot me, I don't want to die," and they
just ducked underneath the covers and I went there and shot them
and my head was really spinning. Then, as I had already committed
murder, I kept on shooting. No sense stopping now.

Corporal Gawthrop — And what about the mother, Victor?

Hoffman — I (blank)[6] jumped out the window and I went around

---

6. The blank was inserted because the tape is unclear.

the other side of the house, around this way. She saw me and she said, "don't murder me." I did, I shot her in the chin. She fell down on the ground and I shot her again.

Sergeant Fraser — Was there anyone with her?

Hoffman — She had a baby. I didn't shoot the baby yet, and I didn't want to shoot it. I went back in the house and finished off the rest of the girls. They were still screaming and they were making funny noises. They weren't dead yet. They didn't die, the bullet in the head just didn't want to kill them. I didn't want to shoot them anywhere else, I wanted to shoot them in the head because I could cut the heads off and take it with me. Then I'd have them bullets with me. But, since some of the bullets were going right through the head and out and hit the wall, there was no sense cutting the heads off anyway because the ballistics would be on the bullets anyway.

Corporal Gawthrop — And did you shoot all the children in the house, Victor?

Hoffman — Yes, except one.

Corporal Gawthrop — Why did you not shoot the little girl?

Hoffman — Because she couldn't see me, she couldn't identify me.

Corporal Gawthrop — Where was she?

Hoffman — She was sleeping on the bed, right next to the one I killed.

Corporal Gawthrop — How many girls were on the bed?

Hoffman — There were three of them.

Sergeant Fraser — Did they all stay in that room?

Hoffman — Yes, they didn't move, none bothered to jump out of bed and hide under the bed. If they had of done that, I'd never have shot them, because I had to shoot everybody so nobody could identify my licence plates when I turned around with the car.

Corporal Gawthrop — What time do you think this would have been in the morning?

Hoffman — Six o'clock fast time.

Corporal Gawthrop — And what about the little baby outside?

Hoffman — I went back out there at the last and finished it off. I didn't wanna shoot it, I hated myself for shooting it.

Corporal Gawthrop — Where did you shoot that little baby?

Hoffman — Right in the head, I didn't want it to suffer, maybe nobody would find it for three or four days. It would starve.

Sergeant Fraser — Have you, did you know who the people were before you went to the house?

Hoffman — I didn't know these people.

Sergeant Fraser — Have you ever been there before?

Hoffman — Never.

Sergeant Fraser — Have you ever been to Shell Lake before?

Hoffman — Never.

Sergeant Fraser — Had you ever heard the name before?

Hoffman — I've heard of Shell Lake.

Sergeant Fraser — Had you ever known Petersons lived there?

Hoffman — No.

Corporal Gawthrop — What did you do with the expended cartridge cases?

Hoffman — I started collecting them, I collected 17 of them. I counted them right there in the house on the sewing machine. I figured there had to be some more missing and I looked and looked and looked and couldn't find no more.

Sergeant Fraser — Where did you, where are they now?

Hoffman — I threw them all away.

Sergeant Fraser — Where did you throw them?

Hoffman — Behind the garage in the grass.

Sergeant Fraser — Who's garage?

Hoffman — At home there.

Sergeant Fraser — Your house?

Hoffman — Yeah, the same day the cops showed up and picked up the gun.

Sergeant Fraser — The baby was the last one you shot?

Hoffman — Yeah.

Sergeant Fraser — Did you go back in the house anymore after that?

Hoffman — Yes, I did.

Sergeant Fraser — And what did you do?

Hoffman — I looked for cartridges.

Sergeant Fraser — How long did you stay there?

Hoffman — Till about 6:30.

Sergeant Fraser — And then what did you do?

Hoffman — I drove home, I was real sick. I was just about sick enough to shoot myself for what I had done. I didn't know where to shoot myself, where I would die quick. Because I saw the way they died, they died so hard, they didn't want to die. I don't even know where my heart is. It's here, isn't it?

Corporal Gawthrop — Was the door to the house locked when you went to it?

Hoffman — No, it was open, wasn't locked.

Sergeant Fraser — Was he awake when you went in?

Hoffman — Yes.

Sergeant Fraser — Did you have the big rifle with you too?

Hoffman — No.

Sergeant Fraser — The .22 is the only rifle you have?

Hoffman — The .22 is the only rifle.

Corporal Gawthrop — Where is that .22 rifle right now?

Hoffman — The police have it.

Sergeant Fraser — What clothes were you wearing at the time?

Hoffman — Same clothes I have now.

Sergeant Fraser — Same shirt?

Hoffman — Same overalls.

Sergeant Fraser — Same hat?

Hoffman — Yes.

Sergeant Fraser — What about footwear?

Hoffman — I had rubbers on.

Sergeant Fraser — You had rubbers on?

Corporal Gawthrop — And where are those rubbers now?

Hoffman - Cops got 'em.

Corporal Gawthrop — Did you ever want to do anything like this before?

Hoffman — No, just those few minutes there. It just popped into my mind, just like that. Do you think I could get rid of it? No, sir, I just went and done it anyway.

Corporal Gawthrop — What, now can you explain how this popped into your mind, what went through your mind?

Hoffman — I looked over at the house, there, I wasn't driving too fast. I was driving slow, just looking at the land. I just looked at the house there, he had a T.V. set there and everything. Figured they were kinda rich, maybe. When I walked beside the house they were penniless and poor. I don't know what ... made me shoot them.

Sergeant Fraser — Did you need money?

Hoffman — No I didn't, I had plenty.

Sergeant Fraser — You had plenty of money?

Hoffman — Mm Hm.

Corporal Gawthrop — Did you take anything from the house?

Hoffman — Yes, I took away a jar of shells and poured it in my pocket. They were .22 shorts and .22 longs mixed in.

Corporal Gawthrop — Did you take anything else?

Hoffman — Seven dollars.

Corporal Gawthrop — Where was that seven dollars, Victor?

Hoffman — There was three dollars in one purse and another purse I found had four dollars in it, but I don't kill for money anyways, so it didn't matter.

Sergeant Fraser — Were you interested in anything else in the house?

Hoffman — Nothing.

Sergeant Fraser — Did you look for any guns?

Hoffman — I looked for guns in the house but I didn't find any. I thought they were out in the shed somewhere. But, I didn't look for any.

Sergeant Fraser — You didn't go to the shed to look or did you?

Hoffman — No.

Sergeant Fraser — And so, you picked up all the cartridges you could find?

Hoffman — Yes.

Sergeant Fraser — You put those in your pocket?

Hoffman — Yes, in my right pocket.

Sergeant Fraser — In your right pocket, and this would be about 6:30 you were finishing up?

Hoffman — Yes, then there was a coyote came out of the bush. A big yellow coyote. He had a bushy tail. I thought maybe it was the dog. I looked at the tail and it was bushy. It was straight out, it had to be a coyote.

Sergeant Fraser — What field was that in?

Hoffman — That was, that was right by the window where I killed the man. I killed the boss of the house, Mr. Peterson. That window, right there on the south side. I could see the coyote outside there.

Sergeant Fraser — Did you get in your car or did you walk around?

Hoffman — I walked around some more still looking for cartridges. Lots of times I walked, I walked everywhere. I even shook the blankets to see if I could find any.

Corporal Gawthrop — What was your reason for picking the cartridges up?

Hoffman — Because I knew they could be tested for markings.

Sergeant Fraser — Do you read some gun magazines?

Hoffman — Yes, I knew about that, Jim Peake told me about that. Robert Peake told me too that empty cartridges can be ...

Corporal Gawthrop — And what about bullets, the lead bullets, did you think about those?

Hoffman — Yes, I thought of them too. I thought I would change the rifling with grinding compound.

Sergeant Fraser — Where did you go to try to buy the grinding compound?

Hoffman — At Hector's and Cheyne's.

Sergeant Fraser — At Hector and?

Hoffman — Cheyne's.

Sergeant Fraser — Cheyne's, in what town?

Hoffman — Leask.

Sergeant Fraser — Did they have any?

Hoffman — No, but dad had some anyway. He told me about it ...
I didn't sleep very good last night either.

Sergeant Fraser — Have you told anyone else about this?

Hoffman — Nobody.

Sergeant Fraser — Nobody?

Hoffman — No, that's all.

Sergeant Fraser — Have you told your father?

Hoffman — No, I wanted to tell him.

Sergeant Fraser — You wanted to tell him?

Hoffman — Yes.

Sergeant Fraser — But, did you?

Hoffman — No.

Sergeant Fraser — Did you tell your mother?

Hoffman — No.

Sergeant Fraser — Did you tell your brother?

Hoffman — No, I knew I had to get rid of the gun, but how could I without him suspecting me of the murder. I should have got rid of it anyway, and the boots, I waited too long and then the cops drove up.

Sergeant Fraser — Have you ever felt like this before? Have you or have you not?

Hoffman — Never.

Sergeant Fraser — Never felt like this before?

Hoffman — Never.

Sergeant Fraser — Did you feel this way when you were at Peakes house when you saw that girl?

Hoffman — No, she even invited me in the house even. I didn't stay in the house for long. I went outside, and I started talkin' to the cat, stuff like that.

Corporal Gawthrop — Is there anything else you want to tell us, Victor?

Hoffman — Just that I know I'm sick in the head and that's all. But I could never kill again, I know that.

Corporal Gawthrop — How many shots do you think you fired all together?

Hoffman — 22.

Corporal Gawthrop — 22?

Hoffman — Yes.

Sergeant Fraser — When did you load the gun for the first time?

Hoffman — I loaded it at home.

Sergeant Fraser — At home, how many shells did you put in then?

Hoffman — All I could get in.

Sergeant Fraser — How many does it hold?

Hoffman — About nine, I guess.

Sergeant Fraser — What type of shells did you load that time?

Hoffman — Longs, there was some shells in the gun anyway.

Sergeant Fraser — There was some shells already in the gun?

Hoffman — Yes, but I wasn't planning on killing anybody at that time.

Sergeant Fraser — What did you load the gun for, do you know?

Hoffman — I just filled it up in case I see something. I'm not supposed to carry a loaded gun in the car but I always do.

Corporal Gawthrop — And the cartridges you picked up in the house, where did you say you put them again?

Hoffman — In my right pocket.

Corporal Gawthrop — And then what did you do with them? The expended shells that were fired?

Hoffman — I took them home with me. I emptied my pockets on the bed at home.

Sergeant Fraser — And then what happened to them?

Hoffman — I left them laying there and then I picked them up and I put them on (phone rings and tape recorder stopped). TAPE RECORDER BEGINS AGAIN.

Sergeant Fraser — We were speaking of the cartridges you picked up at the house.

Hoffman — Yes.

Sergeant Fraser — You took them home?

Hoffman — Yes.

Sergeant Fraser — And then what did you do with them?

Hoffman — I emptied them on to the bed.

Sergeant Fraser — And then what happened?

Hoffman — I put them up on the cupboard made out of boxes and

I left them there for a couple of days, until about Thursday, I think it was, no, Friday. That was the day dad came home from town with the story. I put them in my pocket. I took them outside, went to the garage out there, and threw them in the bush. I thought maybe the cops would put two and two together if they found 17 cartridges and five expended ones which were left at the scene of the crime. They could put two and two together then.

Sergeant Fraser — Did you just drop them or did you throw them?
Hoffman — I threw them.
Sergeant Fraser — You threw them?
Hoffman — So they couldn't be found.

COMPASSION and horror mingled in the packed courtroom. There were looks of revulsion. Robert nearly broke down and wept. Stella sat in a state of shock. All eyes, many hostile, were focused on the accused. There was pity. This boy had shot a diaper clad infant in the head because, "I didn't want it to suffer."

This killer, was not even sure where he had been born.

"Either Prince Albert or Shellbrook."

It was pathetic. After murdering nine persons, this shell of a human had remained in the house with his victims.

"I collected 17 cartridges. I counted them right there in the house on the sewing machine."

CORPORAL Edgar Arthur Kuhn was the eighth Crown witness to be called. He was followed on the stand by identification officer Corporal Roderick McKenzie. A photograph of footprints on the floor near the body of Jim Peterson was entered in evidence. Three pieces of linoleum, spent bullets and spent casings were also tagged as exhibits.

Constable Michael O'Donnell was called to show the continuity of the exhibits. A member of the RCMP identification branch, he told the court that he had taken evidence from the

Peterson home. Following this he related how he had accompanied the bodies to Prince Albert.

Corporal Charles Nolan was the next to testify. He told how he had visited the Hoffman home and seized a .22-calibre rifle. It was loaded with seven live rounds and one spent cartridge. The Corporal also said that a pair of rubber boots had been taken for evidence. During cross-examination it was learned that a neighbor had told police of Victor's mental background. That he had been released from The Saskatchewan Hospital in North Battleford less than three weeks prior to the crime.

An elderly man, who was witnessing the proceedings, shook his head. He was recalling what the trial judge had told the all-male jury. It was their duty to satisfy the people of Saskatchewan and the rest of Canada whether Victor Ernest Hoffman was guilty or not guilty of slaying Mr. and Mrs. James Peterson. The fact that seven children also died would have no bearing on the deliberations. Nor should the fact that there had been a vast amount of publicity.

Sergeant Gerry Fraser, who had previously been called on the voir dire, preceded Staff-Sergeant Shane (Rip) Kirby in giving direct evidence.

A ballistics expert, Staff-Sergeant Kirby told the court that at least one slug had come from the .22-calibre rifle that belonged to the accused. The witness said the examination had been conducted at the RCMP laboratory in Regina. He said the rifle, which was seized August 18th from the Hoffman farm — the one with the modified firing pin — was also the weapon to which several cartridges belonged.

The evidence continued to mount and seemed to leave little chance that the defence could produce any witnesses who would alter anything that had so far been said.

Testimony from Sergeant Frederick Tweed was also forceful. He told the court an attempt had been made to alter the rifling on the gun barrel.

Victor had said earlier, "I thought I would change the rifling with grinding compound."

The 15th Crown witness was Beverly Jean Long, a civilian employee with the RCMP. She was followed on the stand by Sergeant George Robert (Bob) Mooney. Sergeant Mooney, who had testified at the preliminary hearing as a Corporal but who was promoted in the interim, gave evidence concerning a pair of rubber boots that were seized at the Hoffman home. He told the court the boots left prints that matched the marks found in the blood that soaked the front portion of the body of Jim Peterson.

The Crown closed its case. Sixteen witnesses had been called.

Members of the audience who jammed the small room of justice were not surprised to learn how the accused had been found out. Corporal Nolan emphasized that information from a neighbor led him to the Hoffman farm. He said the tip led to the subsequent discovery of a .22-calibre rifle that had recently been fired. The informant knew the accused had been released from hospital such a short time before the fatal consequences.

The defence would call four witnesses.

The mother of the accused, Mrs. Stella Hoffman, was the first to testify. The short, sturdy red-headed woman took the stand. She said her son had told her the day before he entered The Saskatchewan Hospital that the previous day he had killed the devil.

She knew her son had "killed all of that family."

Shaking, the now even tinier looking mother of seven left the stand. She gazed at her impassive son. He was staring hopelessly from the prisoner's box, his mind dormant.

Dr. Stanislaw Jedlicki took the Bible, raised his right hand and swore to tell the truth. He had treated the accused from May 29th to July 26th. Dr. Jedlicki told the court he had diagnosed his patient as a schizophrenic, "undifferentiated type." Schizophrenia was defined as a long standing disease of the mind. A malady, that among other things, causes the sufferer to have hallucinations. Dr. Jedlicki went on to say that he released the accused when twelve electro-shock therapies and other treatments apparently restored him to his senses.

Robert shook his head, "apparently restored Victor to his senses and yet less than three weeks later the killings took place." Slowly, he buried his face in his wide hands. "Hard to believe that Victor could have been released so soon after the doctor said he was very sick."

The testimony continued by Dr. Jedlicki.

He said that during his interviews with Victor the patient described "psychotic incidents that occurred from the age of six years."

He said the accused told him that he saw the devil for the first of many times when he was six years of age. The doctor delineated how Victor had told him that the devil talked to him about his soul.

The devil had urged the youth to "sell your soul to me or suffer a million times."

"The angels and God were also seen by the accused. God told him He would look after him and there was no need to make plans for the future."

The court was noiseless. Dr. Jedlicki forged ahead.

"He used to get messages from God who told him he would go to heaven some time in October. The boy was very withdrawn and preoccupied with sex."

A reporter leaned over and whispered to another.

"It's as insane as the killings. Why was he ever released?"

Court was told by the doctor that a week after treatment started, his patient told him he was very happy and at last free of the devil.

Looks of wonderment flashed around the congested room.

Robert began to think back.

"It was a week after treatment began that Victor told the doctor he was all right. It would have been such a short period from then that Victor would have written the letter saying he could come home. So sick, and yet they decided so fast to let him go."

The head of the psychiatric department at the University Hospital in Saskatoon was called to testify. Dr. McKerracher told the court that after interviewing the accused three times (August 23rd and 24th, and January 8th) he concluded that Victor was suffering from acute schizophrenia.

"He had to kill and kill and kill."

Victor had been having a struggle with apparitions for 10 years. The slaying of the Petersons was his way of pleasing the devil without bowing down to him. According to the witness, Victor believed he was acting on a divine injunction by shooting the family. The doctor told the court it was his opinion that when the accused participated in the killings he did not appreciate the implications of what he was doing.

"He would not have it in his mind to know it was wrong to do what he was doing at precisely the time he was doing it. The thought of wrongness just would not have crossed his mind."

Dr. McKerracher said that schizophrenics often are jolted back to reality by a severe shock and perhaps the sight of all the bodies lying around had brought the accused back near realness. He said that from the 11th of August until halfway through the killings, Victor was in a different world.

The psychiatrist told the court that the urge to kill suddenly drained from the accused with the shock of returning to reality. It was this, according to the witness, that saved Phyllis.

After the murders the accused became frightened and tried to pick up all the empty rifle cartridges. During the interview with Dr. McKerracher on August 23rd, Victor broke down and wept.

"He showed great remorse over the killings."

The three interviews by Dr. McKerracher had been conducted at the request of Crown prosecutor Kujawa. They had revealed the murderous impulses that Victor had experienced. It was made known again that he had entertained thoughts of killing his own family.

"On August 11th he know he was going to kill somebody. He had to kill and kill and kill."

A second psychiatrist from Saskatoon, Dr. Abram Hoffer, told the court that Victor began feeling an impulse to kill when he was 10 years of age. He said the accused made this known to him during interviews September 12th and 13th. The interviews had been requested by defence counsel.

Dr. Hoffer testified that Victor told him he thought of killing his parents on August 15th but instead went for a drive. The doctor said that three days before, on August 12th, Victor thought that if he could actually kill someone it would prove his manhood to the devil. The psychiatrist continued. He said that on the morning of August 15th the accused awakened about three o'clock in the morning. He began to "imagine things" and then hopped in his car and left the farm. During the drive, Victor often wanted to stop and kill. When the Peterson farm came into sight the feeling was overpowering. The defence witness told the court that the accused decided to drive up to the house and "kill everyone in it." Dr. Hoffer said Phyllis had been spared because the urge to kill had been washed out of the accused, "he said he could never kill again."

The psychiatrist advised the court that Victor told him that the victims "looked rotten, they were pig-like."

"I'm convinced," the doctor stated, "that he saw the devil. He was real to him. He heard voices. He felt disembodied hands touching him."

Court was told by Dr. Hoffer that over the preceding decade, Victor had been engaged in a conflict. A battle between instructions given him by angels and by the devil. He had delusions of people watching him and hating him. He felt that robbery was evil and against the law but killing people was not. Victor did not feel guilty after the Petersons died. He was a young man who had felt the urge to kill strangers since he was 10 years of age. At that age he began to be cruel to animals.

He imagined the devil as a pig — a very large animal, over six feet tall, weighing around 300 pounds, black in color, and without any clothes.

Dr. Hoffer told the court, "I don't think Mr. Hoffman clearly separated in his mind the difference between killing birds, cattle or people. He thought he was killing pigs."

The witness believed that Victor was aware of what he was doing and thought he had the approval of God. He did not, however, know that he was doing wrong.

The doctor offered, "The killings were a series of random events that happened at that time."

Victor did not go to the farm to kill a family he did not know. The psychiatrist told the court that when the accused awakened he was unable to get to sleep again.

"He imagined things, like his whole body had been cut in half without pain. He thought of killing someone."

A professional killer hired to do the job or a robot programmed to kill and not get caught could have committed the act. That was Dr. Hoffer's comparison.

He went on, "What was being done was not determined in the normal sense of right from wrong."

The accused, he repeated, felt like killing strangers from the age of 10 years. Instead of killing people, he killed animals. He clubbed cats to death. Once he caught a cat in a magpie trap and kept it imprisoned without food or water for three weeks. This was the state of his mind until the early morning hours of August 15th. Then — the James Peterson family took on an animal-like appearance to the accused. They were slaughtered like pigs.

"He was acting mechanically. I don't think he was capable of feeling any emotion," Dr. Hoffer testified.

Both Dr. McKerracher and Dr. Hoffer gave evidence that Victor had told them he did not tell anyone at the hospital about his urge to kill someone. They testified that he revealed it for the first time after his arrest on August 19, 1967.

Stella still wondered, "Why wasn't he helped as he should have been?"

She knew that he was not right when he was discharged from the hospital. Her husband also knew that Victor was still sick.

"The doctors said Victor felt hands trying to choke him. They said he told them, that once he tore the blouse off an angel. He said he was protecting her from the devil. He even wanted to kill us."

Like most people, Stella knew very little about mental illness.

"When the hospital said Victor could come home what could we do? We would have done anything the hospital asked but they never even discussed Victor's sickness. There was never any advice. Sure, they said Victor must take the pills but they didn't say how important it was. If they only took the time to explain to us. It would have been only a matter of seconds and Victor never would have killed those innocent people."

THE submission of evidence had concluded. The jury would be addressed by the prosecution and defence counsel. Following this, the members would be charged by Mr. Justice MacPherson. Deliberations would follow, the jury would hand down its decision, and the response of justice would be known.

Jurors were not segregated from the community. The only exception was when they were in the courtroom, under police guard. The power to exercise such discretion was in the hands of the trial judge who chose to allow them to return to their families when court recessed. This power of non-sequestering was not available in charges of capital murder but could be exercised in a non-capital murder case.

Mr. Justice MacPherson said of the jury members, who all lived within an 18-mile radius of Battleford, "I don't like to lock a jury up if I can help it."

This practice was not uncommon in his courts. It prompted a statement by Crown prosecutor Kujawa that the procedure was not common elsewhere in the nation. He added though, that the approach was carried out by other justices of the High Courts in the province.

The trial was nearing completion. In less than 24 hours the verdict would be known.

CROWN prosecutor Kujawa addressed the jury for 36 minutes. He said that when a person causes the death of another person and means to do so, this is non-capital murder.

The prosecutor expounded, "There is no doubt in this case that the accused caused the death of Jim and Evelyn Peterson."

The court was then told that Victor possibly knew he was shooting but the question remained whether he knew he was shooting people and that the act was wrong. This was the question that rested with the jury.

DEFENCE counsel Noble took just more than 40 minutes for his address. He said the defence had no quarrel with the evidence of the Crown. Evidence that Mr. and Mrs. James Peterson died as the result of gunshot wounds. Wounds suffered from a gun in the hands of Victor.

The court was told that at the time the Petersons were shot, the accused was not responsible for his actions. That he was legally insane and because of this was entitled to a verdict of not guilty on ground of insanity.

The decision-makers were apprised, "You will have to search the Crown's evidence in vain to find out why the horrifying event of that day took place."

The reasoning behind the murders contained no rational answer, except one.

"The accused was insane, completely insane."

Both the Crown and the defence had concluded their summations.

MR. Justice MacPherson advised the jury that the question was, whether the accused was insane when he shot Mr. and Mrs. Peterson within about eight or 10 minutes of each other.

He said the jury should not concern itself with the credibility of witnesses. "There is no real conflict of evidence. There is no evidence before you of any eyewitnesses. What you have here is a circumstantial case."

The jurors were told that the defence of insanity could only be applied to the defendant's state of mind at the time the acts were committed. The Criminal Code states that no person can be convicted of an offence when he was insane.

The Trial Judge, referring to the time element between the killings, stressed that it was "critically brief."

The decision would be whether the accused appreciated the nature and quality of the acts. Whether he knew that wrong had been committed. The court was reminded that psychiatrists agreed that the accused appreciated he was shooting and killing. They had also agreed that he did not appreciate he was killing people. Mr. Justice MacPherson informed the jury that it was not necessary to prove that murder had been committed. He said that in this case, there was no motive.

At 12:24 p.m., the deliberations began. Jury members seeking to find Victor Ernest Hoffman guilty or not guilty by reason of insanity. It was now only a matter of time. The defendant had been described as a lunatic who in no way could be found responsible for the horrible crime. Yet, the possibility remained that the jury would decide that he was accountable. Victor's father waited for what would seem the longest time in his life. So did Stella. The evidence was insurmountable. There was no doubt their son had committed the crime. They found it impossible to understand how Victor could be so hopelessly deranged, as the psychiatrists had testified, and yet less than a month before the murders the hospital said he was all right.

"Why didn't the hospital keep him? Why would they risk releasing him? Couldn't they have taken just a few seconds to explain what was wrong with him?"

It was their son, in a stupor, without sentiment during the four-day trial, who now faced the prospect of life imprisonment because of his premature release. Robert and Stella endured. They were not the only ones. There were thousands who were following the case who impatiently awaited the outcome in unhurried time.

The jury had to decide: whether to find the accused guilty as charged in the death of James Peterson; guilty as charged in the death of Evelyn Peterson; or not guilty on both charges, because of insanity. It was about three and one-half hours before a decision would be reached.

T HE verdict when it came was not surprising. Victor Ernest Hoffman, charged with two counts of non-capital murder, had been found not guilty by reason of insanity.

All eyes were on the wooden prisoner's box. His vacant expression did not change. He showed no visible emotion. Seated, with bowed head, puffy face, and dulled eyes locked to the floor, he swallowed a tranquillizer. The medication, taken occasionally throughout the proceedings, was at the insistence of defence counsel Noble following the preliminary hearing.

"He was pretty sick at that time. He was acting up in the jail and I felt he wasn't very rational."

Victor showed no feeling, although he wondered aloud "Where am I going?" when committed to the Saskatchewan Correctional Institute in Prince Albert. He was robotic, machine-like in his torpid state. It was directed that he remain at the institution where he would await the pleasure of the

Lieutenant Governor in council. He would be kept in custody — perhaps for the remainder of his life.

Victor Ernest Hoffman was completely insane when he kept pulling and pulling and pulling the trigger of his .22 calibre Browning pump action repeater rifle. That was the ruling.

Defence counsel Noble was not surprised.

"I think it was the only possible verdict and I thought so from the time I had a look at the facts. Victor just had to be insane. The jury didn't really argue about that question, they worried about the fact of whether or not he would get out. It went the way it should have."

Inspector Sawyer was glad it was over.

"Personally I would like to forget the whole affair. I don't want any more to do with it," he offered resignedly.

After what had been revealed during the trial very few people were surprised at the result. The public, however, remembered the details of the random slaughter. There was dissatisfaction and frustration. Some wanted cruel vengeance.

As a scraggly-bearded service station operator put it, "If the guy had nine lives I'd take every one of them. He sure got off soft."

Helmer Helgeton and Evie, Jim's sister, were outraged. It was Helmer who had driven the school bus that had taken the Peterson children to their classes at the old schoolhouse. They had been so well behaved, so fun loving, and so innocent. Now they were dead and buried.

"If he's not guilty somebody is. I think it's a coverup for the government, the hospital, and the doctors. Everybody I've talked to is so mad and so disgusted. The doctors at North Battleford must have known he was dangerous. Why didn't they know?"

ICTOR'S parents were destroyed. No matter what the decision, they were losers. A family in torment. They returned home from the now-empty courtroom in Battleford. Stella, haltingly, went upstairs and entered Victor's vacated bedroom which some would call a lair. She was by herself, alone with her memories, in the unpossessed space in which her son would never return. Its tidy contents had not been touched with one chair (straight backed) and the old applebox bookcase neatly in place. His sister had made it and Victor had placed some of his cartridges among the books after the killings. The literature comprised Victor's favorite type of reading material. There were many: Popular Mechanics, Sportsman's Guide, Outdoor Life, and a lone copy of Reader's Digest. There were also magazines that he had become so interested in such a short time before. Among them: For Men Only, Real West, Ghost Stories, and various others that showed the direction of his mind. Stella turned and tearfully moved away. As if in slow-motion, she slowly descended the stairs and returned to the kitchen. Entering the deserted room, she sighted the latch that had been put on the porch door following the murders at Shell Lake.

She looked at it and began to weep, "Robert we didn't need the lock. The killer was in our house all the time."

HOME ALONE — The Hoffman house as it looked at the time of the court case. Victor, who never returned, used to jump out his upper bedroom window which is on the left. Stella, not realizing that there was a method to her son's madness, would admonish him. Secretly, he felt that one day he might go to prison and believed that the practice would prove useful if he ever wanted to escape. When shown this picture after being incarcerated for 25 years, Victor studied it intently. It brought back a lot of memories. He said with fondness, "It's lovely, isn't it?"

195

HOFFMAN PROP-
ERTY — *Victor spent a
lot of time by himself in
the outbuildings. Several
times, he attempted sui-
cide in the garage. Later,
behind that same shed-like
structure, he disposed of
crucial evidence.*

THE AFTERMATH

XI

THE lively, vibrant home that once housed the Peterson family was soon barren. Helmer, together with friends, took a whole day to clean the blood splattered structure. The police had cut bullets from various sections of the walls. Red stained linoleum was also taken for evidence. There was a great deal to be done. The walls, floors and ceilings had to be scrubbed thoroughly. A sickening job but one that was felt necessary.

The mattresses were burned, as were numerous other articles. Following the distasteful task, arrangements were made for an auction of the remaining possessions. The idea, that of auctioneer Ted McDougall of Prince Albert, resulted in close to $4,000 being netted for the trust fund. Many contributed: the auctioneer, CKBI Prince Albert and the neighbors who could.

There was scarcely anything left. In the girls bedroom, with its rose-colored walls, were three clippings pasted to the plaster. A picture of Mick Jagger, one of The Monkeys and an article entitled Man & His Camera. In a corner near the front door — a raggedy-ann doll and right behind it, one of Jim's jackets.

Out in the yard — an old combine and a bed. The bed was sold, however the purchaser had not taken it away.

Earlier, on August 18th, members of the news media were allowed to tour the clapboard death-house. At that time there were more photographs in the girls bedroom (The Animals, Elizabeth Taylor, and the stars from the television show Bonanza) as well as personal objects, mostly strewn around. The master bedroom contained a crib and a steel double bed while two steel double beds stood alone in the girls stark sleeping quarters. In the pale green painted living room there was a single bed, chesterfield, television set and two chairs. The kitchen, with a dining area, contained a small electric range, wood-burning stove and a refrigerator. The house did not have complete indoor plumbing although it did have running water.

Inside the building, with its windows and lone door boarded shut, all was now bare. The little farmhouse had a deathly stillness about it.

I T was eight days after the court decision that the government of Saskatchewan issued a statement. It said that Victor would remain under 24-hour surveillance while the adequacy of other facilities was studied. The joint announcement, by Attorney General D.V. Heald and Health Minister Gordon Grant, followed a Cabinet meeting.

The Attorney General said, "If facilities at North Battleford are not good enough, we will have to look elsewhere."

Health Minister Grant said he could not estimate the length of time that Victor would remain in the correctional institute in Prince Albert. He said the government wanted to be sure he received the proper treatment under strict security.

And so it was learned the Saskatchewan Government was making a move. It would investigate whether the mental hospital at North Battleford was equipped to handle the 21-year-old who had unmercifully butchered nine innocents. The government, however, did not see fit to announce at this time whether or not an investigation would be conducted to determine why the patient was ever released. Interest was expressed as to whether facilities at North Battleford were suitable to have Victor sent back for further treatment. The idea that inefficiency or incompetence might have been involved in his original release did not seem to be an issue with those in charge.

True, the Saskatchewan government had inserted newspaper advertisements pertaining to a study of the province's psychiatric care program. The advertisements had been published in September, 1967 — the murders had taken place a month before. Early in September, Health Minister Grant and the Director of the province's Psychiatric Services Branch, Dr. Colin Smith, contacted Dr. Shervert H. Frazier of Houston, Texas. The Saskatchewan health officials requested Dr. Frazier to conduct a study of psychiatric services. As advertised, the terms of reference did not deal directly with Victor Hoffman. The advertisement stated:

Public opinion on Saskatchewan's psychiatric Care Program is being solicited by Dr. S.H. Frazier, Houston, Texas, U.S.A., who has been appointed to review the Program with reference to:

Admission and discharge criteria of in-patient facilities;

Quality of psychiatric treatment;

Adequacy of out-patient facilities and care with particular reference to the follow-up of discharged patients;

Any undesirable practices occurring within the context of the specific objectives of the program.

Submissions relevant to these terms are being sought from individuals and organizations.

Written briefs must be submitted to Dr. S.H. Frazier, c/o Psychiatric Services Branch, Department of Public Health, Regina, Saskatchewan by November 24, 1967.

Oral presentations may be made to Dr. S.H. Frazier, Room 267, Legislative Building, Regina, Saskatchewan, on December 8 and 11, 1967.

Appointments may be made by writing to Dr. S.H. Frazier at the above address.

This advertisement has been authorized by Saskatchewan Minister of Public Health, Hon. Gordon B. Grant.

THE mandate of the probe in no way included an investigation into the Shell Lake case. The broad terms of reference were sweeping. When released February 20, 1968, the report would make two minor references to The Shell Lake killings. Nothing more.

On February 12, 1968, Saskatchewan's Deputy Health Minister was interviewed in Regina. The statements by Dr. J.G. Clarkson revealed the government had learned that security and treatment facilities at North Battleford were inadequate to serve in the case of Victor Hoffman. The Deputy Health Minister stated that his department was trying to arrange to transfer him to another hospital — the hospital for the criminally insane at Penetanguishene, Ontario. The admission that the hospital in North Battleford was ill-equipped to handle Victor was certainly not unexpected. It failed with treatment before the killings — thus it was highly unlikely it would be in a position to provide proper treatment and security for a known mass murderer.

Eight days after the announcement pertaining to the possible transfer of Victor to another hospital, the Frazier Report was tabled in the Saskatchewan Legislature. The review and appraisal of the province's psychiatric services was a stinging indictment. The findings, however, caused no immediate stir. They had been prepared by Dr. Frazier with the assistance of Dr. Alex D. Pokorny. Both medical doctors and both from Baylor University of Houston, Texas. At the beginning of the report there was praise for the psychiatric care program in

Saskatchewan.

"One of the world's more advanced community psychiatric programs. Saskatchewan has for at least two decades been in the forefront of innovations in delivery of psychiatric care; it has accumulated experience with many of the programs and features which most states in the U.S. are just now trying to establish."

The report then reviewed the history of Saskatchewan's mental health program.

"In 1914, the North Battleford Provincial Mental Hospital was opened, serving the entire province. In 1921, the Provincial Mental Hospital at Weyburn was opened, and thereafter it served roughly the southern half of the settled area of the Province ... By 1946 the North Battleford Hospital had 2,000 patients and Weyburn Hospital had a total of 2,600 patients, both far in excess of the capacity for which they were built. At this time plans were being made to build a third mental hospital of 1,600 beds at Saskatoon, but this plan was never effected."

The study continued with information about the relevance of the passage of the Mental Health Act in 1961.

"This has been generally regarded as a model act, and has been copied in other Canadian provinces."

There was also mention of the implementation of the Saskatchewan Plan (the concepts included the realization that to keep one in an institution is harmful) and the fact it had been only partially established.

"Therefore the Province has only partly established the Saskatchewan Plan, and has otherwise continued to operate on a patchwork, transitional program containing elements of the old and the new, plus some necessary compromises and opportunistic arrangements."

Section B, of Chapter Two of the Frazier Report, explained the events leading to the study.

"By January 1963, the inpatient population at the Saskatchewan Hospital, Weyburn was down to 1,519. During the succeeding years, there was a concentrated effort to reduce this population, through increased emphasis on local care, foster-home placement, and outpatient follow-up. The census at Weyburn dropped dramatically to 421 by June of 1966. This was the sharpest decline in population of any hospital in North America or the United Kingdom."

Section B continued to state that three years later, complaints were being received about the rate of discharge and the standards and conditions in homes where patients were being placed. There was word of the formation of the Ad Hoc Committee (outlined in the 1966 report of the Canadian Mental Health Association) and an explanation that its investigations led to additional regulations under the Mental Health Act. The complaints, however, ran on. Grievances concerning the early discharge of patients were prevalent. There was tremendous worry expressed about the resignation of professional workers who were supervising community replacement.

"One type of concern was about incidents precipitated by former psychiatric patients. When a former mental hospital patient was arrested for the murder of 9 persons at Shell Lake on August 15, 1967 this concern became widespread, and contributed to the institution of the present survey."

The terms of reference, as noted, did not include any review of the specific circumstances connected with the wretched file of Victor Hoffman.

The survey, then turned to The Saskatchewan Hospital at North Battleford.

"This hospital has followed a less aggressive discharge policy, and has, at least until the Shell Lake incident, run into far less resistance (than Weyburn) to discharge or community placement.

"We did receive, however, a number of individual complaints

which recorded that patients had been released from North Battleford while still assaultive, unruly and uncooperative. Some of the families perceived this hospital as being overly eager to get rid of patients. Physicians complained that admission to North Battleford was too difficult, taking as much as three or four days of negotiations, whereas discharge was much too easy. Also, it was stated that alcoholics and patients from other diagnostic categories were refused admission. Ambulance service was difficult to arrange.

"The North Battleford Hospital received more criticisms than any other in-patient unit concerning lack of communication, (such as a case summary or letter) to the local clinic or general practitioner. Because this hospital usually contains about 250 patients from Saskatoon, 100 miles away, most of the complaints originated there. The North Battleford Hospital also received its share of comments concerning precipitate, seemingly unplanned and uncoordinated discharges. There is evidence, however, that patients were discharged much more rapidly at the University Hospital in Saskatoon than at North Battleford."

There were two recommendations.

"Better communications, arrangements and understanding be developed between the North Battleford Hospital and the other Mental Health Regions from which it receives in-patients and overflow in-patients. This should include a clearly defined admission policy and procedure, so as to prevent delays, as well as a reasonable discharge policy with prompt notification and communication with the local center, physician, and family.

"That no heroic efforts be made at this time to reduce the in-patient population at Saskatchewan Hospital, North Battleford."

Section 4, Chapter Five was entitled, "Practice of Early Discharge, The Actual Application of Discharge Policy." There were numerous points covered; however, one of the most telling was embraced in the third paragraph.

"There were also criticisms about early discharges of psychopaths and potential criminals; these issues will be taken up in a later section."

Paragraph four was also damning.

"We consider, however, that the early discharge procedure at North Battleford and especially at Weyburn is based on unrealistic criteria and not based on improvement from psychotic symptoms, organic brain symptoms, and acting out and socially unacceptable behavior."

The Recommendation was concise.

"We suggest that the practice of early discharge be brought in line with the principles, so that discharge is not determined by bed counts, "statistics," or attempts to satisfy institutional goals, but by the needs of the patient, his family, and his community. Early discharge is indicated only if it appears that this will preserve family ties, prevent institutionalization, etc., after individual case study."

Section b, Discharge Criteria, also contained a recommendation.

"Discharge criteria should be standardized, though they may differ for the different classes of facilities; they should include a consideration of symptoms, availability of appropriate treatment in the community, and the welfare and wishes of the family. These criteria should be written down in general terms and widely disseminated."

Regarding Facilities and Programs for Out-Patient Care, there was yet another suggestion.

"We urge that prompt steps be taken to increase the numbers of community supervisory workers, and also to increase their level of skill through training, supervision and consultation. There should be at least one staff person for each 50 patients in community placement."

The report was highly critical of "reports of inadequate or even no communication between hospital and follow up programs."

Insofar as public education and public relations in the discharge of patients, the study found one serious concern, more prominent than any other.

"Perhaps the most frequent complaint was that families were not involved, consulted, or even informed."

There were two recommendations, the second is basic.

"A simple form letter, containing admission dates, diagnosis, and recommended treatment (including drug dosage) should be completed and handed to each patient at discharge, to be given to the local clinic or general practitioner. A full summary should be sent only when needed."

Page 32 of the Frazier Report contained the heading, "Undesirable Practices Occurring within the Context of the Specific Objectives of the Program." There were four points listed, two of them pertinent to the case of Victor, even though the terms of reference did not make any specific mention of the Hoffman case.

Some discharges of patients from in-patient care appear to be based on a "statistical approach" rather than a patient-family-community welfare approach.

There was no recommendation for the aforementioned as it had previously been made.

The second feature had little meaning to this writing but the third admitted there were no adequate provisions for the handling of psychopaths, sex offenders and similar individuals. The fourth item warned of an especially unsatisfactory situation regarding mentally ill offenders.

"It appears that, whenever a person is acquitted by reason of insanity, he is placed into custody until released by order of the Lieutenant Governor. This may lead to indefinite detention, far longer than the corresponding prison sentence if the person had been found guilty of the offense. Furthermore, the hospital staff has no power to discharge such patients; they are, accordingly, a completely foreign element in the mental hospital."

The Recommendation followed.

"The statutes which permit what amounts to an indefinite sentence, upon finding of not guilty by reason of insanity or upon a finding of mentally unfit to stand trial, should be changed to prevent what appears to be an unjust and discriminatory situation."

The 63-page Frazier report extolled 47 changes. Those with a relation to the Hoffman case have been outlined. There were, however, two more that were relevant.

"The present system of permits to practise for unlicensed physicians should be continued. We recommend, however, that such permits be for a limited period, such as two or three years. Residents in training programs should be exempt from this time limitation. A liaison committee should be set up between the Department of Public Health and the College of Physicians and Surgeons to research a mutually satisfactory arrangement.

"Clear lines of authority, accountability, and responsibility should be drawn and published. Orders, complaints, investigations, budgeting, and funding should follow these lines."

The study also showed that The Saskatchewan Hospital discharged 251 patients from January 1, 1966 to January 1, 1967. The largest discharge rate for any comparable period in an 11-year study. The hospital had 1,867 patients in 1956 and 10 years later was down to 857. Perhaps even more startling was the discharge rate at the Weyburn hospital. The institution had 1,724 patients in 1956 and was reduced to 443 by 1967. Nearly three-quarters of the population discharged.

The Frazier report was decidedly critical in its summation.

"The Province has gradually drifted into a situation in which it is trying to run a first-rate program on a second-rate budget and this simply will not work. As a result, quality of care is slipping, duties are being reassigned to less qualified personnel, caseloads are increasing and work days are becoming longer, all contributing to demoralization. At the present time the personnel situation is of crisis proportions and must be given top priority."

Health Minister Grant, when tabling the scathing document, said it was a candid and forthright appraisal of the program. He maintained the report would be a key to the expansion of psychiatric services in the province. The Health Minister later made mention of a proposed Ad Hoc committee that would be studying facets of the Frazier findings. What was not mentioned was the harsh truth that another such committee had studied the situation before the Shell Lake killings and yet the tragedy still occurred. Also, there was no mention of the 1966 report by The Canadian Mental Health Association, Saskatchewan Division, to the provincial government. A report that had forecast the very problems that could lead to such an appalling crime. Nor was there mention of a brief that the Canadian government had received in April, 1967 from the CMHA. It was later outlined, in part, in an issue of The Canadian Magazine. Paul Grescoe wrote:

"A medical and social disaster is developing in Canada, the Canadian Mental Health Association warned the Cabinet earlier this year in a brief that sounded as if it had been written by a sensation-seeking journalist. The mental health division of the Department of National Health and Welfare is ineffectual, it said. After-care and rehabilitation of mentally ill patients are becoming acute community problems. Facilities for diagnosis and treatment are distinctly second-class. Canada needs at least double the current number of mental health professionals. The Cabinet duly accepted the brief, but nobody — the public, press or politicians — bothered about it much."

Three days before the release of the Frazier report, I interviewed Dr. Stanislaw Jedlicki. The following is a partial transcript. It contradicts, in glaring fashion, portions of the story told by the Hoffmans.

PT — Did you examine Victor when he was brought in?

Dr. Jedlicki — Yes, that's right.

PT — Would you have told the mother and father that Victor was very sick, that he was seeing the devil, and that he would have to be here, referring to North Battleford, for maybe a year and possibly two?

Dr. Jedlicki — No, I only mentioned it because they wanted to take him in one week's time. They wanted to take him home because he improved. To serve this point I told them that he would be a long time, maybe even one year.

PT — Didn't you mention two years?

Dr. Jedlicki — No, for a long time. It depends upon improvement.

PT — Did you ever explain to his parents the nature of his illness?

Dr. Jedlicki — You know they are very simple-minded people. I explained to them quite clearly about everything. They didn't want to accept it.

PT — You would have sat down with both of them when he was first brought in?

Dr. Jedlicki — Yes.

PT — You would have outlined what was wrong with Victor?

Dr. Jedlicki — Yes.

(The second answer given by Dr. Jedlicki states that he only mentioned Victor's illness "... because they wanted to take him in one week's time. They wanted to take him home because he improved." The doctor's answers to questions five and six affirm that he met with the parents when Victor was first brought in and also that at that time he outlined the patient's illness. The Hoffman version is different. They say that three trips were made to North Battleford before there was even a meeting with Dr. Jedlicki.)

PT — A fellow in a white jacket gave them some pills?

Dr. Jedlicki — You know, that's the head nurse's office. They issue medication for one month.

PT — Robert Hoffman said he was told that Victor should take the pills but it wasn't stressed to him how important it would be. He wasn't told if Victor didn't take the pills how serious it could be.

Dr. Jedlicki — Everybody's informed about them.

PT — Everybody is?

Dr. Jedlicki — Yes.

PT — Robert Hoffman said when he went to the hospital Victor was heavily drugged. He said the boy was very stiff and it took three days before he started to come out of it.

Dr. Jedlicki — This is not true. This was the reaction because he was released. I am sure that he didn't want to take the medication and that was when everything started.

(Dr. Jedlicki was not present when his patient was released.)

PT — In other words you don't think he would have been drugged when he was released?

Dr. Jedlicki — No.

PT — Would you have been there when he was released?

Dr. Jedlicki — No. I told them that they should see me but it was at noontime and they left without seeing me.

(According to the Hoffmans they were told the doctor was too busy to see them when they went to pick up their son from the hospital.

"Can I speak with Dr. Jedlicki?"

"I'll see if I can get him for you."

"The doctor is too busy to see you.")

PT — If Victor was drugged it wouldn't have been by your orders?

Dr. Jedlicki — No.

PT — Would it have been possible that he was drugged and you wouldn't know about it.

Dr. Jedlicki — No! Impossible!

PT — According to Mr. Hoffman he was not informed as to what to do if Victor got sick. He was not told to hide the guns and so on.

Dr. Jedlicki — No, no, everybody's informed because we have clinics and there was one in his vicinity, that means Prince Albert. All papers are sent to clinics for follow-up.

PT — Would they get written notice or just be told?

Dr. Jedlicki — Just told, and Prince Albert medical clinic is informed if such a patient is released.

(According to the Hoffmans they were never informed as to what to do if their son's condition deteriorated. The Frazier report, in one of its recommendations, would tend to back this up. "A simple form letter, containing admission dates, diagnosis, and recommended treatment [including dosage] should be completed and handed to each patient at discharge, to be given to the local clinic or general practitioner." The recommendation followed a paragraph pertaining to discharge procedures. "Perhaps the most frequent complaint was that families were not involved, consulted, or even informed.")

PT — Is it true that there is no follow-up treatment? Once someone is released your job is finished?

Dr. Jedlicki — Yes.

PT — It would have been left up to the father to decide?

Dr. Jedlicki — The family.

PT — You would have been the doctor who would have authorized the release?

Dr. Jedlicki — Yes, that's right.

PT — He signed himself in, would he have to sign himself out?

Dr. Jedlicki — Yes, anytime his parents or the patient wants to be released he puts in his notice to be discharged. He wanted to many times but I postponed it.

PT — Would his insistence have been a factor in your decision to let him go?

Dr. Jedlicki — No, it depends on symptoms. He was quite good when released.

PT — He was quite good?

Dr. Jedlicki — Yes.

L ESS than a month after the interview with Dr. Jedlicki, the Saskatchewan Cabinet passed an order-in-council arranging for the transfer of Victor Ernest Hoffman to the Ontario hospital at Penetanguishene. No date was set. It would be as soon as possible. The agreement with the Ontario health department stressed that the arrangement was not permanent. It could be terminated by Ontario at any time. This did not set a precedent.

It would be only a few weeks before Victor would be transported east. Scant time for his mother and father to visit with him. A great amount of time for the Saskatchewan government to be troubled with him and his tormented soul.

Saskatchewan's Deputy Health Minister announced on March 25, 1968 that Victor had been transferred to the institution for the criminally insane. The relocation had taken place three days before. According to Dr. Clarkson, it would be for an indefinite period.

"They'll keep him there to be assessed concerning the security needs he requires."

The Saskatchewan government was free of its mass killer. It was hoped the slaughter of the James Peterson family would be forgotten. Nine people dead; a little girl orphaned; and a 21-year-old, who had despairingly sought help in his gremlin induced world, incarcerated. It had happened and now it was over. The populace had been moderately pacified with the Frazier report and at no time had the government been forced to investigate Victor's road to madness. In this way blame would be attached to no one, the matter could be forgotten and the government and its hospital in North Battleford saved face.

There was never any move to launch a formal probe into the many disturbing questions surrounding the premature hospital release of the son gone wrong. Quite simply, he was abandoned by the system that earlier had failed him.

VISIBLY SHAKEN — *A reporter, with telling eyes, surveys the children's bedroom.*

— Journal Photo by Dave Reidie

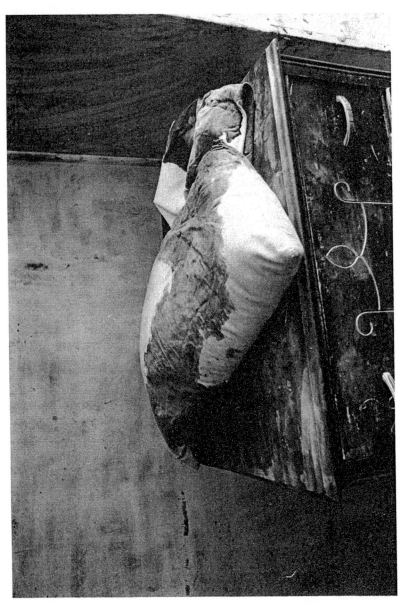

GRIM REMINDER — *The pillow, which replaced personal belongings that once decked the chest of drawers, was burned with other bedding. The furniture was auctioned off.*
— *Journal Photo by Dave Reidie*

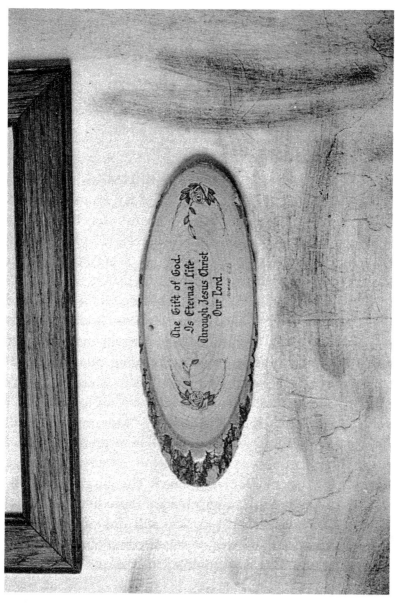

ETERNAL LIFE—This plaque had a prominent place in the Peterson home.

— Journal Photo by Dave Reidie

THE SURVIVORS

XII

C HRISTMAS, 1968 — slightly more than 16 months after the killings — remained an empty time for Phyllis. She missed her large deceased family terribly, especially all of her brothers and sisters who were also her closest playmates. She had no memory of what really happened. The door of the little white house forcibly being pushed open. Her father asking, "Who is it?", over and over. The gun discharging again and again. Her father slumping to the floor and finally dying, punctured with seven bullets. The piercing screams. "Don't shoot me, don't shoot me, please don't shoot me. I don't want to die, I don't want to die." The helpless, pathetic cry, "Mommy, mommy." Phyllis did not fully know the complete meaning of all that had occurred on that early morning of inhumanity. The strange noises. How her mother succumbed. The gurgling sounds. The horrifying manner in which all of those lives and those around them were shattered. She still did not appear to understand why there was so much commotion and then everything was quiet as she huddled underneath the bedding.

AUGUST 15, 1969 — two years to the day of the atrocity — Phyllis continued living with Kathy, Lee and their baby, William. They had moved back to Saskatchewan from Chetwynd and Lee was working his father's farm, as well as the Peterson land. It was a restorative period.

The death-house, an ominous, sorry reminder of the devil's rampage, was vacant.

"The thought of burning it down had been suggested," said uncle Helmer, "we never did and of course now that decision would have to be made by Kathy and Lee."

A monument had been erected in the cemetery at Shell Lake. It served as a grim testimonial to what had taken place. A portion of the $1,700 landmark, some $500, was paid by the Rural Municipality of Spiritwood. According to Evie, "The R.M. wanted to do something and the family agreed that such a donation would be all right."

Fred Peterson, 88, and Martha, 73, could not erase the bleakest day of their lives. Neither could Martha Finlayson, 72, Evelyn's mother. It was their son and son-in-law respectively who visited them nearly every day. He always worried about them. Yet, it was Jim, Evelyn and all but two of their brood who were no longer living.

The Saskatchewan government was continuing to scrupulously contemplate aid for Phyllis. The Crimes Compensation Board, a frustrating two years after the wanton attack, still only had the matter under consideration. The case, advised the sole female participant of the three member panel, was delayed because of evidence that was awaited. Mrs. Joyce Moxley said the hearing on the application opened December 19, 1968. It continued the next day, was adjourned until June 26th and then closed. Mrs. Moxley stated it would be improper to divulge any details as the hearing was held in-camera. She added, however, that an order-in-council directed the board to disregard the private trust fund. It would therefore not take into account donations from a sympathetic public that, according to Helmer, totalled around $20,000.

"Reasonably soon," was the closest Mrs. Moxley would come to revealing when the government would make a final decision.

"It will be difficult to compensate for the loss of nine members of one family," she stated the obvious. Subsequently, the family said it received $3,000. It was paid at a rate of $60 a month.

TWO years from the day of the barbaric deed, Robert and Stella were readying for the annual fall harvest. Allan was preparing to enter grade 10. Victor, 23, was writing home about once a week. He did not send the following account among his letters. Rather, he prepared it later and it is published as received.

I Mr. Victor Ernest Hoffman, Came to Oakridge on the 22/68, in the month of March, and was admitted on B ward. It was a dark gloomy place, and it felt and looked like some ancient dungeon. It was a great shock to be locked up, dressed in a baby doll, that weighted about twenty-five pounds, I arrived at supper time, and I was given my supper, of which I would not even feed to my dog. I paced the room, I had absolutely nothing, but myself, and five walls,[1] and a toilet that stunk and was very old that had been used for a very long time. Hours later I was given a white paper cup. Lucky enough I had a sink in my room.

Two weeks later, I was given my privileges, of which was to walk the corridor and play games in the sun room. I could watch T.V. but I was not interested in that. T.V. did not interest me. Then I met Ed and Tony, and Tonner. I did not know what the hell was up, but I soon found out. Ed made sexual advances towards me, and I knew I had to accept it or get killed. Because he threatened me. If I turned down his offer, he stated, "I will kill you."

---

1. Victor was housed in a corner room.

So as time went on, I was having sexual activities with Big Ed. Meanwhile, others began to get jealous, and want to get some sex too, as turned out, rumours began, and Tonner was really uptight, because the rumours were about him. Things were being passed around that I was saying things about him, and he decided to kill me. He caught me alone in the shave room, came up behind me and pushed me against the windows and then lifted me right off of the floor with his one right arm and told me he was going to kill me. I asked him why? After awhile I talked him out of it, and he let me go. Later on he got mad and so Big Ed called me down to the corridor and pushed me into a room and I saw mad Tonner glaring at me with a world full of hate. They told me to fight him. Then he came at me, so I went at him very quickly and hit him with a right hand upper cut that lifted Tonner right off of the floor, a good foot or more and he smashed into the wall behind him. Then he really got hatefully mad and came at me. I stepped back and tripped over the mattress that was on the floor, and he kicked me out cold. He would not stop kicking me, so they pulled Tonner off of me or I would have been kicked to death. The Staff came by and they wanted to know what had happened, and they made up excuses and the Staff thought it was good enough reason. So now it was time to go to watch T.V. for the evening. The T.V. program was a compulsory program until bedtime.

In the morning I awakened with two shiners and was slapped on the face by Glenn until I told him what had happened and I told as much as could. Later we were all locked up. After a week in lock up we were all let out of lock up.

Then Ed and Tony started playing games with me, the lighter trick was one, and then it was a matter of holding my finger in the flame till the count of four, while he could himself hold his finger in the flame to the count of fifteen, and still he did not get his finger burned, none what so ever. How he did that I do not know and I probably never ever will know. Anyways I had a real burned finger. One particular day I was talking to Tony and he was trying to talk me into killing a guy that just came to the ward, and I would not do it, so he got mad and threw his lighter at the door, it made me jump and yell, and it made a lot of noise. And the Staff came checking and they put every body in their rooms and when they came to my room to question me they soon discovered my burned finger and I and Ed were locked up than Tonner got locked up. A week later we on the loose again stirring up more trouble and suddenly I got transferred to F Ward the training unit.

Victor remained under close guard and it was expected this would continue for many years. As defence counsel Noble reasoned, "In Hoffman's case, where nine people fell in one blow, it takes quite a while before any government has got the nerve to let him out."

SETTING: Shell Lake, 1992. Joe Wong's Sunshine cafe which he had sold to Iris and Cliff Johnstone, the former village constable, is long gone. So is the laundromat which burned down. There is only one store remaining in the placid village but that does not mean it is all gloom. The Teddy Bear Den, a licensed lounge, is open for business at the hotel and Our Lady of Smiles Catholic church continues to administer to the faithful. So does the United church across the street near the Royal Canadian Legion Branch number 15 where Jim and Evelyn, followed by Kathy and Lee, held their joyous wedding receptions. In those happier days, the hall was bustling and not suffering from its present state of decay and peeling paint. The brightest spots in the village, besides the lake, are the nine-hole golf course with its manicured greens, the more than 100 hookups for recreational vehicles and the impressive Parkview Diner. Tourism is big during the summer months. Otherwise, it is a somnolent retirement community that genuinely welcomes newcomers.

Phyllis Melton is the cheerful hostess at the Parkview and vividly recalls the tragedy. She goes back to the time when Joe had the Sunshine cafe and the kids would call him over, as a playful ploy, to fix the unbroken jukebox. Once Joe had it open,

RENEWED LIFE — *Grandma Finlayson, Phyllis and Kathy with her newborn son. This photograph was taken during the first summer that followed the senseless loss.*

the mischievous youngsters would punch in a bunch of free songs. It happened time and again she chuckled, and Joe never figured it out or if he did, never put a stop to the shenanigans.

Phyllis Melton has heard endless rumors about the tragedy and to this day has a host of questions. One of the things that she still finds disconcerting is the way Shell Lake was portrayed by the media. She still frets that people think, "We're a bunch of hillbillies, such a backward bunch of people." With a laugh, she quickly answers her own question as to how you know when you live in a small town. It's easy, "Everyone knows you've been in the ditch before you get out."

Short and wiry, Ed Caplette, who is and looks like a grizzled ex-rodeo performer, still wonders about the events that put Shell Lake on the map. He is puzzled about what became of the killer and positive that if he is still alive and in custody that they should never let him loose.

Minutes away from the diner are the Simonars and with a clear, unobstructed view from their front window, across the highway, what is left of the once vibrant Peterson home. Their location is a constant reminder of the illogical loss of their friends and the narrowest of margins that they themselves escaped finality. Should they put it out of their minds, the morbidly inquiring will guarantee that it returns by stopping in on a regular basis even 25 years later. The peaceful, patient couple recollect how much Jim hated guns and ponder aloud, "Where is Victor?"

The Peterson property is deserted, the house pallid and crumbling. Kathy and Lee never demolished the tiny structure, with its caved-in roof and collapsed floorboards, although they thought about it when Phyllis would get upset while travelling by on the highway. Phyllis did go back afterwards and even played inside the place of many memories — the one that was so hectic on Saturday bath nights, particularly when dad was trying to watch hockey on television — and its bordering tree house. But it just did not seem right. Kathy and

Lee started tearing it down and then fire of unknown origin struck the outer buildings, destroyed two bins of grain and spread to the house. Friends and neighbors rallied around to extinguish it although no one truly knows why.

Today, hunters occasionally traipse onto the property but in other respects it is virtually lifeless.

SETTING: Spiritwood, 1992. It is a quick 20-minute drive for a pre-arranged meeting the next day with Kathy. Before that, unexpectedly, Wildrew walked into the highway restaurant, across from the grain elevators and the railway tracks, and struck up a conversation. A few miles back, we had briefly met at the Parkview Diner but I knew that he was not excited at the prospect of a book on a matter that had caused so much pain. As well, there was no lack of information nor need to disrupt his evening so we just said hello and goodbye. Now, with his keen interest, I invited Wildrew back to my non-plush, showerless motel room to satisfy his concern about how the story would be portrayed. A tall, striking man in blue coveralls, matching cap and large rubber boots, he made obvious his sincere solicitude for Phyllis. He explained that Helmer died of cancer in 1970, that he had married Evie a year afterwards and that she had passed away of a heart attack 17 years hence. It was just recently, he said, that Cyril died, leaving Elsie a widow, after a round hay bale weighing 1,200 pounds fell off a front-end loader, crushing him. Wildrew had experienced his share of agony and he simply wanted to be sure that there was not going to be more. Besides, he had just visited his sister who was sick, had an enjoyable dinner with his adorable mother, and the rest of the evening was free.

With mild eyes and a slow, deliberate voice, Wildrew Lang has had many sleepless nights since the crime.

"I've thought about it lots of times, I've laid awake thinking about it lots over the years," he said.

Wildrew is fair-minded and generally does not know bitterness. However, some things continue to grievously trouble him:

"One is that at the time, at the trial and in the papers, it gave Hoffman sort of a credit for having feelings and this is why he left Phyllis. To me, I think he saw her certainly and she saw him. I think he run out of bullets and plain forgot about Phyllis. I think that's the only reason that he left her alive. It wasn't because he felt anything. He didn't feel anything on the others. He was beyond feeling.

"Why the little children? The boys? It meant the end of a clan.

"If the hospital and the government do not admit the error then they're still making a mistake. When they release somebody like that who has to be on medication, how do you keep this kind of a person on that medication? Somebody would have to be there to make sure he took it. I just think they are responsible for releasing those people before they are ready. I don't think they should be released. I think they need care and we should be able to afford to give them that care ...

"I don't think they would acknowledge any blame, either the government at that particular time or now or the hospital either or the doctors. I think they made a mistake but I don't think they'll ever admit it."

In summing up, Wildrew included the words of grandpa Peterson who concluded at the end of the trial, "He's not guilty but somebody has to be."

Getting a lot off his mind and seemingly satisfied that the story would be told honestly and accurately, Wildrew shook hands and said goodnight. It was close to midnight when he headed home, alone with his thoughts.

THE next morning at the appointed time, Kathy — with a warm smile on her oval face and hair of a color that matched her brown eyes — arrived for our meeting at the same roadside eatery that attracted her uncle the night before. She is a sweet person, just like her mother they say, and on such occasions is not given to an excess of conversation. Strong-willed, this medium-sized mother of five, counting Phyllis, has a history of exhibiting great fortitude in confronting trauma.

Kathy was only recently married when Lee's mother telephoned B.C. with the unfathomable news. The devastating information was sketchy. It was only afterwards, during the frantic 16-hour trip back to Saskatchewan, that Kathy and Lee heard details that only one child had survived. They did not know 'who' until they ultimately reached their destination. The enormous shock was soon replaced with the responsibilities of carrying on and with the superb support of family and friends, Kathy did just that.

Although young, she had been guided well by her parents. She was used to baking, housecleaning and doing a lot of outside work such as helping in the fields or milking the cows. Kathy was also the 'official babysitter in charge' when her folks went to town. Before moving away, she spent a tremendous amount of time looking after Phyllis as her mother was called upon to devote extra hours with William who was not well. Kathy faced resistance when it was finally decided that she and Lee would raise Phyllis but remained firm in her resolve. "I was told I was too young to raise kids. How many 15-year-old kids have kids? It was no big deal. I just went ahead and did what I thought was right."

What she and Lee did was a marvelous job. The two newlyweds, confronted with their own insurmountable loss, nurtured Phyllis until she was 15. They never broached the tragedy, choosing instead to allow Phyllis to raise the subject when and if she desired. Consequently, it never played a big part in her development into a normal, healthy youngster. She was treated no differently than Kathy and Lee's four other children and other than the trust fund money there were no complications. The problem with the donations was the continuous, objectionable involvement by other people in their lives.

"They meant well but at the same time you've always got someone butting in, thinking things should be this way or that way," recalled Kathy. There was interference and an appalling invasion of privacy with inordinate gifts at Christmas, that made everyone feel uncomfortable, and other foolish purchases such as an accordion that Phyllis had no use for and gold earrings that were absolutely inappropriate for a seven-year-old girl.

Kathy, who has a sense of confidence and contentment about her, has some views on the lack of counselling for Phyllis and the amazing ability of her only surviving sibling to block out the terror of the night:

"Basically, all it (counselling) was, was to find out what she knew and she simply wouldn't talk. She had it blocked out and they couldn't get it. There was no getting through and I said, 'leave it alone, what's the point?'

"I'm afraid that someday, something will come up that's going to remind her of it. She never really has talked. She doesn't really remember what went on. I know she does. I know she knows. Four-year-old kids do remember. A lot of people say they wouldn't remember but they do. I know they do."

Insofar as worry that Phyllis could have an explosion in her mind should she experience recall, Kathy is convinced that would not occur.

"No, I don't think so. I think she's accepted things as they are and the only time something like that might happen, she would have to be in the same situation all over again."

Kathy, who has no desire to talk with strangers about the senseless killings, got up and walked out when a travelling salesman introduced it one day. There have been other awkward moments. Her eldest son notices it more than the others because he is the image in looks and manner of his grandfather and is reminded of it often. Her daughter had the case brought to the forefront while taking a psychology class at university. Explained Kathy, "She said 'it gives you a sick feeling to sit there and have them talk about your grandparents who you never knew.' It bothers them too because they've lost a lot, they've missed out on a lot and they know that."

Forced by circumstances to mature rapidly beyond her years, Kathy has some feelings about the cause and the demon-driven individual who single-handedly annihilated her family.

"I was upset that he was let out. I thought, 'they know better than that.' They knew he wasn't well. His parents knew it. They knew it. There was no need for it.

"I thought the man was sick which he was. I felt sorry for his parents and his younger brother who had to deal with all that. Like I said to Phyllis at one point, we were given so much help. They cared. But his family, no one ever thought about them. No one gave them a thought and it still kind of bothers me. They probably felt as bad as he did but they were not the criminals. It wasn't fair."

SETTING: Alberta, 1992. It was the toughest call of my life. Worse than sitting inside a coal-dust covered house in Natal, British Columbia with the fearful wife and family of a miner who was trapped in an underground explosion. He never made it and neither did 14 other workers who perished in the most catastrophic mining disaster in the West since 1930. More difficult than approaching disbelieving parents, being comforted by a man of the cloth, to ask for a picture of their child for the six o'clock news. The toddler's limp body had shortly before been pulled from an abandoned refrigerator.

A full of energy voice spunkily answered and its gracious owner politely listened as I explained what the intrusion was about, that a book would soon be released on the Shell Lake story, that I believed she should be aware of it and perhaps would be willing to allow readers to share her thoughts and feelings. There was only the slightest of pauses and then full vocal agreement with one proviso, "I'd like my husband to be there."

Due to the distance that had to be travelled, we arranged to meet within a few days and did so at a mutually agreed upon restaurant.

Thousands of people would never forget that forlorn picture by Dave Reidie that was flashed around the world so many years earlier when mass murder was an unknown quantity. Yet, to this point, Phyllis had never spoken publicly nor did anyone, other than those close to her, know what had become of that sad, fragile-faced child who had so cruelly been subjected to such madness.

Phyllis, now five-foot one and 3/4 inches and a trim, willowy 115 pounds, was seated at a table with her handsome, concerned husband when I approached. Both are instantly likeable. She is bright, pretty, slender-figured and her once fear-filled eyes are now beautifully crystal clear, sparkling in their aquamarine hue. They invited me to join them and thus began the first of many delightful conversations with this charming couple. There was a 'getting to know each other period' which began over coffee by paging through the manuscript, with the exception of the chapter entitled In Cold Blood, and reviewing the exceptionally graphic pictures of the crime scene. Phyllis, brown haired, red bloused and bespectacled, examined the photographs intently. There was no outward sign of emotion, only a request that photos of Kathy and Lee grieving at the graveside not be used. Additionally, she sought an undertaking that her husband's identity remain undisclosed. In other words, this assured, spirited young woman did not want their normal lives to become a circus but was willing to contribute to the chronicling of the worst random mass killing in Canadian history.

There was much to talk about and our conversation progressed at a tentative, leisurely pace.

Phyllis, with a sense of grace, praised Kathy and Lee as "good parents" who raised her as one of their own. She described Kathy as a "super mom" who was "patient and caring" and who "had what it took."

At the age of 15, those questioning, restless teen years, she moved over to her aunt Norma's, Evelyn's sister, in Carrot River. From the Johnson household, it was a variety of jobs — an old folks home, restaurants, that sort of experience — and then the meeting with her husband-to-be in 1983.

During that time, Phyllis at the age of 19, again cheated death. A powerful car, one of those sturdy, old Cougars, said to be travelling at a speed of 100 miles an hour plus, slammed into the back of her brand new burgundy Chevette. The compact car, purchased a week earlier with trust fund money, hit the ditch, rolled twice and ended up with its back bumper on the front of its tan dashboard. Miraculously, Phyllis walked away with nothing more serious than a cut to her neck.

In 1986, she married her beau — one of those guys everyone likes — and they now have a new addition to their family.

Trusting, congenial Phyllis, who resembles her father with personality plus, was agreeable to taking part in a lengthy, recorded interview. With thin lips pursed and an earnest expression veiling her small-boned features, she was composed and ready to proceed.

PT — I understand with all of the growing up, with Kathy and all of that sort of thing, I understand that you took some counselling?

Phyllis — I don't really remember it. I did take it but I don't remember the counselling. Kathy and Lee, I called them mom and dad. Kathy had children of her own and we grew up as brothers and sisters. Kathy's children and myself, and today we're as brothers and sisters and to me they're my younger brothers and sisters and they think of me as their older sister.

PT — In terms of society, when you were growing up, did people keep raising this matter or talking about it?

Phyllis — All the time, yeah ... I was a person and I was my own person and people didn't care to know, to know the real me. The thing they were interested in was knowing what I remembered. Rather than meeting somebody and you know, you always have first impressions when you meet somebody, everybody already had their impressions made of me so it didn't matter what I did — I was little Phyllis and it made no difference what I did in life.

PT — Did you find that you might have been over-protected?

Phyllis — Yeah, definitely! Definitely! Over-protected and spoiled rotten.[2] Spoiled rotten and that was my biggest problem throughout my entire life as a child was being spoiled and I don't mean to say anything bad about the people who did this. But things like, I was growing up and I was supposed to be a child in Kathy's family and that's how I wanted it and that's how they wanted it. Kathy and Lee, they weren't poor, it was just the normal family type thing. But Christmas time I would get big presents from the trust fund money and it always made me feel bad and it made Kathy's kids feel bad because those big presents weren't there for them. It always made me feel guilty and I always tried to over-compensate her children for it because I was being spoiled and they weren't. You grew up with eight kids and you know what it would be like to have one child being spoiled and the others not ... money was the majority of the problems. In my opinion, what could have helped better was to just leave the money there until I was 25 and just leave it alone.

PT — Is it all gone now?

Phyllis — It's gone, thankfully — I'm glad it's gone. The money was gone before we were married and what we have and what we've done now is strictly on our own and that's the way we like it.

PT — In terms of the night in question, what do you think of when you think of that? What do you recall? You were very young.

---

2. There are those who would contend that Phyllis was spared rather than spoiled. Perhaps being given more than enough reason to believe that life is not all horror-filled despite the early trial that robbed the innocence of her idyllic rural setting.

Phyllis — Your mind is an incredible thing and it has a way of blocking out things and there are, there is very little that I remember of that night and I am sure it's there somewhere, it just hasn't come out yet. But I don't remember very much about it. I remember the policeman carrying me out of the house and I remember Wildrew being there because I knew him from before. I remember going to the Simonars across the road to spend the rest of the day and after that it's just bits and pieces of things that I remember here and there that stuck out but not, not really anything important. Like I remember there being policemen around and that kind of thing but as a child I didn't realize what was happening. I didn't know why the policemen were there. It didn't sink in until I was older as to what had happened.

PT — What age do you think?

Phyllis — I don't think I really started thinking about it really until I was eight or nine, that it really hit — that that's what had happened. To me, it was that my parents had died and had gone to heaven and they weren't there anymore and as a kid they could have died in a car accident and it wouldn't have made a difference to me how they died, they just died. You know, it didn't matter how it happened.

PT — So at the age of eight or nine you began thinking about it?

Phyllis — I thought about it and I … how do I explain it … there was a lot of different feelings and I was really resentful. People used to always tell me that there was a reason why this happened and God always has a reason for why He does things and that's a really terrible thing to tell a child. Because you don't know what God is and so you think if God did this he obviously is not the good person that people are telling me He is. So it took a long time to …: to decipher those things and to realize that it wasn't God who did it — I mean, you know, the devil had a part in it too. You know, and so it took a long time to figure it all out and that's why I left home when I was 15. It all hit and it was really confusing and I was confused and I didn't know what I was supposed to do. I kept thinking. Wow! I'm here for some magnificent reason, you know. Whereas I'm not. I'm here because of some fluke really.

PT — So when do you think you really sorted it out? If you left home at 15 is there some magic moment when a light came on?

Phyllis — I was 20 and that's when things started making sense to me because I had someone who I could talk to, who listened and didn't judge and didn't step in and say, 'Oh but you know, well this happened, and this is what happened', and he just wouldn't and he let me talk and talk and that's when it started making sense. That's when life started making sense and I was here because of a fluke and I'm just a person. I'm not here because God had a special plan for me and I'm not supposed to be something miraculous.

PT — So with the counselling, as you said at the outset, it didn't really twig because of the age and so on but did it continue on?

Phyllis — Very brief counselling.

PT — Do you ever feel you could use more?

Phyllis — Hey, I might some day, I don't know. There's nothing bad about going to counselling if you need it you do. At this point in my life, I don't feel that I do. I feel that everything is fine. I mean, I don't have any bad effects. I don't have any nightmares, I mean, I'm not afraid of people and I think a lot of people out there have that opinion. They think that I should have nightmares all the time and that I should be scared of people and that I should have bars on my windows because I'm afraid someone is going to come in and get me. It's not like that. I'm a normal person and I live a normal life. I mean, I have a dog, two dogs — a big dog and a little dog — and I feel safe with them.

PT — Of course that could be just the farm upbringing too?

Phyllis — It could be anything. We love animals. I don't have the fear that everybody who loves me that I'm going to lose them. It's not a fear that I have all the time. I'm concerned about the people who I love and as everyone else is but I don't dwell on whether they're going to be here today or whether they're not going to be here today. I think one thing Kathy and I both learned is that you have to live life for today and the people may not be there tomorrow. It's like that with everybody but not everybody learns it. Not everybody knows that and people put off telling people that they love them. It's something that we've learned ... it's scary. It's life and when you're four years old and it happens you learn real fast. But that's part of life and there's nothing you can do about it. Yes, I'm sad that a person who I loved died but I can't change that so you don't dwell on it — you go on.

PT — I wanted to ask you, when you figured it out at the age of eight or nine, what sort of feelings would you have had, first of all, if you were aware of this release of this man from the hospital?

Phyllis — At that time, no I wasn't aware of it at that age. Oh boy, how old was I? The thing that I remember the most was when I was in grade nine, I think, and we were having a discussion on capital punishment and this kind of stuff and my teacher said, 'you don't really have to participate', but I do have an opinion on things like that you know and I think that's when it was that I realized that it wasn't anybody's fault and if there was blame to be laid it would be on the government. If people are sick they need to be in the hospital. The government can't say that these people should go back home, you know, steps have to be made that sick people are kept where they should be.

PT — So would you feel that he should not have been released?

Phyllis — Definitely! Definitely!

PT — What do you think of him as an individual? Maybe your answer has given me that answer?

Phyllis — As an individual he's a sick person. I mean, I've never seen him but I'm sure that if he has good days type of thing like some sick people do I'm sure that he regrets what he did, on those good days. If in fact he does have good days. I don't know. I don't know how sick he is. I don't know what his personality is like. I don't really blame him either. It was him who did the actual action but as a person I don't think he had what it took upstairs to be able to lay blame on him. I don't think his mind was there and you can't blame somebody who doesn't have a mind for doing something.

PT — So the blame in your view would be for the release of him? That he never should have been let out?

Phyllis — Yeah, if there's any blame to lay that's where it should be. It's definitely not on his family. I mean, the way I feel about it, I don't know about anybody else in the family, but my views on his family is that they lost their family as well. Their family was torn apart. They lost their son and we had the support of people. We had everyone's support and everyone's sympathy whereas they didn't. I can't say it was harder for them but it was just as hard for them to just go to town, to buy your groceries. I mean, what kind of things must have happened to them, you know, doing simple things like that whereas with us we could go to town and there was 25 people to talk to us type thing. It must have been extremely hard for them and it wasn't their fault. I mean, anybody can raise children and have that happen. You don't know — you take your chances.

PT — You had mentioned all of the support that the family had received, your family, by way of letters and that ...

Phyllis — Letters and people donated money and people who didn't have money donated things that could be sold. The entire family appreciates everything that everybody did and all the support that they gave us and we can't say thanks enough to people like that.

PT — With your new family and baby, what are your thoughts about telling the family history?

Phyllis — Telling our son that?

PT — Yes.

Phyllis — It's not a secret in our family and it never has been. It's something that you grow up knowing. We talk about it. It happened ... it's not something that we shut out. We have pictures of our family. Kathy and I, we have pictures of our parents up and, well yeah, that's grandma and grandpa and this is what happened and they grow up knowing it and at some point they'll be old enough to understand it. I mean, I won't just wait until they're 10 or something and sit down and tell them. It's something that they'll know and when they're old enough to understand it ... maybe your book will help — for that purpose.

PT — Thank you. I'm just wondering in terms of the family. Are there any special occasions, like once a year, do you do any things as a family by way of remembering?

Phyllis — We go and visit mom and dad's grave. We go together.

We don't do anything special. We remember. We'll always remember the day that mom and dad were killed but it isn't a special day. It wasn't a special day that it happened. But we always remember that day and you wake up in the morning and you think about it and then it's sort of gone for awhile. There were special days, special occasions in my lifetime that I really missed the family and there were special times when I really wished that they could have been there to share things with me and Kathy's the same. It's just like anybody who loses their parents, you have those days when you wish they were there to share them with you and that's the same with everyone who loses somebody.

PT — Can I ask how you feel about, you know we've looked at part of this story here and so on, and then of course you've looked at these pictures, how do you feel about revisiting, going back there?

Phyllis — It doesn't bother me that much because I've learned to deal with it. I've been doing it, not in as big a way as this, but with every new person that I've ever met, I've had to go over it again, you know, and so that's not a problem. I think that the biggest thing ... with my close friends I've gone over it. With other people I've just sort of ignored it and tried to walk away from it. The thing that bothers me the most is that I was a kid, I was a little girl, and I don't remember very much of it. It didn't affect me really until I was in my teens. But Kathy was married and Kathy remembered so much more about mom and dad and she had a really hard time of it and people seemed to forget about her. All the sympathy was put on me because I was a little girl and 'Oh, no! What was going to happen to me' and a lot of the support and a lot of the sympathy should have been with her and not with me. I'm not saying that I shouldn't have gotten any of it but it should have been balanced and to me looking back it doesn't seem to me as though it was balanced. I think Kathy should get an award for how she raised me and how she took care of me and what she did with her life because she was 19 and she has a lot of memories and it's hard for her. You know, little things like when I got married, Kathy was there for me. When we had our little boy, Kathy was there for me. When she had her little boy who was really there for her, you know, and that's the part that I can't change but that bothers me. It's that I was too little to be there for her and to me I don't feel that there was really anybody there for her. I don't know. She's my best friend really, other than my husband. He's my best friend but Kathy's my second best friend — and she's my mom.

WHEN all is said and done, there is a powerful chemistry that endures within the two Peterson daughters who remain. They are both what you would call, 'genuine.'

MERRY CHRISTMAS
1980

LOVE
PHYLLIS

SWEET SEVENTEEN — *Graciously, Phyllis agreed to allow this photograph of her teen-aged years to be published. She is now 29 years of age, happily married and wishes to retain her privacy and that of her young family. Phyllis and Kathy have no desire to speak publicly of this tragedy again. Nor do any of their relatives. It is asked that their wishes be respected.*

CONDEMNED

XIII

1992, a quarter-century re-moved from the massacre at Shell Lake. The Sas-katchewan Hospital, across the railway tracks, through an industrial district along Thatcher Drive — designated in memory of the late W. Ross Thatcher who was the head of a Liberal government at the time of the tragedy and the father of a son now serving time in a Federal prison for the murder of the son's wife — has not forgotten Victor Hoffman although the recollections have faded.

"That's the boy who shot his parents, isn't it?", a solitary receptionist in a newly decorated work-station, declared in hushed tones to a visiting reporter. Her head low, her voice a whisper, it was almost as though the question should never have been posed.

No, he was not the boy who shot his parents but he might just as well have been. Things were never the same after Robert was advised that he could retrieve his son and then departed with him down the comforting, tree-lined roadway flanked by the relaxing atmosphere of its neighboring golf course and the wonderful evening view of the setting sun and the resting geese on the river below.

BLAINE Lake, an hour's drive, has retained its small-town atmosphere with coffee shop gossip and opinions flowing as rapidly as the young people depart for the cities.

"I think this town is finished," laments a graying farmer, "all the old people are dying."

Talk turns to a 141 International combine that long ago picked up a stone and then the story of the son-in-law who had a swather and when he took it to the welder it broke again. The men agree on two things: the fixer does good work, even better than the fare served up at a known Chinese restaurant.

"I'm not a racist of any kind," states the senior participant who listened over yet another cup of brew to his middle-aged companion's tale of woe about food poisoning, "I just don't trust them, they'll feed you anything."

All of it is idle talk and none of it relates to the boy who first came into trouble with the courts in this community when he was handed a two-year suspended sentence in the summer of 1964. Victor had been charged with two counts of break, enter, and theft. It involved stealing guns and ammunition from two different stores in Leask and justice was meted out six months after his 18th birthday, a menacing sign of things to come.

LEASK, a short drive east, is where a tired, unforgetting Robert lives, very much alone, behind consistently closed curtains. Stella died, some say of a broken heart but officially it was after a long bout with cancer, in 1974. Her 80-year-old husband, existing in an adequate, subsidized, yellow housing unit, misses her immensely. His chin is firm but his eyes have the look of exhaustion matched by the sound of his voice.

"I used to know many jokes but they're all gone", he reminisces, "when my wife died it was terrible. I liked her so very much."

Love is not a word that comes easily. Neither is reference to Victor.

"I don't even want to talk about it, it makes me sick. I cried for three or four days. Sometimes I feel like taking a gun and finishing myself off but the Lord said you can't take a life, so I can't do it. It's not our life, it's God's gift."

Robert, his arthritis bothering him, coughs a lot. His memory is lapsing and sleep comes easily.

"I'm so very, very tired … I'm finished. I hit my 70's and I could work good. Then it hit me like a club on the head."

He used to write to Victor and send him money but his eyesight is failing and he finds it difficult to correspond or to read as much as he would like. The well-worn pages of the Bible remain close, however, and he sporadically drifts into lengthy monologues, quoting from memory.

Adjusting thick, brown-rimmed glasses and brushing a work-calloused hand through patches of thinning ghost-like hair, he often wishes he was dead. There are no pictures of Victor in the spartan living quarters. Robert had one but is unsure where it went. The cramped living room, with three chairs, two television sets and an antique radio as a reminder of the farm since sold to Allan, displays a photo of his brothers and sisters, grandchildren and the beaming family of the Prime Minister of the day. There is an abundance of religious material, mostly in pamphlet form, scattered in disarray on a nearby rickety table.

"God gave man the freedom to take the rough road, or the smooth road; the straight road or the crooked road or whatever he chooses," he replied with closed eyes riveted to the ceiling when asked to rationalize a world where his own son would be part of the land's murder of a century.

"I don't like to think about it — it's just like a bullet hit me in the head. When I don't think about it my mind is at ease. He was pretty young when that happened. He had a good mind.

He worked in the fields with the tractor and in the bush and hills. Then all of a sudden, something happened."

The elder Hoffman, whose children are married and living throughout the West, lives just a few blocks from the Leask school and within walking distance of the mutually operated St. John's Lutheran and All Saints Anglican church. The saintly, white building, with its green topped spiral, has a sereneness about it as it hovers just off the quiet, tree-adorned street. Half a block away is the Trinity United church and down the road is the place of worship for St. Henry's Roman Catholic parish. There is also another place of prayer to serve the Baptist faithful. It too is close but then, so is everything in a place this size.

The Leask hotel, the dilapidated two-storey focal point on main street, was constructed the same year as the Battleford Hospital for the Insane. It too has rules. It too invites people to leave. The regulations, some with unique spelling, are the clearest thing in the dimly lit beer parlor with lights the shape of wagon wheels:

1. Anyone causing a disturbance will be asked to leave.

2. There is to be no theft, distruction (sic) or defacing of hotel property.

3. Hotel staff has the right to cut anyone off they feel has had too much to drink.

4. Anyone not having proof of age will be asked to leave.

5. Anyone individually, verbally or otherwise abusing another person will be charged.

6. Anyone assaulting bar staff (automatic life).

"Life," the notice states, "means as long as I own this hotel (no exceptions)."

Robert, in failing health and fully knowledgeable about life sentences, is a frequent visitor to Ed Musich's drinking establishment.

"He comes in pretty well every day, has a beer, shoots some pool and then leaves," according to Ed who has owned the black and white carpeted tavern, with its seldom blaring jukebox and always drab vinyl chairs, for about five years.

"You can't stare at four walls," he said of the restless octogenarian who has a reputation for roaming around, buying the occasional beer for some of the native girls and generally not being able to fully relax or find inner peace.

Robert, with drawn features and lined face, has evolved into a rambling man. A wanderer of sorts. Someone who feels he may soon have to go into a nursing home.

Ed has never discussed the insidious days of '67 with Robert although the no-nonsense hotelier, having gone to school with Victor, knows some of the story full well. He understands it better than he does Victor.

"He was so quiet, he wouldn't mix with nobody, wouldn't say anything, just like a wallflower. I never really associated with the guy, he was so quiet you couldn't get nothing out of him. I still think it was over a girl, the old man put the run on him, kicked his ass out and then …"

Musich, 46, is solidly built and comfortable in a T-shirt, blue jeans, black boots and expressing his opinion; even though his motive theory is all wet.

"This used to be a damn good drinking community," he mused, "now the Indians spend their money in one day and the farmers don't have any."

Ed wonders what happened to Victor and remembers the aftermath of the killings and subsequent arrest on the Hoffman relatives.

"He had a cousin and at the ball game they called him 'killer Hoffman', that's how the other teams got his goat and it was a pretty cruel way to do it."

The Paris cafe, the closest most residents have come to the far-away, seemingly unreachable city, has long ago shut its doors. Lamontagne's pool hall is no more and Cheney's has been replaced by Banda sales and service with its bumper-to-bumper service and its faded metal, oval Esso sign. Behind the hotel, Barney's gas bar, confections, car wash and laundry, rents movies. Licence to Kill, Ian Fleming's James bond 007, and Blood Rage are included in the slim selection.

One promises "a terror filled movie about a psychotic young killer who stalks the streets of New York's decadent Times Square area ... It's about a vicious mass murderer who expresses his pent up anger through a series of violent, cold-blooded killings."

In his ongoing quest to escape loneliness, Robert is a regular visitor at Barney's. His visits are not necessarily to rent movies but to join the other fellows in a game of cards and drinking gallons of coffee. He drives out to the farm every so often, past Rogerson Motors Shell service station which now has another very old, slow-moving German Shepherd on the premises. In some respects, so much has changed in Robert's world of tractors, combines, Case, International and New Holland implements. Yet, so few of those haunting memories of that terrifying mid-summer have been blotted out. His sense of humor remains but inside this almost fanatical, deeply religious man are his darkest feelings that become too readily apparent during the course of a lengthy conversation prior to a reporter's visit with his son.

"Say hello, there's nothing wrong with that," he concluded, "tell him that I'm dying."

PENETANGUISHENE, population 5,533, is a few miles from the picturesque town of Midland, twice its resident base, about 90 minutes north of Toronto. Both Simcoe County communities are a vacation planner's dream, offering an historic past — this is Huron country — and unparalleled scenery among the 30,000 islands sparkling Georgian Bay. The Huronia museum, a wildlife centre and palisaded outpost of the Jesuit priests, among the Huron Indians, beckons visitors and succeeds in attracting several thousand annually. There is also the Martyr's Shrine church, built in 1926, which serves as a tribute to eight pioneers who met agonizing death.

The Penetanguishene Mental Health Centre, situated on 320 acres of parkland sweeping down to the majestic bay, has two separate divisions: Oak Ridge, the only maximum security psychiatric hospital in the province and the Regional Division, which is the local psychiatric facility for South Central Ontario's half-million population.

Oak Ridge, a striking red-brick structure built in 1933, has a 300-bed capacity but those numbers have been reduced to nearly one-third. With high-perimeter fencing, heavy metal gates and barred windows, the outside world for its ill inhabitants becomes but a distant recollection replaced by a jungle of psychopaths. Forty-six percent of those admitted are suffering from schizophrenia — Victor Hoffman among them. His fellow patients, those not in the same category, are a collection of odd people suffering personality disorders, effective psychoses or such maladies as sexual deviance or organic brain damage.

Victor will never forget the trip that brought him to this place of misery. Under RCMP guard, he was transported 226 miles to Regina, flown 1,659 miles to Toronto and then driven, blindfolded part of the way he claimed, the remaining distance. Among his memories is the profound belief that one of his escorts had sex with a pretty, mini-skirted stewardess while the aircraft winged its way eastward. He confessed that he did not actually see the encounter but remains convinced that it happened because, "I could smell it."

I had written Victor a few weeks prior to this 1992 visit and had no idea what condition he was in nor that there was any reason to suspect that he was anywhere other than in maximum security. Upon arrival, after earlier receiving confirmation from the hospital that he had agreed to meet, I was directed to Brenda Knight who, five days before, had been transferred over as the Director of the Brebeuf rehabilitation unit from Oak Ridge. Brenda, with ready smile and shampoo sparkling curly hair, greeted me and introduced Sandra Staruch, a pleasant, plump nursing assistant assigned to the Hoffman file. Instantly, Victor — newly moved to the 34-bed minimum security unit — appeared. We looked at each other with mutual apprehension and I opened by saying, "Victor, I've thought about you a lot over the years." Thick-necked with thighs the size of tree-trunks, he stood there, somewhat bashfully, in his leather-belted blue jeans, orange T-shirt and brown work boots. His chunky face and paunchy belly overshadowed the paperback in his rear pocket, the brown cigarello packages in his shirt and the hint of perspiration under his dampened armpits. He had never met me before and it would take a little while to get comfortable. We both knew it as he nervously smiled and warmly said hello.

DAY ONE: We advanced past several gawking faces into the Director's office, with its magnificent view of the waters below, and discussed how to proceed. I wanted to talk with Victor, then with Brenda and then return the next day, Saturday, for another visit. The plan was agreeable but first it was time for lunch and the patients had to be punctual. Victor and I progressed to the cafeteria, no different than any other except for the diners, where soon his name was called and he went up to get his tray. Meals are pre-selected and Victor, wanting to shed 50 to 55 pounds of the ballooning 230 he carries on his frame, returned with the vegetarian dish. With his false teeth in storage, he began gumming his food and talking about all of the "awesome books" on the wall-mounted shelves. The atmosphere was relaxed despite the strange cast of characters who exhibited persistent hacking, sloping shoulders and vacant looks. He shut it all out but to the visitor; the Buttonman, covered from head-to-toe with his pin collection, and the Purple-Skirted Lady wondering aloud if Wayne was

still mad at her for bumping into him days earlier, it took some getting used to — this routine scene of abnormal people trying their best to co-exist.

Victor, competently switching his fork from left hand to right, explained that at one time he was drinking up to 30 cups of coffee a day with sugar and cream. Because he is dieting, he now consumes it black but that is rarely and his beverage of choice is diet Coke given that its competition, Pepsi with its new look and claim of "same great taste," is unavailable. He mostly smokes Old Ports, the little cigars, because he reasoned they last longer than cigarettes, save money and, "I can think and dream all kinds of things." He once had a pipe but lost it. His left hand, trimmed with a silver-strapped Cardinal time-piece with big black numbers, and nicotine stained fingers, shakes. His lips tremble and his right eye tears.

"I was born to be a night truck driver," he said. "Maybe someday I'll be one but I don't know. I'm capable of falling asleep at the wheel."

Dribbling a touch of food on his shirt — it is not easy eating without teeth — he chatted about a host of subjects ranging from Europe ruining the grain market, to the ozone layer, to the government making money on crime. "It's criminal," he declared, "but they don't see it that way." He talked about his writing and his art work.

"I could become a great artist if I wanted to be but I'm a better writer than a drawer. I chose writing, it gives me more pleasure."

Numbers are important to him. He rattled off the serial digits of the gun he adapted to kill nine people and laughed when he recalled that his old school, the one at Kilwinning which is long gone, was number 1392.

"When I told the police 1392 they didn't know what the hell I was talking about. They said, 'you weren't born in 1392.' I could become a mathematician easily. I'm very good at poetry too. It would interest a lot of people. It may interest the whole world."

Blue-eyed Victor combs his faded red hair forward in order to cover the bare spot he caused by pulling it out when he was younger. If it gets too long he will still tug at it. The ideas flow non-stop with the patient devouring his mid-day meal.

"I plan on memorizing all the sonnets of Shakespeare. I'm capable of doing it.

"My goal is to write a book better than the Bible. I'm going to check the style of Hitler and write a Bible for atheists, for man.

"I'm going to collect literature on all governments and write a book for the younger generation. You've got to have democracy and dictatorship. With the death penalty, everybody should decide and the guy (accused) should go on T.V. everyday till they vote. If they cross a line or don't make an X they should get fined or go to jail. People don't fool around and throw chalk. If you get 75 percent or more you should get a reward (money) so the parents can't use it.

"We have freedom to the point of tyranny. It's ridiculous you can't make a point about other people.

"We should have a gum chewing area. I'm going to write a letter to the CBC to put it on the news. I don't know when I'm going to do it. I have so much to do."

Lunch was finished and the next step, several actually, was into the smoke lounge for a break before moving to the staff room, off the corridor, for the taped interview. The pasty-faced Buttonman from the cafeteria, disoriented Knitting Momma and the Babbler — known to staff as the Chatterer — were all killing time inside the hazy space. The fan was whirring, the window open and the television blaring as we entered. A skinny fellow, unshaven, unshowered and unaware, was rocking to his own beat as he perched atop the biggest table in sight. He kicked his shoes off, flicked his lighted butt in no particular direction and curled into a fetal position. Another lost soul shuffled over and asked Victor for a cigar.

"My cigars are holy to me. I gave you one, one time and you broke it. Cigarettes are expensive," he admonished.

The spaced-out intruder sauntered away in her mismatched socks to her favorite spot in the corner. Then, the Rocker, spotting Victor's pocketbook about the life of Jesus, which was resting on the arborite surface, hurled it against the wall. Calmly but sternly, Victor warned him, "Don't throw a book like that around. God will throw you on the floor."

We talked more about Victor's plans to write a Bible. He hopes to have it written by the year 2000 and released in 2010, "When society is ready but I might never get it written so who knows."

It was time to go into the staff room. On our way, a female patient with a paper cup of cola in her hand, apologetically announced to all and sundry, "The only time I drink it is when I get thirsty." It made a lot of sense — more so than many of the comments bantered about.

PT — I've got it (tape recorder) going here. So it's been a long time since you came from Saskatchewan?

Victor — Yes, 24, 25 years.

PT — 25 years, do you miss Saskatchewan?

Victor — Sometimes I will. Sometimes I have memories where, what I might be doing on a certain day. Like cleaning the barn and loading the manure onto the stoneboat, using lots of strength and almost breaking the handle on the fork because I was strong enough. It only took minutes to clean the barn you know, where it would take my dad an hour, you know.

PT — Your dad says you were a very hard worker. You were a hard worker.

Victor — Yeah.

PT — When do you think, I think you were six years old when you started feeling not quite 100 percent. Is that accurate?

Victor — I think it was earlier than that. There were incidents in my early childhood when my headspace was diminished. Where it was insane, where there was something wrong with me and my brothers and sisters would let me know about that. So would the hired man and he told me that some day you're going to prison or you're going to go away for a long time. [laughs] ... He kept talking like that. [laughs] ... It came true.

PT — *I think that you sort of, uh, did you kill any cats and that sort of thing?*

Victor — *I did, yeah.*

PT — *What would make you do that kind of stuff? Why would you have to do that? I'm just wondering.*

Victor — *There were a number of reasons. One reason was there were too many of them and dad wanted to get rid of them.*

PT — *Oh, your dad wanted to get rid of the cats?*

Victor — *Yeah, so I had to get rid of them that way. Other times, I would just love them to death. I would play with them so roughly that the cat would lose its love for me and would just die. The next day I would find him dead. A cat is an animal that can really fall in love with you and once they lose that love it's very depressing. The pressure can kill them.*

PT — *So do you figure you killed a few of them?*

Victor — *Lots.*

PT — *Anything else?*

Victor — *Then there was the other time when I was hypnotizing them with a mirror. Cats you can hypnotize easily because it will stare back at the mirror or a bright object. A dog will attack, will want to bite you. You can't hypnotize a dog but a cat you can because it will stare. So I did this and walked out and came to the barn with my dad and my mother and brother and when we opened the door the cats were going in every direction. They were hitting the walls, bouncing off the walls, the ceiling and the mangers and everything and finally they made it out the door and I never saw them again.*

PT — *Oh, so you hypnotized the cats?*

Victor — *Yeah, I hypnotized them.*

PT — *How long does it take to hypnotize a cat?*

Victor — *It only takes a few minutes. It doesn't take too long.*

PT — Why would you do that?

Victor — I was into hypnosis when I was a young kid. I bought a book on it too and afterwards my mother took it away from me.

PT — Oh, so after she took it away then you still sort of …

Victor — Oh, I still had the memory about how to do it.

PT — Oh, yeah, and then I guess you liked to hunt birds and the odd deer?

Victor — Yeah, I did. I didn't like hunting deer but my dad wanted me to hunt deer. He wanted me to be a man and I didn't like hunting deer because they were beautiful animals. They were animals that I admired because I lived to enjoy their beauty and their elegant behavior. They would run nicely, they would walk around, they would look nice, they would pose nicely, they were beautiful. I didn't want to shoot anything that beautiful. Squirrels are something else again. They are like a rat. They carry around diseases so you've got to keep the numbers down. So I did that. I hunted for the hides. I don't know if I'll ever regain that state of pleasure with that state of mind where I'll want to hunt again. I'd rather hunt with a camera instead. Take pictures of the animals and just watch them and enjoy their presence. That would be more interesting to me than anything else. I think I would enjoy that to a great extent. More so than killing the animals. If I were to kill an animal now I would be very upset.

PT — You were a really hard worker, you know. Your dad says that you were just the best worker he ever had. What else did you do other than work. I mean, did you just work, work, work? Did you play sports or what did you do?

Victor — I didn't play very many sports but I had a ball glove and we had a baseball. Not a baseball but a softball and we had a rope on it and spun it around in circles and took a bat at it. It was a lot of fun and sometimes people would come over and we would do that. Then dad got kinda cranky about that because he had to drill a hole into the ball and onto the rope, because we didn't really know how to put a rope on a ball and so we did it our own way which we thought was right and he wasn't agreeing with it and got uptight about it, that we were wasting money, and my dad wouldn't let me spend my money the way I wanted to spend it. I earned my money. I had every right to spend it and he, once he gave you the money for your payment, for your work, he wanted to spend that money the way he wanted you to spend it. That is no darn good. I don't believe in that and to this day I think my old man is still that way. If you buy something and then ruin it or break it or whatever it may be … If I bought a Coke and spilled it I'd hear about it for the next five years.

PT — *So what did you do to have fun? Like you'd play with a ball the odd time but did you ever go to dances or stuff like that?*

Victor — *No.*

PT — *I guess you'd go over to Jimmy Peake's house the odd time?*

Victor — *I used to go over there. He became unfriendly about two years before the crime.*

PT — *Because you left school and he was still in school?*

Victor — *Yeah.*

PT — *So you didn't see each other?*

Victor — *I don't know what happened there. Something happened there anyway. I guess he was aware of my insanity. He knew I was going crazy and I was dangerous and he sort of just dropped me. He probably wanted to leave me alone because I was getting into trouble. I kept coming down there to see him but he wouldn't talk to me very much. Sometimes he would and sometimes he wouldn't.*

PT — *Did you know yourself that you were starting to go?*

Victor — *I knew, I knew. I used Jim Peake as a sounding board to release my feelings. Like a man uses his wife. Tell her everything, you know. I would use Jim Peake just like a sounding board to release. Just like a garbage dump. Dump everything on him. Then go back and do my own thing.*

PT — *You didn't think you could talk to your mom or dad?*

Victor — *No, I couldn't talk to them about that sort of thing. Sometimes I could talk to my mother but my mother, she would squeal to the old man and get things all twisted up and then the old man, he'd get uptight and then there'd be a battle in the house.*

PT — *Did you think your dad was tougher on you than the other kids or about the same to all of them?*

Victor — He was the same to them all. He was more rougher on brother Richard than anything else, my older brother, because, uh, my brother Richard was smarter than my old man and he let him know. [laughs] ... So the old man didn't like that. So if he ever had a chance to nail him, he'd nail him really good.

PT — And you were a hard worker and the oldest one left at home?

Victor — Yeah. He left home when I was 14 or 13 or something like that.

PT — Did you ever take out girls? Jim Peake had a sister I think?

Victor — I never took any girls out. I had one incident where I spent an afternoon with a girl, with her and her brother, rich brothers and that was when I was about 10 or 11 years of age. I went down to their house. I had dinner there and then her parents went into town on the Saturday night, it was on a Saturday too, and reported to my dad I was raising hell with their daughter and so my old man had a talk with me and this and that and just like a sieve it went right in one ear and out the other. Sometimes he would give me heck and it would bother me for a long time.

PT — Did you ever think of taking out more girls?

Victor — I took this one girl. I phoned her up one time but I couldn't go through with it so I just hung up on her. But she went and phoned back and my mother answered the phone. [laughs] ... My mother was in the room when I phoned her up. I was interested in her.

PT — Yeah.

Victor — I think deep within my unconscious mind, when I was a young kid with the hired men, talking about marriage, they talked about it that if they had to do it all over again they'd never get married. Never get married, and I tried to be like that. Always a free man. Never get tied up with a woman. That stayed with me and it still bothers me this very day. Whether I'll get married I do not know. I don't think I will. I may if I meet the right woman and she has the right kind of personality and the right kind of body, same interests, good interests and can intellectualize things, it'll be O.K. It'll be a different story then. It's very unlikely that will ever happen though but it could happen.

PT — Sure it could. You know, most kids 13 or 14, growing up, that sort of thing, think of sex a fair amount.

Victor — Yeah.

PT — Did you spend a lot of time thinking about that?

Victor — Yeah, I thought about it. I had some sexual fantasies but I put that all away now. I don't have fantasies at all anymore. In 1980, oh it was 1990, in January, I stopped fantasizing completely and I only had five or six fantasies afterwards throughout the whole year. And every time I had a fantasy it would make me ill. It would always make me sick because I would always have such a big fantasy. It would go on for hours on end. So I don't fantasize at all. I haven't had a fantasy for about six months now.

PT — Oh, good. Why do you think you got ill and not the other kids in the family? Do you ever wonder about that?

Victor — I think it was something to do with the diet. The food we eat and it could be my dad through religion and Sunday school and other kids, children, my brother and sisters; I couldn't get along with them. Sometimes I got along good with them and other times not. My brother Richard would squeal on me. I would confess to him. I was a confessor you see. I was a confessor at Oak Ridge too when I was in therapy. So I would use my brother Richard also, like a therapeutic situation. It had some kind of therapeutic value and I just pursued it for some reason and I was laying goose eggs, like at Oak Ridge between truth and fact and everything would just come right out. So he would report that to my dad and my parents and I'd get heck you know. So fine, I wouldn't do it any more. Every now and then I would and then once I started talking I would never stop until it was all out and then I would be in trouble. That bothered me. It made me feel kind of bitter and untrustworthy of other people. I used Jim Peake as a sounding board so I could get my releases out — then mental pressures.

PT — So when your dad got mad he'd just yell or scream or did you come to blows?

Victor — He would do all the talking and I would do the listening. I wouldn't react towards him. I wouldn't say nothing.

PT — Did you respect him?

Victor — There was one incident where I talked back to him. I told him, I really don't like working here and he said, 'you can leave the farm and go off on your own.'

PT — Were you afraid to go off on your own?

Victor — I was. I wouldn't survive on my own. There was so many things you have to know when you're out on the street or out living by yourself. There's so many things you have to do. There's so many responsibilities that I was unsure if I could handle them and I just wouldn't leave home. That's one reason. Even after the crime was committed I couldn't even run from the law because I didn't even know how to do that. I could not run. I knew the problems I was going to run into. It was far better for me to just remain there and wait until I was arrested because if I ran I would be shot. They'd shoot me down and they would not even ask questions. They would say you're under arrest and just open fire and that would be the end or they'd probably wait for me and I'd be in a situation where I wouldn't have no cover whatsoever and then gun me down. I knew that. I knew that for sure so I just waited.

PT — I just wanted to get back to that hypnosis. Why did you buy that book? How did you hear about that?

Victor — I got it from the back of a newspaper ad, the Free Press Weekly. I think I got it from Winnipeg. Some company in Winnipeg.

PT — In any event, we've sort of gone through your childhood and then you weren't feeling well and your dad took you to Prince Albert, to the doctor?

Victor — Dr. Jed, Jed, Jedlicki, Jenkins.

PT — Yeah, then you went to North Battleford and then I understand, what did Dr. Jedlicki say, somebody was saying you had to be there for at least a year or was it more?

Victor — I don't know how long he said I'd have to be there but when I was in the Saskatchewan Hospital they told me I was going to be there for the rest of my life.

PT — When you were there?

Victor — Yeah.

PT — And I guess they gave you shock treatments and pills?

Victor — And medication and work. I was the only one who could handle the big machine they had in there to clean the floors. When they brought it into the building, they had to bring it in by pieces you see, it was too big to bring through the door. So when they put it together they left a screw out of the clutch and the clutch wouldn't work properly. So you had to push it and the machine was very heavy and very hard to push and I was the only one who could do it.

PT — So your dad says you wrote him a letter a few weeks after you were in saying that you could come home and he could come and pick you up?

Victor — I don't know. I don't remember that at all. I don't think it was. I think it was Dr. Jedlicki who made that arrangement. I don't remember writing a letter.

PT — I see. Your dad came and got you and then you went to the fair and were you surprised to get out?

Victor — You see, if I wrote a letter home, if it was all right for me to come home, that wouldn't work anyway because the doctors have to clear it. The system at the Saskatchewan Hospital could deny my request to go home. I don't know the reason they took me out of the Saskatchewan Hospital. I was in bad shape. (Blank[1]) was my closest friend there and I wrote a letter to the Saskatchewan Hospital to see if I can get in touch with him but I can't. Whether he's not available there, the letter didn't come back and I didn't get no letter from him. But he was my friend there and I talked everything about it and he told me before I left, 'Don't kill anybody whatever you do, don't kill no one.'

PT — Did somebody in the hospital tell you where this house was in Shell Lake?

Victor — No, I don't remember that, no.

PT — Yeah.

Victor — There was somebody there talking to me about something. I don't know his name. It was something about a farmer firing this guy. He worked for him and he did something wrong and he

---

1. A blank in this transcript represents a deleted name.

wasn't able to work properly, he smashed the tractor up or something and was ashamed before his family and whipped by James Peterson and uh. ...

PT — Somebody told you this story?

Victor — Someone told me some kind of story but I don't remember it very clearly at all.

PT — And it was after the, after the ...?

Victor — It was before the crime.

PT — It was before the crime?

Victor — I was in the Saskatchewan Hospital before the crime.

PT — Right, that's right. Yeah and somebody told you a story about Jim Peterson beating up somebody or something?

Victor — Yeah, something like that, yeah. But I don't remember making any promise like that. Why did I pick that family? I was just on the road. I just happened to be there. It could have been anyone else as far as that goes. If I would have picked another family, people would say the same thing. 'Why did you pick that family?' I didn't know them. James Peterson seemed to be an accidental thing. He seemed to be like destiny. It just had to happen that way. Just like the supernatural had some work or power and control over me when I was doing that. I don't know.

PT — Yeah, because actually when you went down the highway, there's the Simonar home. Remember that one? There's the Simonars and you slowed down there and just turned into the Petersons.

Victor — I was going to stop there.

PT — Simonars?

Victor — I was going to stop there and go home. Even as I opened the gate to the James Peterson farm I hesitated and thought I should just get in the car and drive home and take that gun and throw it in the ditch and leave. This is a stupid and foolish thing to do. But then I gotta do it and went and did it.

PT — But why do you think you had to do it?

Victor — I don't know why, I don't know why. I think the reason was, if you look at all my illness and the pressures of them and the trouble I had with my family and people in the area, it was more to

*escape reality completely. To escape them, leave them, hurt them too
and shock 'em. I think I wanted to destroy my dad's name more than
anything else because of the way he treated me. It wasn't just that,
the way he gave me heck and that. It was mainly his bad eating habits.
Ever ate a meal with him?*

PT — Uh, I just had coffee.

*Victor — He made the same sound as the pigs do in the pig barn,
in the pigpen, the same sound. They had the same sound and
language in both of them. I would listen to my dad and I would listen
to the pigs and they made the same sound.*

PT — For goodness sake.

*Victor — And he was really making lots of noise and I couldn't
stand it and it would always drive me up the wall every day and I'd
be so mad I'd go into the garage and pull the doors and get into the
car and start the motor up and try and commit suicide that way. He
would come back out of the house and open the doors and give me heck
and threaten to call the police if I did it any more. Now I did that, I
tried to commit suicide maybe six or seven times. I don't know, by
carbon monoxide poisoning.*

PT — And your dad was sort of aware of that and ...?

Victor — And so was my mother.

*PT — But you didn't really go to the psychiatrist, Dr. Jenkins,
until afterwards?*

Victor — It was after about six months or so.

*PT — Do you ever think back to the Peterson house at all? Do you
ever think of it at night around here? As a flashback?*

*Victor — I think of the T.V. set that was in the house. The T.V. set
was a very large T.V. It was too big a T.V. for uh, something like that
would have to be specially ordered. I don't think they make T.V. sets
that big. That was an oversized television set. Then there was no T.V.
aerial on top of the house so I don't know what happened to it. My
mind was so impaired. I don't think I've even got the scenery of the
Peterson property registered within memory or anything like that at
all. It was all screwed up.*

*PT — So then when you left Phyllis there, which was pretty nice
...?*

Victor — Yeah, well she was on her belly. Sleeping on her belly and her head was leaning to the side and she had a smile on her face and I figured, uh, I'd let her go. And the dog, I didn't kill the dog either. The little dog in the house.

PT — Then there was Larry, the little baby?

Victor — The little baby is something else again. It was, uh, like it was not a boy. It was a girl. I examined, I removed its diaper, I examined its sex and it was a little girl not a little boy and how I ever got that mistaken in my mind I don't know how come a person's sexuality could be totally opposite, so my mind was very impaired.

PT — You thought the baby was a girl?

Victor — Yeah, cause I checked its diaper. I wanted to know whether the baby was a girl or a boy. I didn't know that. So I checked it. When I checked it I found it was a girl. But then according to everybody else it was a boy. That's how impaired my mind was. I wasn't seeing things properly.

PT — If you had thought it was a boy would you have spared it?

Victor — I don't know I would have killed it anyway, I don't know.

PT — So how did you leave? By the front or the back?

Victor — The same way I came in.

PT — Off the main highway?

Victor — Off the main highway, yeah.

PT — There were some tracks in the back, you know, and somebody was telling me the next night they thought they saw your car in the district. Parked on a side road. Did you ever go back?

Victor — No I didn't.

PT — Never went back?

Victor — No.

PT — So when you went home, how did you go home? The same way you came or over the back roads?

Victor — I came home the same way I went there.

PT — So then you went home. Were you able to sleep O.K.?

Victor — I slept O.K. I had dreams about the crime all night long. Before the night I had dreams and every night until I was arrested and then I never had no dreams until 1987, '89 and '90 I had a dream.

PT — When you think of it now, do you feel badly about that night?. What do you think of that?

Victor — I don't feel bad about it. I think I've accepted it and sort of forgotten it. It's more or less tucked away in memory not to repeat that sort of thing anymore. Not to let any kind of feelings or thoughts or desire or idea to repeat that sort of thing anymore and behave normally and acceptable in a sane way. To be law abiding. Like after I committed the crime I knew I was on the other side of the tracks with the law and that was a hard feeling. I didn't like that feeling.

PT — No. So did you ever think of doing something like this again? Do you ever get upset that you feel like ...?

Victor — Not any more, no. At Oak Ridge they'd really put the pressure on me. They'd make me so mad sometimes I'd say things like that but never meant it. I would say things about crime but I decided never, ever to commit that crime again. Not mass murder. At the Ridge they talked about things, wild stories but I've forgotten all about that. I've forgotten all the procedures. So I don't think about them any more. They had such great ideas at the Ridge about how to rob a bank and it was so inviting and desirable that it's, uh, so simple to do and everything was laid out so real nice. You know everything could go right. Nothin' could go wrong but even that, I've given that up too. With me, if I were to do that something would go wrong.

PT — If you could ever talk to Phyllis, you know the little four-year-old, she's about 29 now, what would you say to her? Would you say that you're sorry or what do you think you'd say if she walked in here?

Victor — I don't really feel sorry about the crime. I think I benefited from it. It helped a lot. I'm sorry that her brothers and sisters are dead and her parents. I imagine that I could apologize to her but I don't believe that would do any good. They're already dead anyway so what's the sense of saying you're sorry. She'll say, maybe you're sorry but when are you getting out. [laughs] ... And that'll probably be never.

PT — Well, what do you think. Do you think you'll ever get out.
Victor — I don't know.

PT — Would you like to.

Victor — No I don't want to.

PT — You're happy here?

Victor — Very happy here. I've got my writing still to develop. I like to write. I get a lot of pleasure out of writing and someday I'd like to write a very good book. Maybe a bestseller. Who knows? Maybe I can become one of the best writers around.

PT — You've read a lot of books all of your life and you told me you buried one. What was the name of that one?

Victor — Enemies the Shield. Enemies across the top. There's a big picture of a grave and a shield and a broken sword and a helmet hanging on the end of the shield.

PT — Why did you bury it? I'm just interested.

Victor — I don't know. It was something about me.

PT — You buried it with Jimmy Peake's boots too?

Victor — Yeah. [laughs] ... I buried his boots too. [laughs]

PT — So they'd still be there?

Victor — Yeah.

PT — Do you think that you shouldn't have been let out of North Battleford?

Victor — No, I shouldn't have been let out of the hospital for two or three years, at least until I was ready. Another thing I feel is that I never should have been allowed to go back home.

PT — Because of your dad's influence?

Victor — Yeah, yeah. My dad was very religious and very strict and I don't think he was, uh, he was a good provider but I don't think he was a very good father to his sons. One thing he did when he gave me a father/son talk, he started to give me a father/son talk and then he chickened out and said, 'just watch the animals,' and that was it. That's not a father/son talk.

PT — Oh, in terms of sex?

Victor — Oh yeah, 'watch the animals and figure it out,' yeah, yeah.

PT — It's not too in-depth.

Victor — Humans are a whole lot different than animals.

PT — *Did your dad ever tell you that he loved you or did your mom ever tell you that?*

Victor — *Not when I was on the farm. No.*

PT — *Ever use that term love?*

Victor — *No, not that I ever remember.*

PT — *Ever hug your dad or mom?*

Victor — *When I was a young kid I did. I loved them then.*

PT — *Yeah, some people find it hard to express emotions.*

Victor — *Yeah. He used to be a very important person in my life when I was a young kid. I still remember when I'd hear him coming home from the fields. I'd run out of the house and meet him and be talkin' to him and I'd be talking like a real man to him, trying to impress him. [laughs] ... Then after he'd be finished eating he'd be chewing gum and smoking and I was really enjoying it. I really enjoyed that snapping sound, the way he'd snap that gum, you know. Then, just one day, just like that, I couldn't stand it. I couldn't stand that sound. I tried to get off his knee and he wouldn't let me go and I was cussing and screaming and crying and everything and I ran away and I pushed him and I went down to the pigpen and saw the real pigs and I was cursing mad.*

PT — *You were never abused?*

Victor — *No, not by members of the family.*

PT — *By anybody else?*

Victor — *Yeah, it happened.*

PT — *What's the background to that Victor?*

Victor — *I best not mention any names. It happened at school. I got raped in the boys washroom. There was a big fight over it too. I fought them. I didn't get hurt though.*

PT — *How old were you?*

Victor — *Sixteen, 17 something like that ... It happened in '62 because it happened in the fall.*

PT — *But he must have been a pretty big guy?*

Victor — *He was the same size as me. Maybe an inch taller but he had a lot of help from other guys. There was a whole bunch of guys who helped him.*

PT — *These guys stood and watched this happen?*

Victor — No, they helped to hold me, to fight me, to restrain me.

PT — *And this guy had sex with you?*

Victor — Yeah.

PT — *Oh, geez. What did the teacher say about this?*

Victor — Well, the principal of the school said I could press charges but I just didn't want to.

PT — *So is that why you quit school?*

Victor — No, I forgot all about the incident and never even thought about it for years later. I didn't think about it until I was back at Oak Ridge. It just dawned on me that it happened. I never had a memory of it before. It was just out of my memory.

PT — *So you would have told your folks about it or would you bother?*

Victor — I never said nothing to my folks about it.

PT — *How do you feel today? Are you feeling a lot better than ever before?*

Victor — A lot better. It's like the difference between black and white. When I was at the Ridge I was very sick and I got sicker all the time because they didn't have the right kind of medication for me. They still don't have the right kind of medication. The medication is good for the mind but it's not good for the body. It gives me the shakes. They have different types of medication but I don't know if I even want to try them because I don't know what to expect from them. Every kind of medication has a different kind of side effects. I don't want bleary eyesight because I like to read especially. When you have a change of medication there's always something that happens with the eyes. You get bleary eyesight. But this medication that I've got right now doesn't cause bleary eyesight. But what it does, when you get the drug into your system, it surfaces and the mind comes like a T.V. set. You dream while you're awake but you've got to have your eyes closed. You're dreaming consciously awake and that takes about three weeks and then after that you can sleep without dreaming while being awake. But every time you change the medication the dreaming comes back consciously. I'm not the only one to experience it. There *are other people at the Ridge. People here at the hospital who are on that drug will experience the same thing and I know they experience the same thing because I've talked to them and they've told me what they've experienced. There are different kinds of schizophrenia.*

PT — Again, why do you think you've got it and other members of the family don't? Do you ever wonder about that?

Victor — Well you see, in our family my dad has it too but one thing is he uses it for work. He used it for business. I used it to play with. I played with my mind, you see. I went along with the dream and I started seeking religious things and when you seek religious things you're going to get into a lot of turmoil and it becomes a disaster area.

PT — You went to church every Sunday in your life?

Victor — No, I didn't. Dad may have said that but it's not true. I used to run away from home on Sundays. I used to run away from home.

PT — You know, another thing your dad was telling me is that, well one of the things he said was that, well, Victor was never in trouble. But I guess there was a little break and enter.

Victor — At Leask. I stole guns and ammunition from Mansell's hardware store and another hardware store.

PT — This was the same night?

Victor — No, it was a different time. Whenever I'd run out of ammunition I'd go back and raid it again.

PT — Then the RCMP got you?

Victor — Yeah, what happened was I had the guns and the ammunition stored in an old house and my brother Allan had a friend coming over to see him and they went over to the rafters in that building and they found the guns and ammunition. I knew they had found it but I left it there for another week and went back to get it and it was gone. Was I ever upset then. Then I knew it was coming. I went to look for it and came pretty close to finding it too. But brother Allan and his friend raided my ammunition stockpile and hid it by the fenceline. I remember, the neighbors checking the fence found it and phoned us up and we denied it. Allan denied it too and so did I and the cops came. They put two and two together.

PT — You got probation?

Victor — I got probation for two or two and a half years, something like that.

PT — You had to go and see a probation officer?

Victor — Yeah, at the time of the arrests I was a kleptomaniac. I had to steal just for the sake of stealing. Now, to get out of that, I had to work hard to get out of that problem. I had to steal little things. I would go raid old buildings, old abandoned buildings and steal cans or lamps or books or magazines or anything. Then it would be a little bit less and less and finally I wouldn't steal nothing. I got away from it.

PT — How many times did you get in trouble with the police?

Victor — Just that once and then there was the crime of murder and then that was it.

PT — Your dad knew about the stealing of ammunition and that?

Victor — Yeah, he said he suspected it. I was doing way too much shooting. [laughs]

PT — What were you shooting, birds?

Victor — Anything; tin cans, rocks and stuff like that you know.

PT — You know, your dad was telling me too that he never saw you drunk. Not once. Boy, that's amazing.

Victor — I was drunk at Christmas time when they had me drinking some wine. I didn't like wine but I had to drink because I had to be social. I didn't like being drunk.

PT — Did you ever drink that much?

Victor — No, I didn't drink that much. I got drunk one time when Allan put something in the Italian wine. He put something in there. He didn't want me drinking it. I just took one little drink and I was sick. I became very dizzy. I lost my balance, had to climb the stairs on my fours all the way from the basement to the top stairs and crawled onto my bed and went to sleep. I slept for about an hour and I recovered. I know he put something in it. I know he always gave me heck every time I went into that Italian wine. I know he put something in it but I don't know what he put in there.

PT — So you never drank much?

Victor — No, I never drank it after that.

PT — What about beer?

Victor — I had a little bit of beer. In July, I liked to come home from work. I worked in the fields or in the hay slough, wherever it may be, and have a glass of beer. After I came out of the hospital I was a little bit different thinkin' wise. I was a little bit more bold and didn't care what my old man said. Like if I drank all of his beer and he got mad. I wouldn't give a darn and hurt wouldn't bother me none at all. I'd just give him the money and he could go buy some more. So I drank about a glass full. I couldn't even finish it.

PT — But a lot of guys, when they're growing up, you know, go and get a box of beer and you go jump in the car and go somewhere. But you didn't do any of that did you, with Jimmy Peake?

Victor — No, I didn't.

PT — Never used drugs at all. There wasn't a lot of drugs then anyhow, I don't think. Marijuana and stuff like that?

Victor — I was into medicating the cats and animals. I'd make my own drugs. Did dad ever tell you about that chemistry set that he once found? [laughs] ... I told the police about that.

PT — Your dad? He owns a chemistry set?

Victor — I had one. I stole one. My mind was impaired. I don't remember which store I stole it from but I know I had one and what irks me over that is that I don't know either but I did make my own medication. I would give it to the animals.

PT — Did you take it yourself?

Victor — Not much of it.

PT — What was in it?

Victor — Something that really makes you sick. I took 10 cc's of it one time in October.

It was in '63. I don't know how I learned this but you know, you take a tea towel and wrap it around your head and hold it in your mouth with your teeth for a knot. I knew how to do that but I've forgotten how to do that now. But I did know how to do it at the time. I took 10 cc's of it. But I knew this drug was going to do something for me very good. It was going to either kill and if it didn't kill me it would make me insane. But once I overcome my insanity I'd become very well and I'd get more well and get weller and weller and weller and very potent like — and that came true.

PT — *It seems to me that you were looking for an escape. You didn't want to run the farm?*

Victor — *No, I didn't want to run the farm. Not with my old man there.*

PT — *So you were looking for a way to get out of the situation?*

Victor — *I was suicidal for one thing. There were a number of reasons for committing that crime but they were underlying. They were unconscious reasons. They were not consciously available for me at the very time. They became consciously available after thinking about it at the therapy program at Oak Ridge. One of them is I tried to commit suicide a number of times and every time I failed. So if I committed murder I would have no choice but to commit suicide. But even after I committed murder I was still unable to do it. Another reason is I wanted to escape my dad. His bad eating habits, his bawling out and the people in town, the people in church, the people at school, the girls. I just wanted to go away for the rest of my days. I knew I would go away for a long, long time. I almost had it when I went to the Saskatchewan Hospital. They said I'd be there the rest of my life. That was a shock.*

PT — *Did it make you happy when they said that?*

Victor — *No, it was a shock. It scared me. I wasn't expecting it. I was expecting to be there only a short while and do well and then I'd be O.K. But they didn't keep me there long enough. They should have kept me there for at least two or three years. At least a year or two until I stabilized so they could at least observe insanity. They say there isn't a cure for insanity but there is a cure. Let's say you have bad thoughts and a desire to kill somebody. Right away you begin thinking, this is against the law to want the other side of the fence. It's not the right thing to do. It's not God's wish. It's not the way of man. It is an evil thing to do and go on and on and on like that until finally it don't come up anymore. Everytime it comes up you gotta keep doing that. That's exactly the cure right there. You break the circle that way and also make observations on people around you. That helps break up the fantasy world. The fantasy world can't operate then. That breaks up the schizophrenic world.*

PT — You know, when they let you out of North Battleford did they say take these pills, you gotta take them, if you don't take them you're going to be in serious trouble? Did anybody tell you that?

Victor — I don't know if they told me that or not. I don't think I paid attention when they were talking. My mother made sure I was taking them. She said many times that I wasn't taking them.

PT — But you didn't know what would happen if you didn't take them?

Victor — I don't think they were the right medication for me anyway.

PT — Do you ever have flashbacks about the incident? I've asked you that before, I don't want to go around in circles but ...?

Victor — No, I don't. I'm free of it. The only time I can have any regress or fears or bad feelings is if someone brings it up in a bad way. If they say he's the killer of nine people then it comes back. But it hurts me only with what they say. People ask me about my crimes at Oak Ridge. I say I was carrying on in all directions. Another time, someone said I was just charged with one charge of non-capital and one charge of capital. That's what it was you know. I was just charged with two charges. I don't say I killed nine people. I just say two charges. It's not too bad, you know. It works out O.K. [laughs] ... But if they get a little bit more nosy, like, well maybe I say it's none of your business. I don't want to talk about your crime. I'm not interested in your crime why should you be interested in mine. Just stay out of my life, you know. I want to live my life, you live yours.

PT — So you never talk about it?

Victor — Sometimes I do with (blank). He knows of my crime. We talked about it. But it was talked about in a different way. He believes that I was framed because of the way I told it at the Ridge. I always believed I was framed because I couldn't remember the crime. I couldn't remember it. So I went to town and I was feeling very bad and heard about it there. I pieced it together, well it's gotta be me. I told the police when they arrested me. They wouldn't believe me when I told them so I just told them what they wanted to hear. I told them that later on. [laughs]

PT — Well I guess they had the boots and everything?

Victor — Yeah, they had everything. Yeah, they had the evidence. They had the gun, the firing pin, that was the gun all right. The thing was, in court they said there was a blood stain. That when I shot Evelyn Peterson the blood shot right out of the gun barrel. I tried to remove that blood. I couldn't remove it. But the police said that was paint. How it become paint for some reason I don't know. Maybe somebody covered it with paint, maybe somebody put paint on it, maybe dad did it, I don't know. But they said it was paint. I don't remember putting paint on it. So someone must have disguised it. I didn't disguise that gun barrel but they said it was paint.

PT — Is there anything that I haven't asked you that you want to add in or talk about or that you've been thinking about?

Victor — I also tried to commit suicide that night. The very night of that crime. What happened was, I was working on the engine in the garage and, uh, I worked on it for about an hour or so and all of a sudden I just didn't feel like working on it. I just felt like I was split in half. So I decided to put the engine back together as quickly as possible just so it wouldn't get rusty or get injured in any way, shape … just so I could … what was I working on it, I was working on it for about three weeks. I tried to put it together and do you think I could do it, I couldn't do it. The crankcase and the block wouldn't fit together. It just wouldn't fit. No matter how I tried it, it just wouldn't fit. There was something wrong. My mind was always changing. My vision was screwed up. Maybe it was the medication and the beer I had that night, I don't know. Maybe it was too much medication. I took five pills, so, and the beer may have done that. My dad's car wasn't in the garage either. It was not in the garage. It wasn't outside the garage either. I wanted to commit suicide but I didn't know how to do it. So I took the alcohol and tried to swallow back but I couldn't do that. So I spit it out, it was awful. So I dropped the bottle, I don't *remember dropping it but I must have dropped it. Dad found it anyway. It was all empty. Whatever happened after that I'm not sure. I didn't know which gun I was going to use. I remember when I was thinking, after I decided that I was going to commit murder, that I would do it now or never. I'll do it now and get it all over with and get it out of the way. That's what schizophrenia is. It's something like an individual inside you. It's like the unconscious. It makes up its mind and you gotta do it.*

PT — Do you ever hear voices still? You used to hear voices quite a bit?

Victor — It's petering right out. Back in October, I think November, November 22nd it began to peter out at level five. I became free.

PT — What about hallucinations? You used to dream a lot or hallucinate about the devils and angels?

Victor — It depends what I see. If I'm looking in the dictionary, looking for a word and I come to a picture of a snake or an alligator or a dinosaur or something like that, I may, I may if I look at it too long. Sometime if I'm going through a book or a magazine and see a picture of an ugly snake or something like that and it really looks outstanding, really looks alive, I will produce it. But I will not see it with my eyes. I will see it with another vision within the eye, the imaginary part, the invisible part of it. You know it's there, you can sense it, it's there, it's real — it's not real to you and me — but it's real to the imagination and it's alive.

PT — But when you go to bed at night ...?

Victor — It's like a nightmare. I have nightmares every now and then. I had two nightmares on level five where these two guys, one guy was from the outside, he was in the room. He attacked me and said 'are you going to come around now and do things that we want you to do?' and I was saying 'no'. I was fighting them. Then I wouldn't fight them so I just woke up. That was a nightmare.

PT — So you had a few of those?

Victor — I could feel it. You know it's a dream but you just wake up. But when you're awake consciously, sitting on a chair or standing on a chair reading a book and come across a snake or see a snake, what can you do then?

PT — Yeah, right.

Victor — You've got to live with that snake. But you know if it can bite you it can't kill you. It may sting a bit but that's about all.

PT — But the devil? You never think of him anymore or who or whoever? You used to?

Victor — I meditate and try to figure it out, what it really is and there's no such thing as God or devil. Where man came from I don't know. What I think, what Genesis really is, is just that it all began when the he/he met the she/she and everything developed from thereonafter. That's about all there is. There's no devil and no God. So when you get into the Bible and start reading about devils and angels it's easy to get into imagination with them, you know. Those dreams I had before, I've never had them enter my mind anymore. They do not go through my mind anymore. I have them in memory but I don't think them. They're just a thought of memory. I don't tune in on them.

PT — You're reading that book? You showed me that little Bible. Do you think there's a heaven up there?

Victor — No, I don't think so.

PT — Do you think you'll run into God some time?

victor — I don't think so.

PT — No?

Victor — No, I don't know what caused us, whatever put us together or whatever put this thing together but whoever did it is bad at it. See, I think, my theory is He created Himself. If He created this universe He knew that it was a trap for Him. He created everything here. He knew what He created. But He knew that if He come to this world or any world in the universe that He'd be stuck here and it would be like a pit to him, like a trap. That's what I believe. That's my theory and that's the reason He's not around. God created the heavens and earth but he doesn't participate in the functions of it. He doesn't rule it. The people invent things. Prophets had dreams they're talkin' to God but they're not talkin' to God. Not the God the creator or the God it says in the Bible. Humans are gods because they know the difference between wrong and right and they can be intelligent and they can perceive things with understanding and reason and create knowledge and do things with knowledge.

PT — Yeah, I follow you. I was just thinking that if, uh, and this is hypothetical so you can tell me to butt out, but you know when people die and I guess we all are going to eventually and if there is a heaven that we go to …?

Victor — If there's a heaven it's in the grave.

PT — So there's nobody to talk to after that or to explain any actions.

Victor — There could be. There very well could be. The whole world is a grave. But I think it's all in the mind. But the mind goes out when you die. Like it says in the Gospel to St. John, uh, the light of man, no, the life is the light of man. I'm not sure exactly how it goes. We can look it up.

Victor — (Then starts talking about astral fighting) It's done with the hands and legs. Like, I can't come out of my head, I'm stuck in there. But I can come out of my arms and legs. So if they come inside me I can always cast them out. I can throw them right out. I can beat the heck out of them. I never met one person yet who can outfight me except (blank). He fights astral fighting. He can really fight. He's really strong.

PT — Are you talking a physical fight? About throwing punches?

Victor — Yeah, but it's a duel. I can sit here and I can fight and you wouldn't even know it. It's invisible. That's what happened at the Ridge when I fought these false Jesus Christses and the devil advocate, and God, the devils and the demons. I fought them and I beat the heck out of them and they can't outfight me. I always win.

THE first portion of the interview nearing completion, Victor added that he has had few visitors over the years, his brother Richard about a dozen times and his sister Bernice once. He also has had a friend of patients, a volunteer, who visits once or twice a month, bringing in a magazine or two and a present at Christmas. He said he planned to write his dad but when his father dies does not expect to shed a tear.

"Because what I gather from what my brother Richard said, he's suffering quite a bit from his arthritis and he's getting old and he's ready to die and I've already accepted his death and when he dies I don't think I'll feel anything at all. I don't think I'll shed a tear or anything. I'll probably be happy that he's died. I didn't shed hardly any tears at all for my mother but it was a shock. When my dad dies I don't think it will hurt me ... I still love him, I still love him. I still respect him very good for one thing, for a very good upbringing. A very good upbringing except for that there father/son talk. Everything else was pretty good. He helped me to be honest and truthful and work and when you work put your mind to it. Work hard, do the best you can. I always do that sort of thing."

It was time for a break and we continued visiting with more cups of cola in the smoking lounge. Victor had lots to talk about. He said he somehow always knew that he would go to jail, school or get married and it was clear to him that he did not want to go to school and he certainly did not want to get married. He talked of memorizing every word in the dictionary, reading about Oak Ridge a week before the killings and no longer having an interest in magazines about guns. He emphasized, "guns are very dangerous. If you carry a gun you're going to have an accident."

Victor paused to give one of the patients a drag off his cigarette, related how the voices seemed to have departed his head some weeks earlier and then agreed to allow his picture to be taken. He preferred that any visual record be done without his teeth, "so people won't recognize me." Victor said he was hoping to some day get a brand new set of teeth so he would have a nice smile and be able to whistle just like (blank).

"Don't ever use his name," he warned gently, "he almost killed me. I was strong but he was stronger. I went for a second cup of coffee and he bumped into me. When I'm mad, he can't handle me. I can't get mad like I used to get."

Victor, who is only interested in sports on television if he happens to bet 25 cents on the outcome, has an income of slightly more than $200 monthly. It is fairly evenly split between a 'comfort allowance' and the shop 'incentive wage.' This day, Friday, he booked off work for my visit and it was now about time for us to return for our pre-arranged appointment with Director Knight who is an occupational therapist by profession with several years experience in the mental health field.

PT — The first question I want to ask you is about Victor Hoffman's illness. What is the illness?

Brenda — He's got paranoid schizophrenia.

PT — And the paranoid, does that mean the type?

Brenda — That's the type. It's a form of schizophrenic illness and paranoia is a strong element in the illness. That's why the label.

PT — When it comes to paranoid schizophrenia, is that the worst type? Is there a worst type or are they all equal?

Brenda — I guess it depends on the individual. The fact that there's paranoid features often leads to dangerous sorts of behaviors or thinking so that makes it dangerous from that point of view. There are other types of schizophrenia or thinking patterns along with schizophrenic illness that might be self-abusive or self-destructive in nature, so that makes it dangerous from that point of view.

PT — What are the symptoms of paranoid schizophrenia?

Brenda — Well, schizophrenia has symptoms of hallucinations, delusional thinking, ideas of reference, various other kinds of odd thinking patterns. The paranoids tend to have persecutory thoughts. That is they think that people are thinking about them or they believe harmful things are going to happen to them or they think about doing harm to other people in order to protect themselves or to avoid situations. In your case, Victor, it was more of, you had some strange thoughts about devils and angels and control and ...

Victor — Government.

Brenda — *Government, yeah, and each individual has unique thoughts that reflect their own upbringing, their own concerns.*

PT — *Are there degrees of paranoid schizophrenia?*

Brenda — *Yes, there are definitely degrees of it.*

PT — *And what degree would Victor be at today?*

Brenda — *Today he would be considered paranoid schizophrenia in remission. Controlled by medication. I think he was definitely out of control and he was in a very serious form. A very serious state at the time of the crime in '67.*

PT — *If it's now controlled and it's in remission is there hope for a release? What does the future hold based on what is known today?*

Brenda — *I think anyone with a similar illness to Victor's who can take medication and that medication is helpful in terms of controlling the symptoms of hallucinations, delusional thinking, paranoid thinking, with supervision and appropriate monitoring — again individualized to the needs of the patient, they can live in the community in a relatively normal existence and enjoy a reasonable quality of life. In Victor's case, I think his medication has been the real answer. Once stabilized, you've been on?*

Victor — *I've got to have it changed. Look what it's doing to my arms and legs.*

Brenda — *Yeah, we can talk about the risks and the side effects of it but the medication, the sort of major tranquillizers or psychotropic medication that he's on, does help control the symptoms of schizophrenia and the paranoia. So, his thinking is clear, he is competent to make decisions for himself, he's got good judgment, he demonstrates insight, he can solve his own problems generally, you know, when to ask for assistance. So he demonstrates what one would expect of a responsible adult. The trouble with these medications is that they produce side effects.*

PT — *As we can see. There's some shaking?*

Brenda — *Yeah.*

PT — *A little movement in the lips?*

Brenda — *The knee jerks.*

PT — *Tearing, if you will, in the eye. Would that be a result of that?*

Brenda — Not necessarily.

Victor — I've got eye problems.

Brenda — He's got eye problems. What we call them are extra-paramidal side effects and that's what you're seeing. It's similar to people who may have Parkinson's disease and that part of the brain — people who have Parkinson's — is affected by the medication. So the dopamine receptors are somehow affected by the psychotropic medication. There are different medications that reduce those symptoms but in Victor's case he's pretty dependent on his mental state and dependency on that medication to keep his mental state in good order. So he resists changing the medication because he also runs the risk of experiencing physical discomfort when coming off the medication, mental discomfort, a lot of worry. Is that fair?

Victor — [laughs] ... I know that's true.

Brenda — Any purposeful activity tends to stop those side effects.

Victor — And leave permanent damage.

Brenda — But it can leave permanent damage called tardive dyskinesia and I think at your last Board that was addressed specifically. One of the psychiatrists on the Board pointed it out. We're aware of it but we're also aware of Victor's strong concern about changing medications. I think we're at a point where we're going to have to look at it. There are new drugs on the market. Maybe with some combination, with some change and close monitoring, we'll be able to help them.

PT — What is the drug that is used today?

Brenda — The medication he's on today is called fluphenthixol decanoate.

PT — Is that taken by way of pill or a liquid?

Brenda — This is an injection every three weeks. So it's a long acting medication.

PT — There's no pills now?

Brenda — Yeah, procylidine. That's taken daily to assist with the side effects, to help reduce them, the discomfort. What happens, what you're seeing now, is that he's sitting here with the shaking or the quiver of the lips but there's also a tendency for muscle stiffness.

What do you experience if you don't take it?

Victor — (Talks about movement in the lips) ... nervousness and when I'm standing I can't stand still.

Brenda — A feeling of agitation all the time. If you can imagine sort of being hyper on caffeine and it's something Victor has accepted as a fact of life in order to maintain his mental stability. On the other hand, from a medical point of view, I think there's tremendous concern about this. Long term and irreversible effects if not treated and changed. Throughout your stay here you've been on different medications because of that and certainly with the more modern medications there's less risk of it. But there has to be a constant awareness and change.

PT — Is it fair to say that there's no cure for this disease? Only control? Is that accurate?

Brenda — Yes.

PT — I was very pleased to hear that Victor tells me he doesn't have any hallucinations or see the devil anymore or angels and also, which is great news, that he doesn't hear voices anymore. I'm just wondering, does that stack up with ...?

Victor — Yeah, I'll have one every now and then. Like November 22nd, I was sitting in the smoke room on level five and all of a sudden, it was about eight o'clock at night, it was beautiful. It was like my schizophrenia was coming to an end. It petered out, you know. I felt free, relief and everything.

Brenda — You wrote me a letter about that.

Victor — It was beautiful.

Brenda — I remember you writing about that.

Victor — Yeah.

Brenda — I think what Victor is saying is that he doesn't hallucinate regularly. He doesn't have voices regularly, and that's what we mean by the disease under remission or control. Medication control. But he'll always have experiences like this periodically but understands it, knows what it is, isn't frightened by it and deals with it. He's got his own internal psychological methods of control, don't you, really? And isn't afraid to talk about it. He's usually very open and up front about it, so when staff see something different, they normally can approach him and he'll talk about it and let you know that he's feeling a little unstable or a little different. But that instability doesn't mean that he's dangerous at that moment. If he stops medication, if it's left uncontrolled, then I think the risk of dangerous behavior becomes increased ... And Victor knows that and I think is very frightened of that. He knows what he did and he knows the wrong that that represents.

PT — One thing that always bothered me and I'm not a doctor or anything but schizophrenia and there's lots of mysteries surrounding it and so on, I understand is a cluster of disorders. You know, there could be shyness, there could be antisocial behavior, there could be the internal ego to the outside reality, there could be environmental and those sorts of things. Would the file indicate anything that there might be one of those disorders that is more prominent than the others. If you follow what I'm saying here, you know, Victor's history, there were the cats and that sort of thing ...?

Victor — Yeah.

PT — And then the shyness about the girls and all of that and then of course with your dad, you know, your dad is a tough boss ...

Victor — Of the situation.

PT — Bawling out and so, there's a lot of things that fall within schizophrenia. So my question is, is there more than any of the others?

Victor — In my attitude, my feelings ... and the way I perceive reality and the way I felt about it and the way I felt should be done about it. I reacted towards society and I made myself into what I am and I didn't do it because that wasn't me, that wasn't me. Reality is very bitter, life is bitter, people are cruel and children really cruel. Now sometimes when you try to do something good to somebody it can be very cruel to the person receiving it. But the person who is handing it out is doing a real wonderful job. My teacher, my father; my father made it tough and he was doing the right thing. I did the same thing to my brother Allan. It was not the right thing. He said I would get it some day.

PT — Allan said that?

Victor — I bawled him out for something he was being irresponsible for because someone made a mess in the garage and I bawled him out for it and I hurt him worse than my dad did because I could really bawl people out. And I don't do that anymore. I never did that since I've been locked up.

PT — And brothers do that. I know the same thing happened with my brothers. The older one would yell at the younger one.

Victor — And my brother was doing things the same as me. If I was doing something in the garage he would do the same thing as me but he would make a mess, he would wreck things. (Tape unclear but Victor talks of his brother making a mess out of a camshaft and he thought his dad would blame him) ... [laughs]

PT — You know, one thing that Victor told me and I was quite surprised, but at school one time at Leask, some boys attacked him.

Victor — They raped me in the high school washroom.

PT — Victor's dad had never mentioned that but presumably that would be in the file?

Brenda — Yeah, that's going way back.

Victor — That hurt me one heckuva lot, you know. It made me feel ashamed going into town.

Brenda — Speaking to your point and going back to your question, I don't think I would describe schizophrenia the way you did.

PT — I took it out of a psychology book but again I'm an amateur.

Brenda — If we knew what caused schizophrenia or could describe it in any easy definition we'd all be geniuses but I think it's an illness that might be biologically ...

PT — Hereditary?

Brenda — Hereditary and biologically based. Where it comes from and why does one of seven get the disease is very unclear, however, yes you're right, there are a lot of influences from the environment, from the rearing, parenting practices. I think in some cases there's just a personality or predisposition that comes through. Like any of us, we are products of our environment. There's all these theories about the second child or the middle child of the group. You know, it was a farming family, they had to work hard, perhaps didn't have the advantage of higher educational opportunities, there may have been some intellectual impairments along the way so that ...

Victor — (Tape unclear but essentially talks about birth and mother and that she complained to neighbors that it was the worst experience she ever had ... back to quotes.) When I was born, I was born with a very small head.

Brenda — There was likely some sort of birth trauma.

Victor — But they also said it was a healthy pregnancy. They state that in my file.

PT — Oh, good.

Brenda — And a normal pregnancy. So we don't know for sure. That's the bottom line — we don't know. I don't think anybody does. I mean, Victor's referred to a clairvoyant mom and his brothers had some clairvoyant dreams. Are they clairvoyant or is there an element of illness somewhere? Is there just a general shyness, I mean, you worked all day, did you have much time to play? Were you very old?

Victor — I did all kinds of work. Dad would send me out to the country, I'd go out there, I'd take the gun and I'd walk for miles all day long. I'd go down to the lake and all around the country and not even go home for supper, come home about nine o'clock, wait for supper but meantime he's working all day long. [laughs]

PT — That's interesting. So you don't feel cheated that you worked all day long and didn't have five minutes to yourself. It sounds to me like your dad went and let you play?

Victor — Oh, yeah. I had a wonderful time.

PT — You were O.K. that way?

Victor — Yeah.

Brenda — They were pretty isolated activities I gather. You spent a lot of time on your own?

Victor — A lot of time in the field, going up and down the field in the tractor. Like in the field on the tractor I experienced mirages, you know. (Tape unclear but essentially one time in the field Victor saw three big waves of water coming at him) ... [laughs] ... It scared me but I knew what it was. When it got close to me it just vanished.

PT — The family history. Victor indicates he doesn't believe there was any evidence of any problems. You know, the mother, father, any of the siblings. The father tells me all the kids turned out. They're all scattered around the West.

Brenda — O.K. I mean, our bottom line is there is no history of family mental illness. A summary in his report is: birth normal and development normal. The child was considered to be a healthy boy but inclined to be quiet and shy. He lived in a happy home and there was no quarrelling between his parents nor financial worries. With schizophrenia there's usually an age of onset and a seemingly normal individual changes and his, I gather, was an early adolescent onset.

PT — He talked about the age of six where he started hearing voices?

Brenda — He repeated grades three and nine.

End tape.

Notation — Victor's I.Q. at 92 is described as average.

Afterwards, Victor elaborated on the sounds preying on his mind. "… over the years I've heard a voice coming from the ground, crying, 'Why did you kill your younger brother?' … Who is speaking?, I would ask … 'It is I, Able, the shepherd of goats and sheep and you were the tiller of the soil. God did not like you!"

DAY one with Victor and his keepers was almost over but before it would end there were two more telling quotes:

"Space is a vacuum. There is a black hole. The Earth is a plate and when you reach the end of it you fall down. Why are we always checking out Mars? You have to believe in basically some things that can't be believed.

"Did you see the latest on Jason and Freddy Krueger? His head went flying across that stage. It was amazing. An amazing tribute. Quite the show."

The boys in Midland's Highland Inn lobby-bar, which exults "Exquisite Charm," were sharing their words of wisdom. Just a short drive away, Victor had turned in for the night. His thoughts were on the memories brought back from an intense day of interviews. Tomorrow there would be more to talk about and he had already prepared some thoughts in written form. The separate writings, printed as received, dealt with his development and the subject of 'Phantom Fighting.'

On behalf of my growth, as a small boy, I was a very active child, roaming the fields and woods, hoping to find someone who may teach me those interesting tricks that had been performed before my eyes. There were other things besides that, hoping to find those appearing and disappearing monks, that could reveal more interesting ideas in the fields of immorality. Also, I looked for the boogie man that would take me far away and eat me up. This was stated by my father, mother, and hired man. They tried to strike fear into me, to keep me out of the woods. I would take with me my big dog[1] for protection.

I wanted to know more about my name, of who I really was before I became Victor E. Hoffman. For I have met many monks who would not accept me with the use of my name, Mr. Victor Ernest Hoffman.

I did behave as though I were going far someday in the future, and that did happen. I went to Oakridge for twenty-three and a half years in the province of Ontario.

This pursuit led me into having nightly dreams and also daytime dreams when asleep. I did have dreams about being in Egypt, and also had dreams about travelling in space, especially the other side of the universe. A lot of my dreams were religious and very negative. I did not know that in the later years of my life that these dreams would become a very serious problem area for my insanity and my crime.

---

1. Remembering his dog, Victor said: "I could hear conversations as good as my dog. I could hear people in Leask better than my dog." Prosecuting Attorney Serge Kujawa described Victor as, "The craziest man in Saskatchewan." Clearly, Victor had taken leave of his senses. He was unable to perceive the external world by sight, hearing, smell, taste and touch. He had lost the ability to think or reason soundly.

These dreams had a background scenery of my dad's farm mostly. When I turned twenty-one years of age, I wanted to know what these dreams meant. I did talk to certain people about them, and they thought and said that I was very strange and insane. As time went on I got very ill mentally; I did not hallucinate much. I had hallucinated wild game, and had fired my gun at them, but to my surprise the bullets would go right through, but would not kill them nor injure the animals in any way, shape or form.

On the day of my twenty-first birthday, I became extremely ill after I had experienced severe chest pain on my left side. For moments I thought I was going to die. What caused the pain is not known. Afterwards while walking, standing, sitting, or laying down, I could feel a heavy dark and negative lump in my chest. It was so vivid, that within my mind I could almost see it for real. The incident caused me to start reading chapter after chapter of Revelation of The Holy Bible. That was my big mistake. I got all the more worse. I even began to pray, that too was bad. Then the memories of the dreams began to go through my mind. I was going in circles in thought, and I did that till 1982, after being placed on a drug. Afterwards I began to make some progress.

PHANTOM FIGHTING

Phantom fighting is the art of fighting without the use of the flesh body, but with the phantom body, or you could call it the soul, or still yet call it the astral body. The battles can be experienced by those who have a sensitive mind to pick up on it. The fighting is invisible, not to be seen by the naked eye of the flesh. Fighters will do that before they fight their adversary, to feel him out, to find out his weaknesses. A fighter is capable of fighting in the flesh as he also fights like he does soul wise.

How is it done? It is done by astrol projection of the inner invisible body. It is very simple and is very easy to develop. For fighters that all comes natural. In closed places like prisons like Oakridge everybody does it and there are hundreds of fights that go on daily. It is like being on a battle field at the time. It's an art that should not be allowed, but to control such behaviours the system would need special trained men, to enforce peace and control over such evil art.

Author. Mr. Victor E. Hoffman
Pen Name Shakespore

MINIMUM SECURITY — *The rehabilitation unit does not have any bars. Victor, days before his 46th birthday, had just returned from a stroll on the grounds. He made sure he was back on time.*

RELAXATION — *The interior of the building is no different than most modern schools. The view of majestic Georgian Bay is even more spectacular through Victor's binoculars.*

MANUAL LABOR — *The patients workshop is housed in this castle-like stone building. They are assigned various tasks including the packaging of products. Victor sometimes feels that he would like to quit so he could concentrate on the things he likes. He knows, however, that then he could not complain about a lack of spending money.*

THE EYE OF
THE STORM

XIV

DAY TWO: It

dawned as it should and began to unfold in kind. A dead of winter sky, cool, crisp temperatures and a brief cab ride past the fortress-like Oak Ridge facility to the low-slung single-story Brebeuf rehabilitation unit. Visitors can see its occupants walking the halls, or shuffling as the case may be, in street clothes. Victor, in freshly washed shirt and neatly laundered slacks, was anxiously awaiting my arrival. There was a lot more to discuss and some of his writings — evidence of the inner workings of his mind — to pass along. As he excitedly showed me examples of his typewritten views, he explained that his pen name is "Shakespore" but in future he might use "Shakespiel, unless someone takes it from me." Two of the following literary efforts were honored through a second place award stemming from a competition held by the Prison Arts Foundation. It is significant to remember that Victor, when he permanently entered the mental health system 25 years ago, had only part of a grade nine education and had just randomly murdered nine people. Since then he has been heavily medicated with various psychotropic drugs.

LIFE, DEATH, TIME, REALITY AND ETERNITY

Hegel had been developing a philosophy of history, by starting a project of trying to identify death for people. Hoffman believes that there are certain persons who have a desire to die. Actually, they do experience the death-wish at a certain point in their life. It is not necessarily a result of certain people giving up on life or trying to escape life's burdens that a lot of suicides do, but it is an overwhelming feeling that puts them into a state of thinking and desiring to be dead. However, this desire consists of other unknown phenomena.

The one that I am interested in is the one that has a strong attraction of wanting to die even though life for those individuals is going just fine. The death seems to appear to be a flight from point "A" to point "B". Where does this attraction come from? No one really knows for sure and it is quite likely that scientists never ever will know until more research work is done upon this type of phenomenon. Is time really negatively, and is it a fact that negativity is known widely as extroverted death? It appears to be both a conscious and an unconscious death instinct, because I believe it takes both minds or all of the thinking processes to be in harmony with the ego and the id.

It appears to have the quality of an inseparable unity i.e. life and death ride hand in hand because both are absolutes; two opposites, producing a balance of control. It also may be a vicious circle or cycle for the living and also for the dead; once alive, one must die, once dead one must become born again.

It may also have something to do with a fulfillment. Like reaching a certain point in life when one is ripe with living or ripe with knowledge and the subject wishes to be elsewheres instead of being here.

Author Mr. Victor E. Hoffman

A MATTER OF LIFE AND DEATH

Today, abortion can be looked upon as a crucial event. It is an issue that concerns everyone.

As the scientific medical research advances, it can produce biological facts that can be used. Then the government will be able to base their decision-making upon our personal life.

We now need rapid growth to develop our abortion laws. This will not be an easy task, yet it has to be done. Society is screaming.

How often does the doctor choose abortion as the solution in dealing with the difficulties.

The justified abortion laws of the traditional grounds are being stamped upon. However, we need new grounds to deal with this present problem area.

In terms of evil and goodness, the moral choice aims for justified satisfaction, of which will make society happier.

Men today must act to maximize the value of life. They must actualize their potential as a giver of life, or be their executioner.

Men have always exercised power over one another. Should this power over life and giver of death be permitted? That question has been raised many times by many. Should it be one for many, or many for one?

What right have we to be born into this world of choice? A world that is torn between love and hate. A world that is full of war, crime, and condemnation. We today have a society of indecency. Troubles and nothing but troubles, yet a child may be born who may change this world; also, many will be born that will abuse this world too.

Who should be born and who shouldn't be born? We are not God, so let's not behave as if we are God. That which can be born, let it be born. That which is crippling, let it be so, because they have other gifts to give.

We are equal for self-preservation. We come into this world of good things and other things of wrong, and evil things happen afterwards.

Author Mr. Victor Hoffman
Aug. 22/91

ACTORS AND ACTRESSES HAVE TO BE VERSATILE

Upon the stage of life; I have this to say,
with means to take part; as an act of an actor,
with the uses of the natural required understanding.
I must be fully aware of many advancing evils.
Under those certain conditions; I am conscripted to strip,
to the purpose, the good measure, the circumstances, my honours.
To the measures of extremes, my balances, the honours.
When I win the awards, for being the best,
I do welcome the honours; from here, and the extremes.
I like my state of mind; when involved I feel independent.
I've found out in my experiences, of those certain matters,
"I just love to feel the touch of astonishments,"
When giving out my services of my act;
I often feel ashamed of my parts,
even so, I do my part; doing my performances.
The daily workable experiences of: mannerism, images, chastity, and
     greed-should I blush?
The rotten dew does melt away at the mortal openings.
The scars of it (I do remember), I to straighten out my act!
Acting is hard work; at these, my conscience does return.
When I do fail, I can wear a gown of humility!
After resolving the problem areas; I can function better,
When carrying out my duties, my conscience does not betray me.
With love to the destiny; to bring home a score.
I too live to feel free upon any stage of the act in living.
So it fits this life of hysteria;
the emotional outburst of imperfect conception,
restricted to the proper particular attitude,
stopping only at certain places,
the forces of law, acting in treatment centres,
to the utmost liability in restricted areas.
To the ones who strives; he is appealing to the intellect,
the dancers go by; passing right on by,

of them all, feeling self-contained.
Walking hand in hand, sharing kisses,
than I knew I was the bad actor,
existing, making hopes impossible for my love.

                                   Author Mr. Victor Ernest Hoffman

OUT OF THE CHEMICAL TRAP

INTRODUCTION

This is a short article that is about modern farming and all about the troubles that keep arising yearly; crop failures, the insect invasion, drought and the use of chemical fertilizers.

Small farmers are turning back to the old horse power to produce organic foods for two main reasons, to produce healthier foods and because of high expenses.

There is also soil failure by the loss of crop nutrients. The conditions today are very alarming by the use of chemicals. These conditions are the result of modern farming. By the use of newer things, herbicides and pesticides are leading the farming situation into three great big problem areas; moisture loss, wind erosion and pollution. It is very alarming because the organic content of soils has declined by 40%.

Some scientists are worried because they think they are losing the battle against the insects.

There is a reason why many farmers do not stay away from the use of chemicals, and the answer to that is economics.

OUT OF THE CHEMICAL TRAP

Many big time farmers have been noticing that it takes more fertilizer each year to get a similar yield on the same land. The cost of the use of fertilizer is increasing each year by 20% and still yet grain prices were only increasing at half that rate.

The fact is that good soil is declining yearly in the plant nutrients *and the soil conditions are very necessary for plant growth. Soil fertility is being degraded, the physical loss of the soil's components through erosion increases salinity and loss of moisture of which causes the loss of a good crop yield. There is no profit today in farming.*

Shunning the use of all chemicals, some 40,000 farmers are returning to the old ways of agriculture. These farmers have reached the point that any more use of chemicals will defeat the land and their pocket book completely, so there is no alternative but go back to the old ways of farming in order to survive.

There is a strong demand for healthy organic food and farmers know that they can win by the world's expectancy of healthy foods for babies, children and themselves. This is more desirable and is coming into demand as other big time farmers will be out of business and will have to do the same as the organic food producers.

The scientists are now very worried about the fact that the war on insects is now lost. Some experts say, "monster bugs are evolving, of which cannot be stopped by any product on the market." The insects have developed a resistance to the pesticides (I.E. the Colorado potato beetle has been treated with 15 different insecticides since 1950 and is now immune to all of them). Nature has a way to make a strong come back on human food production of foods. Farming nowadays, when viewing the arising problems, it is becoming a nightmare to the farmers and scientists.

With today's high cost to farming, we see the farmers and the scientists defeated. Modern ways do not work now. Farming business has gone down the drain. It is impossible for us now but hope that we are wrong in using modern methods and now we must side with nature.

What can we be afraid of? — just take it step by step and work to make daily needs be. Facing the situation with brave acceptance, we hope to find the workable solution. We cannot give up, but do battle as men should, for men are intelligent and must never be defeated because when all men are defeated, civilization of modern times ends.

Author Victor Hoffman

RECEPTIVE READING FOR ANYONE

In short, the dictionary could put into your brain, a fortune of treasure. The information data could very much paint your works in writing, spelling, knowing to understand big words, and do much verbal intellectualizing. Both the reader and speaker will gain much insight into what you have written and whatever you say. You will be able to express yourself with understanding. You may be recognized as an expert, being on top of all things. You may become very receptive to all problems, that are occurring in society. By making ideal opinions, with better ideas than anyone else. The dictionary can be productive. All you must do, is use it everyday. Besides that, go nowheres without one. There are pocket-size dictionaries that one can make good use of, when waiting for the bus, or when one is travelling on a plane. So be not without one, or you'll miss out on a lot of things.

There's always something new to learn. The idea is always in reach of one. Buy a lot of them, for all occasions. They come in all sizes. This is not an ad, but an essay.

October 14/91
by Mr. Victor Ernest Hoffman

VICTOR'S interest in words means so much to him that he once traded a clock radio for a typewriter. He plans on writing plays, once sent a song to the United States for publication — "they wanted $90 American to publish it and I don't want to be a sucker". — and keeps thinking about authoring a Bible or whatever tale he can assemble.

"There's all kinds of stories but it's hard to collect them around here because they won't talk about them. At Oak Ridge they would talk about all kinds of things out there but if you write things they're going to steal it from you. I did all kinds of writings but they stole it on me."

The conversation returns to his childhood and he related how he almost injured or killed his mother on three different occasions. "Once I was throwing darts. She almost walked right into it. Did she ever give me a scare. Another time she went to get the cows. I took a gun and shot at the magpies. The bullets ricocheted off the granary and just missed her. One time I threw the crowbar. I had super strength. I saw her and screamed, 'Mother, stop!' I threw the crowbar like a javelin."

Victor is proud of the strength he had while living on the farm. "I could bend horseshoes and iron bars. I showed them to the police." [laughs]

He remembers his jailer, before his move to Ontario, who did not like, "my crime I did. He said, 'Who are you, some superman?" [laughs]

It was in 1987 Victor recalled, that he was watching wrestling on TV and began to growl like 'The Hulk.' Then there was the time when there was a movie featuring Bruce Lee.

"Christ, I had a fight with him. He hit me in the ribs. It's hard to beat up a guy like that. I blocked most of his blows but he would get me with a trick one." [laughs]

VICTOR'S bedroom, which he shares with mood-swinging Harold who he met at Oak Ridge, contains two metal beds trimmed with wooden headboards, two dressers and almost all of his worldly possessions. It is next to colorless with a white ceiling, walls of light pale green and a faded, pinkish door, backed with a full-length mirror. There is a sleek, black two-speaker radio — only one works — and a picture of three small boats and an exterior view of more brick building. In the tight accommodation without frills and inside his personal hallway locker are various books. There is also an impressive drawing of a beautiful woman with bright red hair. Victor was the artist and the picture, quite accurately, reminds him of a certain female patient when she bends over. He has a diary and as it is opened on his bed, with the blanket stamped "MHC" in black, the name Marc Lepine surfaces. Lepine, with a pre-planned destination and pre-meditated attack, killed 14 women in what is known as the 1989 University of Montreal massacre. Asked why he thinks the killer undertook the grisly rampage that set off a stormy debate about feminism, Victor replied: "It was the way he was brought up. The way women treated him and the way society treated him. Society is a cruel beast of hell."

Victor, who at one time thought of becoming a mercenary, a policeman or a security guard, believes the approach to war, with nations fighting with their best, healthiest citizens, is wrong.

"They should fight with their weak, with their criminals, rats and the insane," he reasoned, "so the strong aren't killed off and they can rebuild. There's a problem though if everyone does it."

When it comes to the opposite sex, Victor feels, "eventually I will have a woman … If I don't get caught I'll be OK."

It was not that long ago that he thought aloud that a woman acquaintance of his, also a patient, "looked better dead than alive." His privileges were lifted.

The conversation turned back to his memory of August 15, 1967, how he got up in the middle of the night, tried to kill himself with pure grain alcohol and heard a voice, "Victor, you do not know what you're doing — don't do it." He recalled driving out of the yard without his car headlights on, the clear sky and a highway sign leading up to the Peterson property.

I T was time for some fresh air and Victor signed himself out so we could go across to the canteen, in a separate building, a short walk away. It too is full of blank, hollow-eyed inhabitants but the atmosphere in the large, open space is inviting, with pool and Ping-Pong tables, a space invader video game and comfortable furniture for lounging. Many of the languishing occupants greet Victor. He expresses concern because one of his friends has suffered a relapse and he offers a cigarette to another of those filling their endless hours on a slow, lazy Saturday. Victor, who enjoyed playing the video diversion — the first time he had ever done so — then made it known that perhaps he should have become a lawyer or a politician.

"I could say nothing and talk lots. Mulroney (Prime Minister of the day) could be a professor, teaching men how to become politicians."

We were interrupted by the 'battle of the radios' which broke out when two patients both insisted on their own trumpeting music. Finally, one of them relented and reverted to earphones. Victor continued. He talked about his upcoming birthday and his plan to prepare "a little speech" in case there was "a surprise party." He talked about staring at the sun when he was a child, "I had such an attraction, such a desire. I was told I could go blind." And he talked about writing "a good love novel" that he would call "Kill The Duck And Save The Pig." He also recalled many months earlier when the thought of escaping crossed his mind.

"I couldn't get a plan to work. It made me sick in the belly. The only way is if I was invisible. It's unbelievable but it can be done. Only about six people succeeded. I did exercise but I can't tell you because it's top secret information. The devil advocate from the church in Rome will come after me."

Victor glanced at his watch. It was time to return to the rehabilitation unit and he knew it was important not to be tardy.

THE smoking lounge was packed. Tidyman, who looked like he could have been a successful executive in an earlier life, was continually picking up cups, lids and imaginary pieces of paper that he was convinced were buried within the overflowing ashtrays. As he doggedly went about his time-consuming mission in his trance-like state there were occasional outbursts of wild laughter — totally unrelated to anything apparent in the room.

Victor was reminded again that it was too bad he was let out of the Saskatchewan Hospital. He replied: "It was a real shame. The girls there were on the horny side and a nymphomaniac had her eye on me. They kept us separate but I saw her in the laundry area. I was always shy of girls. I could have got over my problems but Oak Ridge caused more for me."

He told me that his surroundings were like a holiday. "It's a picnic. They're not making me suffer, they're doing me a lot of good. I'd like to quit the shop and write or draw. I could quit my job but I couldn't complain that I'm out of money."

He remembered that a preacher once said, 'If the hand sins, chop it off,' and afterwards when Victor kicked his sister, "I took the axe and chopped my toe quite deeply. I don't know what foot it is."

His family album was thrown out long ago. "I had too much stuff. I was tired of those pictures. One paper had me on the front page and Diefenbaker (former Prime Minister) on the second."

Victor then reflected on the day when he was disciplined for the one experience he had with a girl. He claimed he was 11 and she was a year younger.

"I was raising hell with (blank) in the hayloft. She was making moaning sounds. I almost blew my stones. Her mother came in and kicked me off. I stood up and came all over her mother. I pleased her and she came. She had an orgasm. Her mother was upset."

Victor wanted to visit the Friendship Centre to check on some batteries he had ordered. When we returned there would be a message from one of the patients who eavesdropped as the hayloft experience was so intimately divulged. The complainant may have been estranged from life as it is known to be real but she had not lost her sense of decency.

THE Friendship Centre is an old, white house with hardwood floors. A cozy building where patients and visitors can purchase greeting cards, birdhouses and various other knick-knacks. There is a kitchen area, where the patients can cook, and a warm living room to relax, read a book, have a coffee or kiss and hug as was the case with one dazed couple.

Victor was welcomed by several patients who recognized him as a friendly face. He was polite and interested, telling one co-patient that he did not have any radio batteries to lend him and offering to light a cigarette for another worrisome soul who was frantically playing a number game as if his very future depended on the result.

There were not a lot of jokes in this room although Victor remembered one from his school days. "Confuscious say, woman who fly airplane upside down have crack up. The girls laughed and the teacher handed it back. I was exposed." [laughs]

He then referred to a female patient and said, "I can't understand her. She's a perfect woman for a nag. I had to drop her."

Victor requested that any names that he made reference to, not be used in this book.

"Give them a number. You can use my name and I won't sue you. I'm not afraid to die as long as they don't cripple me. I'm not a coward. I faced the odds before when I went to school. Life is a choice. You can be whatever you want to be."

He then grabbed a book from an overloaded shelf, The Fourth Horseman by Will Henry, and pointed out the line, 'Trouble is a word spelled woman.'

Then, for the first time, he revealed that 'official concern' was shown for his bizarre behavior long before he was ever given treatment.

"The school nurse thought I should be in reform school and so did the teacher. My parents argued against it and also the cost of drugs. You don't fool around and hope the kid will get better."

Victor, who stressed he gets more satisfaction from writing than from women, had an idea of what his house would be like if he ever had one.

"I would have a room with a sign 'Passion Over Reason' with the word 'love' all over the place. We would write our problems in a book and leave them in that room."

ON the way back to the Brebeuf Centre from the Friendship building, Victor told me he has had a very good life. Once, he said, he was in an airplane before his trip in custody to Oak Ridge. He had gone as far as Buffalo Narrows — a desolate community of 700 about 240 miles northwest of Prince Albert. What he did not know was that the remote settlement, shortly after his Shell Lake deed, would also be the scene of a mass murder.

Nineteen-year-old Metis laborer, Frederick Moses McCallum, was charged in the January 30, 1969 axe-slaying of seven people. He had hacked away at eight humans but miraculously one of those bludgeoned managed to survive. The victims, members of the Thomas Pederson family and a house guest, were discovered in their blood-spattered dwelling. McCallum was arrested nearby while drinking a cup of tea. When informed that he was being taken into custody, the accused told RCMP Corporal Jack Fraser, "Sure I killed them, so what?" Corporal Fraser, in later testimony, said he found Mr. and Mrs. Pederson in their bedroom, "The upper parts of their bodies completely saturated with blood. The heads were very mutilated." He told the court he discovered a long-handled fire axe standing against a wall with blood and hair adhering to it. The accused was eventually found not guilty by reason of insanity and committed to a mental institution. As was the case with Victor, Frederick McCallum had sought treatment for his worsening mental state prior to the night that he finally cracked. Psychiatrists thought he was simply 'an angry young man' and he was not hospitalized.

INSIDE the rehabilitation centre smoking lounge, Victor, who did not know the details of the horror at Buffalo Narrows, was telling me he considered stealing the plane that took him there in order to escape from the horrendous crime he had committed.

IT was at this point that all hell broke loose. The patients had been coming and going from the lounge — with its incessant booming noise from the high-volume television and portable radio — to get their regular dosages of medication. Suddenly, Knitting Momma began throwing a fit. Swaying back and forth in a chair next to me, she started moaning and then yelling for a nurse. The tempo picked up and she hurled a flood of obscenities at the Jesus Woman across the room. It was sheer bedlam. Back and forth it went:

"God says to be quiet."

"You crazy cunt, you be quiet!"

"Ah, shut up."

"Who's talkin' to you."

"Shut up, do what you're told."

"You're a fuckin' murderer."

"God told me to talk."

"Fuck off."

"You stink like a murderer."

"You fuckin' bootlegger."

Then — Knitting Momma jumped to her feet and menacingly with legs bouncing, lunged towards her target. A third woman, who had only moments before made her appearance, blocked her path. Eyes locked, they stared at each other. There was more blue language, clenched fists, and it was only then that both retreated to their own space.

IN the midst of it all, in the eye of the storm, Victor, his capacity to wreak violence dissipated, never flinched. Neither did the others who had learned from harsh experience that one of the cardinal rules of survival in a place such as this is to mind your own business.

Outside the tension-filled arena, the Jesus Woman was now crying hysterically to one of the caring hospital workers. It was just one of those many irrational explosions among the disoriented and it had crushed the woman of mindless religion, reducing her to tears. Some say that those inside are merely part of a junkheap of minds — battered, bruised and in a lot of cases beyond repair. The patient who was subjected to the vicious, verbal onslaught was being comforted by a professional who knew otherwise.

IT would soon be time to depart but before that, Victor candidly described his goddess of love, beauty, victory, triumph and all of those wonderful things. "Calwhoelea (Cal-i-hoola), she'd be my goddess. She would be 6'8 1/2", weigh 245 pounds and have golden-red, long hair. She'd have big breasts, real nice, full uptilted, and have a thin 36" waist and 44" hips. If a man was 6'8 1/2" forget it. If he's 6'8", I can beat him."

Insofar as Calwhoelea's nationality, Victor was unsure. He chuckled, "from the other side of the universe."

Victor had a message for his father as we were nearing the end of our two days together: "Tell him I'm glad he brought me up well, honest, obedient and hard-working — it paid off."

When asked, he offered some titles for this book. Rapidly, he reeled off four suggestions:

— Madness Strikes at Shell Lake
— The Expression of Evil
— A Man Who Had No Faith in Himself
— The Man Without God and Calamity Resulted

Victor, with a certain reassuring calmness about him was

ready to go for supper and it was time for me to leave.

"It was really nice meeting with you," he said, "you're like a friend."

"Look after yourself," I replied.

He said he would.

When the taxi pulled up a few minutes later, Victor, flashing his toothless grin from his chair in the cafeteria, waved good-bye. After his meal, he had said, he planned to settle down and do some typing.

As the cab, its radio playing 'I Can See Clearly,' left the darkened, deserted hospital grounds, I couldn't help but think that it was a shame Victor — a clash between nature and nurture — didn't have more friends, sooner. He had a troubled life from the age of six, slipped through the cracks of the mental health system and sadly, the Peterson family paid for it. Proper treatment would have made the difference. Friendship might have helped.

A GOOD WORD —
Victor's interest in books and writing occupies much of his time. He talks of writing another Bible and memorizing all of the words in the dictionary.

20th Annual Prison Arts Competition

Second Prize

Creative Writing

Victor Hoffman - "Out of The Chemical Trap" - "Actors and Actresses Have to be Versatile"

Congratulations! Your entries merit Second Prize in our Young Offenders division in our Annual Prison Arts Competition. This brief essay succeeds in describing the vital necessity of protecting our food chain through the use of better farming methods and the banning of harmful chemicals. Actors and Actresses Have to be Versatile, written as a soliloquy, succeeds as a probe into the roles played by people in daily life. Its use of language and meter give this poem an energetic texture and a solid structure.

Writing - General Comment

The entries in the competition this year deal with a wide array of subjects in a straightforward manner. The material ranges through cultural transition as experienced by natives serving time, the rigors of survival on the inside, reflections on love, and a strong ecological concern.

These entries once again prove the power of the written word to overcome limitations imposed by confined space, when the geography of mind and spirit becomes a priceless asset.

Keep writing and good luck

Alfred Hushton
Creative Writing Adjudicator

Michael Johnson
Executive Director

June, 1991

A WINNER — *The Prison Arts Foundation recognized Victor for his writing efforts.*

NEATNESS — *His room, with its dresser-top full, is neat as a pin. His roommate, who also has been incarcerated for many years, knows Victor's background. They get along well.*

LOOK-ALIKE — *In disguise, with hair combed forward and part of a comb held under his nose, Victor feels he bears a resemblance to Hitler. He asked that this picture be taken.*

Epilogue

STANISLAW Jedlicki, 63, retired to Saskatoon in 1975 from his job at the Saskatchewan Hospital. Eight years later, in the month of March, Dr. Jedlicki died of respiratory failure.

An official of the institution, Al Blais, reflected long afterwards, to the time when Victor was first admitted. He told me: "The hospital is a situation of last resort. It is the last stop. Everything else has failed. Those seeking help usually settle down quickly and if they are compliant with their medication the emphasis is on out-patient care and reintegration into society. You might say, they were victims of that type of thinking."

BARRY Richards, who often wonders why he was "chosen" as the first policeman to be at the scene of the massacre, will never forget the carnage that he witnessed nor the little girl who survived. He was a father himself, of twins, aged two. "I think of it quite regularly, the date and the time," recalled the former officer who retired as a Staff Sergeant from the RCMP and makes his home in the city where the force trains its members.

INSPECTOR Brian Sawyer left the RCMP to become Chief of Police for the city of Calgary. He later served as Ombudsman for the province of Alberta followed by an executive position with Canadian Airlines. Now retired, he makes his home in the community that hosted the 1988 winter Olympics.

DEFENCE counsel Ted Noble was appointed a Court of Queen's Bench Justice in Saskatoon in 1976. The Honourable Mr. Justice Noble is also chairman of the Lieutenant Governor's Advisory Board of Review. The provincial Board is charged with the responsibility of customarily evaluating persons incarcerated in mental facilities via Saskatchewan warrants.

RETIRED Crown prosecutor Serge Kujawa, as the longest serving member of such a review panel in Canada, visited Victor routinely over the years as part of the process with those being held in custody at the pleasure of the Lieutenant Governor. The mighty lawyer, who successfully prosecuted Colin Thatcher in the celebrated trial that spawned 'Love & Hate' — the network television movie based on the novel 'A Canadian Tragedy' by Maggie Siggins — knows much about the distorted minds of those who run afoul of the law. His experience tells him, "More than 95 per cent of those charged with horrible crimes have had involvement with the psychiatric system before the fact. It's interesting to see how little psychiatry knows about humanity." Mr. Kujawa, a Member of the Saskatchewan Legislative Assembly who counts himself among few seniors who can do one handed push-ups, was the first Director of Public Prosecutions in Canadian history and in charge of not only the Hoffman case but the courtroom drama that followed the multiple axe-murders committed by

Frederick Moses McCallum. At 67 years of age, with a talented daughter the same age as Phyllis, he vividly recalls his countless conversations with Victor. As to why the killer went back inside the house and then returned to kill the baby, he was told, "The baby wasn't going anywhere." When he asked Victor why Phyllis was spared, the response was, "I wonder about that so goddamned often," with Victor then pointing to a psychiatrist with the statement, "He should know." Serge Kujawa, who was born in Poland and speaks fluent Ukrainian, remembers Victor telling the review panel about hospital dances where the female participants were old, fat, shapeless and ugly. But as Victor told the Board, "I'm no Prince Charming either."

I N 1989, the reviewers addressed the issue of Victor's residency. In 1990, it was decided that the killer of nine would retain permanent status within the boundaries of Ontario. The reason, according to Brenda Knight, was because, "It wouldn't be in Victor's best interests or the interests of the public to have him return to Saskatchewan's jurisdiction."

T HE Supreme Court of Canada, in May 1991, struck down the law dealing with the criminally insane. It declared that legislation allowing indefinite confinement — without regard to whether a person was a danger to society — contravened rights and freedoms. It would not have made a difference* in the Hoffman case as those found not guilty of murder

---

* The change in law did have an effect in the case of Donna Lynn Trueman of Manitoba. In the autumn of 1991, with her 11-year-old daughter nearby, she choked her four-year-old son Skylar and then plunged a broom handle through his head. Court was told that the mother, 32, thought her child was the reincarnation of Adolf Hitler. She was placed on anti-psychotic drugs and acquitted of murder. Within the space of five months, Ms. Trueman was set free, with conditions, to the care of her parents. Victims of Violence, a national advocacy group, and others were outraged. The woman's estranged husband, noting that his wife sought treatment for the mental illness before the senseless tragedy, publicly disagreed with a psychiatrist who said he would not have a problem if the killer was his neighbor. The father, still grieving over the loss of his son, questioned, "How'd he like to have her babysit his kids?"

by reason of insanity could still be incarcerated for life. It is interesting to note, as outlined earlier in this writing, that the Frazier Report, 23 years earlier, termed the existing law, "unjust and discriminatory." There are those who allege that the wheels of justice turn slowly. They are indisputably correct.

SEPTEMBER 10, 1991 saw the annual review of Victor's case by the Ontario Board. Lieutenant Governor Lincoln M. Alexander, two months later, issued a warrant with orders for the hospital and its infamous patient. It allowed for Victor's December transfer out of maximum security, provided unsupervised ground privileges daily and permitted supervised recreation and socialization visits into Penetanguishene and Midland and an area of approximately 120 miles surrounding those communities. The hospital could use its discretion, stated the Lieutenant Governor, keeping in mind that anytime it was exercised the local police had to be notified. There were four rules for Victor:

a) to return to the Hospital each night and remain therein overnight;

b) to permit disclosure of your clinical record by the Administrator of the Mental Health Centre, Penetanguishene if the said Administrator deemed such disclosure to be necessary for the protection of the public;

c) to abstain absolutely from the non-medical use of alcohol and drugs or any other intoxicant, and,

d) to refrain from having in your possession absolutely any firearm or ammunition or other offensive weapon or being in the company of any person possessing a firearm other than a peace officer.

FOR Victor, the prospect of a move — even though it was an escape from maximum custody where he had spent the majority of his life — was frightening. He later confessed:

"It was a great pleasure to release the progress proof, however, after receiving the walking ticket I did not want to leave. I could just not tolerate a transfer and so I turned it down." Reluctantly, his fears somewhat disquieted, he did accept and has not looked back. In his words, "Now, things are different."

PERIOD: 1992. Wildrew Lang, 60, will remember his discovery until he no longer exists and possibly beyond. He is asked, what he would think if they said, any one of these days, "We think he's better and we're going to release him?" Wildrew, in his measured way, replied: "Oh boy! I don't know that I've ever thought about that. I just assumed that the man is never going to be better and never going to be released. I would say that if he suddenly was sane and then read or heard what he had done that he would no longer be sane because no sane person could do that and live with himself at all. I just couldn't see that happening to anybody."

KATHY Hill, 45, who has never received an apology for the premature hospital release of the patient who eliminated her family, is asked what she would feel if he is again given his freedom: "I think it would scare me because there is no cure for that type of thing. They haven't found a cure for it. There's nothing saying he won't go and do the same thing again. He's been under care for that many years, he's not able to deal with the outside world. It's just been changed too much."

PHYLLIS, 29, was not only miraculously spared during the madness of the night but amazingly has suffered no mentally debilitating after-effects. As defined by the masses, she is perfectly normal. Again faced with the horrific events of that fateful time, in the final few weeks preceding publication of this chronicle, her mind-blockage is nearly complete. "I don't remember any screaming or crying," she told me, "I do remember a man talking to one of the kids."

PT — *I was just thinking, if Victor Hoffman, and he's been there for 25 years, if in the view of the doctors he was sane — he was recovered — would you have any feeling on whether or not they should let him get back into society?*

Phyllis — *Well, I think if someone's sick enough to do something like he did that they're not ever going to get better. I mean, yeah, I would definitely have a view on whether or not he should be released. I would have an opinion on that, as I'm sure not just my family but everybody has an opinion.*

PT — *What would the opinion be?*

Phyllis — *That definitely, no! I mean, people go to jail for less crimes than that and they come out and do it again so I certainly think he should stay where he is.*

IF you passed Victor Hoffman on the street he would appear to be a normal person. If you happened to be within the vicinity of Penetanguishene that could happen. In fact, had you been in the nearby Legion during a 1991 Christmas meal you would have been in his company as he was there on an escorted temporary absence.

Victor — *I was not looking forward to it but just the same I did want to find out what a Christmas dinner would be like at the Legion downtown. Once I arrived, I felt lost and scared for about 10 minutes or so. Then I met my friend and his wife. We went and sat at a table and chewed the rag (talked). We had a great time. The dinner was good and it was a lot of food but did not fill me. I would have eaten doubles or thirds but there was just the one helping. I received a present which was a book, a good book about ships and battles at sea. When I left, I felt happy and contented.*

PT — *Maybe this is premature to ask because you (Brenda) can't predict the future and of course it's up to the Board to decide to a large* degree the permanent release if that ever happens. What do you foresee happening or do you have a feeling or what do you think? You know, Victor's now been here for 25 years?

Victor — It would depend upon the medication I'm put on and how I react to it. It depends on whether I ever need medication. I might not even need medication some day. But that is very unlikely. It's quite likely I will always need medication. I will always need some kind of supervision for my status where I might happen to be. I might be able to go on a trip to Florida some day, for a week or so and come back. Maybe I'll go to a group home in about five years time.

PT — Yeah, I guess that's the next step?

Brenda — Yeah.

PT — If that day arrives, would there be a group home? Do you agree with Victor?

Brenda — I wouldn't venture to say out loud what I would think would be an amount of time. I think that Victor has a very serious illness. It's controlled by medications. He likely, as he said, will require medication to control his illness for the rest of his life. The risk of dangerous behavior is higher with Victor than with other patients because of the degree of the illness that he suffers, when he is unwell, as is evidenced by the crime. I mean, that was a very serious crime relative to someone else who is thinking in paranoid ways and holes up in the basement of their home when they feel paranoid.

PT — The magnitude?

Brenda — The magnitude, the extent to which he went to relieve himself of his concerns and ideas, the fact that he possessed firearms, has a knowledge of firearms. He's on such heavy medication that he can't risk alcohol or drugs or any of the other sort of thing. On the other hand, he's demonstrated very stable, responsible behavior over a long period of time now. Never been considered an assaultive individual within the institution. In fact, I would say you're a bit of a mediator. You'd like to see problems solved between people.

Victor — Right, I even help them out.

Brenda — And helps out where he can. But I think you've learned to mind your own business and stay out of issues that you can't fix, are not his to fix. I guess what you're asking is there a time? No, there's no time. I think it'll be based on clinical judgments, on *assessments of his dangerousness to himself but particularly public safety. That risk has to be evaluated very carefully and annually. My guess is that there will be an element of supervision in his life forever and I think that Victor is probably very close to what his life will hold. Probably, eventually a group home so that there's supervision but that supervision although there, may not be evident 24 hours a day. My guess is that he will be able to live, run a fairly normal life, probably have his own space, live a nice quality life, perhaps work in some sort of setting ...*

Victor — Writing. It may lead to my profession. I may just become a professional script writer. And then again, I might fail at that too.

PT — Well, the thing about that is you never know until you try, right?

Victor — Right.

Brenda — And regardless, he's also talked about farming somebody's land or becoming an assistant. So I think there's some reality to that. Victor likes his writing and I think dreams of some sort of significant future and is working towards that and has some goals and is going to school.

PHYLLIS, with the advent of this true story, took it upon herself to contact the Hoffman family for the first time since the tragedy. Her initial telephone approach was to Allan but he was not home. Obtaining Eileen's number, she dialed, waited and then — the words flowed, "Hi, are you sitting down? Please don't hang up ..." There was a pause, Eileen listened attentively and heard, "There are no hard feelings." The unexpected call, "part of the healing process," was followed by other long distance discussions with Brian Sawyer and Barry Richards.

As stated at the outset and as you have come to share, Phyllis is a rare, remarkable human being. Deservedly, she gets the final word: "If he is ever released the public has a right to know. They should let Kathy and I know. I wouldn't want him living next door to me. I am hoping your book opens some eyes. Kathy and I are not holding grudges. If we're not — the rest of the world shouldn't."

If you wish to join the procession
Go to your car immediately following
the Service

When driving in the Funeral Procession
please keep your head lights on bright
For safety.

APPRECIATION

On behalf of the Family, we wish to express
our gratitude for your many kindnesses
evidenced in thought and deed, and for
your attendance at the memorial service.

MacKenzie Funeral Home
PRINCE ALBERT, SASK.

W. T. BEATON   H. J. JORDAN

MR. JAMES F.R. PETERSON

MRS. EVELYN M. PETERSON

JEAN: MARY: DOROTHY: PEARL

WILLIAM   COLIN   LARRY

PASSED AWAY

Shell Lake, Sask:
August 15th 1967

PALLBEARERS

Legion Members   Neighbors

Mervin Madsen   Earl Loseth
Alf Vaagen   Wildrew Lang
James Walter   Alex Lang
George Lucier   John Clarke
Axel Erickson   Keith Clarke
Albert Bellisle   Alvin Simonar

IN

REMEMBRANCE

FUNERAL SERVICE

Shell Lake Cemetery

2:00 P.M.

Saturday, August 19th 1967

OFFICIANTS

Reverend G. Spence
Canon D.A. Gregory

INTERMENT

Family Plot Shell Lake

Graveside Service for the late
James F. Peterson conducted by
Royal Canadian Legion, Zone 4
of District 6, Sask; Command

*IN REMEMBRANCE — An expression of gratitude given to mourners. It
thanked them for: "Your many kindnesses evidenced in thought and deed, and
for your attendance at the memorial service."*

PORTRAIT OF INNOCENCE — *An angel who was allowed to live.*

Chronology:

VICTOR ERNEST HOFFMAN

- <u>Born</u>   January 15, 1946
- <u>Hospitalized</u>   May 29, 1967
- <u>Released</u>   July 26, 1967
- <u>Committed mass murder</u>   August 15, 1967
- <u>Arrested</u>   August 19, 1967
- <u>Charged</u>   August 21, 1967
- <u>Trial</u>   January 8, 1968
- <u>Verdict</u>   January 11, 1968
- <u>Eastern transfer</u>   March 22, 1968
- Minimum security
  <u>Escorted absence</u>   December 1991

CHANGING FACES — A page in the life of a once promising child who has been locked up longer than he has known freedom.

Author's Note

FOLLOWING the extensive interviews at Penetanguishene, the audio tape transcripts were forwarded to the hospital. The procedure had been promised and was designed to ensure accuracy. They were reviewed and returned with two letters on February 25, 1992. Each contained a telling response.

"Let me say that the interview, but more importantly, the reading of his transcript was most disconcerting for Victor. He found it rather difficult to see the brutal truth of 25 years ago, once again, brought before his eyes. I think the reality of having his story in print at this time in his recovery process has hit home."

— Brenda Knight

"I do not know how I may handle that situation, specially the crime. It may change my whole lifestyle here at Brebeuf. It may make me very ill."

— Victor E. Hoffman

Reference:

MASS MURDER

MULTIPLE murders, prior to the mid-1960's, were a rarity that invariably involved victims known to their killers. Public massacre was an unheard of quantity — family annihilation of the immediate kind was not. Such was the case on June 28, 1959, a scorching summer day, when police discovered seven decaying bodies of the Albert Raymond Cook family in the grease-pit of a garage attached to their Stettler, Alberta property. The eldest son, Robert Raymond, born in Hanna — a short drive southeast — had recently been released from prison where he had spent much of his time since graduating from the ranks of juvenile delinquency. Bobby, 21, was arraigned in connection with the slayings and sent to Alberta Hospital Ponoka for an assessment of his mental state. He was then embroiled in a sensational escape and massive police search. Subsequently, reporters who had flocked to the manhunt zone, including my brother Michael of CKY Winnipeg, reported on the capture which came four days after the daring dash for freedom. Mike recalled his radio story filed from the scene: "The accused was hungry, almost starving, exhausted and half-naked. Robert Raymond Cook, a mere shell of someone described as a ruthless madman, was the epitome of a frightened child when he was arrested while cowering in a pig barn less than one hour away from where his family was buried." Bobby Cook, proclaiming his innocence until the end, was found guilty of murder and sentenced to death. A noose was placed around his bull neck just after midnight on November 15, 1960. He was pronounced dead at

12:14 a.m. although as I later witnessed — the wide rope burns indelibly seared into his cervix remained long after Bobby, with his brush cut and trademark blood-shot eyes, departed at the youthful age of 23 years.

MASS MURDERERS

Richard Speck
July 14, 1966
Chicago, Illinois
Murdered: Eight

■ A new era dawned in the summer of 1966: the age of mass murder. It began when Richard Speck with "Born to Raise Hell" tattooed on one arm, broke into a townhouse in south Chicago — repeatedly assured nine young nurses that he only wanted money and was not going to hurt them — and then methodically proceeded to stab and strangle all but one. Authorities were unable to determine a motive for the actions of the drifter who represented the first truly high-profile multiple murder case in North America. Speck was sentenced to death in the electric chair but the U.S. Supreme Court struck down the decision. He remained in prison until December 1991, suffered chest pains, was taken to the hospital, and died one day before his 50th birthday. A sister of one of the victim's was quoted as saying, "I think that it's a shame that it's taken this long for him to leave this earth." A retired policeman, one of the first to witness the July 14th carnage, added, "Judgment day has finally arrived for that sucker, he died an easy death — he should have suffered a lot more than he did."

Charles Whitman
August 1, 1966
Austin, Texas
Murdered: Sixteen

■ Two weeks after Speck's brutal rampage, Charles Whitman climbed to the top of a tower at the University of Texas. Sixteen people died before he was finished shooting. He became the 17th fatality when gunned down by police.

Victor Hoffman
August 15, 1967
Shell Lake,
Saskatchewan
Murdered: Nine

■ Canada entered the realm of mass murder — thus we depart the United States where the list has grown — on August 15, 1967 with the emergence of Victor Hoffman. The Peterson family — staring death in the face — did not have a chance. Victor is now allowed temporary absences into the communities surrounding the mental hospital where he still resides.

Frederick McCallum
January 30, 1969
Buffalo Narrows,
Saskatchewan
Murdered: Seven

■ Frederick Moses McCallum, charged with the January 30, 1969 axe-slaying of seven people in Buffalo Narrows, Saskatchewan, was returned to society in Central Canada although it was not announced nor acknowledged by those in charge. They say they cannot comment due to confidentiality cited in the Mental Health Act. As the law with the mentally ill stands, the public is denied information when mass killers, cured or controlled according to the experts, are allowed back on the streets. Canadians are kept in the dark about the strangers beside them because the rights of privacy are deemed more important than the sanctity of knowledge. McCallum, with previous convictions for break and enter, theft, and prison breach — as well as psychiatric treatments before he went on his wild night of abhorrent violence — is married and has been living with his wife and child in the West. He has been ordered to stay away from alcohol. Since his secretive release, after close to 20 years in captivity, he has not added to his criminal record.

Dale Nelson
September 5, 1970
Creston,
British Columbia
Murdered: Eight

■ Dale Merle Nelson, 31, went berserk September 5, 1970 and savagely murdered eight people in the southeastern British Columbia community of Creston. One body, that of a child, was so mutilated that it took police several hours to determine who it was. The atrocities included putting his face into the ripped stomach of an infant and eating undigested cereal from the gaping cavity. The heavily-built lunatic, released from a mental hospital in January of that year, was a man known to violence. It may as well have been his name. In June, less than three months before the horror that some described as "inexplicable", a psychiatrist warned that "something would happen" if he was not sent back for treatment. Dale Nelson was sentenced to life in prison and more than 20 years later remains behind the walls of a penitentiary in his home province.

David Shearing
Wells Gray Provincial
Park, BC; August 1982
Murdered: Six

■ David William Shearing, 23, was an unemployed lone wolf who lived at Clearwater, British Columbia. On August 16, 1982 Bob Johnson, 44, was reported missing by his employer. Afterwards, a berry picker stumbled upon the burned-out shell of a car in Wells Gray Provincial Park — just down the road from Clearwater. Inside were the charred remains of Mr. and Mrs. Johnson and their two daughters. They were accompanied by the corpses of grandparents George and Edith Bentley. David Shearing, claiming he was looking for work, was arrested more than a year later. He pleaded guilty to six counts of second-degree murder and was sentenced to six concurrent life terms with no eligibility for parole. Justice Harry McKay, now deceased, had earlier sentenced serial killer Clifford Olson to a life behind bars. Noting that Shearing had murdered for the victims' possessions, the Judge wondered aloud: "What a tragedy, what a waste, and for what?" David Shearing is imprisoned in Saskatchewan.

Marc Lepine
December 6, 1989
Montreal, Quebec
Murdered: Fourteen

■ Marc Lepine, a loner who despised women and was consumed with hatred and feelings of rejection from the University of Montreal, stormed its engineering school on December 6, 1989. The resulting bloodbath left 14 females dead. Lepine, with a troubled history, then shot himself. Parliament later declared December 6th a national day of commemoration. On the second anniversary, a survivor was quoted as saying, "I have read many books ... I'm trying to find out what the reasons are that can push a person to do such an evil act."

PERHAPS this account of the Shell Lake Massacre — documenting the advance warning signals emitted by those whose warped minds were in the process of snapping — will help. All were deeply disturbed — None were adequately addressed. They were what you would call, walking time bombs.

SERIAL KILLER

Clifford Olson
1980-1981
British Columbia
Murdered: Eleven

▼ The criminals who authorities call "killing machines" — those within the category of serial killers — are almost totally foreign to Canadians. The lone exception — Charles Ng sought refuge in Canada but committed his wicked deeds on U.S. soil — is Clifford Olson. The married father of one admitted to police, after securing payment of $100,000 for his confession, that he had beaten, strangled or stabbed to death 11 children. It happened in British Columbia between 1980 and 1981. Clifford Olson, well-known to authorities prior to his killing spree, remains in a maximum security penitentiary.

GANGLAND slayings are also a part of this historical roll call of mayhem. Richard "The Cat" Blass died in a January 24, 1975 shootout with police. He was a prime suspect in a multiple murder at the Gargantua night club in Quebec which claimed 13 lives. The victims, including several underworld figures, were locked in a small storeroom of the second-floor party place which was then set ablaze. Bottles of cognac helped fuel the flames. A second suspect was later released because of lack of evidence. Eleven years later, Michel Blass — "The Cat's" younger brother — admitted being part of a dozen killings going back to 1974. He was sentenced to 12 life terms in prison.

Publisher's Message

THE contents herein, as signified at the outset, are protected by the laws of copyright. Prior to publication some news agencies expressed specific interest in material contained within the section entitled, "Reference: Mass Murder."

General permission is hereby granted to recognized news organizations for use of same provided the following credit line is included.

Source: Shell Lake Massacre by Peter Tadman.

— John T. Gorman

Names:

AUCTIONEER
Ted McDougall

CAFE PATRON
Ed Caplette

CAFE WORKERS
Cliff Johnstone
Iris Johnstone
Phyllis Melton
Joe Wong

CHURCH WARDEN
Ernie Frank

CIVIL SERVANT
Dr. J.G. Clarkson

CORONER
Dr. Calvin S. Lambert

CORONER'S JURY FOREMAN
Ed Simonar

CRIMES COMPENSATION BOARD MEMBER
Mrs. Joyce Moxley

CROWN PROSECUTOR
Serge Kujawa

DEFENCE LAWYER
George E. (Ted) Noble

EDITOR
Karen Sulz

HOFFMAN FAMILY
Allan
Bernice
Eileen
Lorraine
Marion
Richard
Robert
Stella
Victor

HOFFMAN NEIGHBORS
Jimmy Peake
Robert Peake

HOTELIER
Ed Musich

JUDGES
Mr. Justice M.A. (Sandy) MacPherson
Magistrate J.M. Policha

LETTER WRITERS
Margaret Butcher
Walter Kreutzer
Mr. & Mrs. H. Pion
Esther M. Sanders
Mrs. L. Schoonover
Phyllis & Peter Skish
K N Snasdell
Jean Weberg (Mattock)
Mrs. Rita Whalen

LIEUTENANT GOVERNOR
Lincoln M. Alexander

MEDIA
Associated Press
Broadcast News
Canapress
CBC
CFCN
CFQC
CKBI
CKY
CTV
Bob Colling — Canadian Press
John Dauphinee — Canadian Press
Andy Garrett — Canadian Press
Ashley Geddes — Calgary Herald
Paul Grescoe — Canadian Magazine
Don Kew — Edmonton Sun
Steve Makris — Edmonton Journal
Ross Munro — Canadian Magazine
Gillis Purcell — Canadian Press
Regina Leader Post
Dave Reidie — Edmonton Journal
Saskatoon StarPhoenix
Southam Inc.
Standard Radio News
Vancouver Sun
Winnipeg Free Press

MEDICAL
Dr. Shervert H. Frazier
Dr. Stanislaw Jedlicki
Dr. R.E. Jenkins
Brenda Knight
Dr. Oliver G. Lane
Dr. J.R. Michaud
Dr. Rathana Nakintara
Dr. Alex D. Pokorny
Dr. Colin Smith
Sandra Staruch

PETERSON FAMILY

Colin

Dorothy

Evelyn

James

Jean

Kathleen

Larry

Mary

Pearl

Phyllis

William

PETERSON NEIGHBORS

Wildrew Lang

Mr. & Mrs. Mervin Madsen

Alvin Simonar

Marjorie Simonar

POLICE

E.R. Blatta — Staff-Sergeant

Ken Ferguson — Staff-Sergeant

Gerald Fraser — Sergeant

Arnold (Gus) Gawthrop — Corporal

Shane (Rip) Kirby — Staff-Sergeant

Edgar Kuhn — Corporal

Beverly Jean Long — Civilian Member

Ken MacLeod — Staff-Sergeant

Roderick McKenzie — Corporal

George Robert (Bob) Mooney — Sergeant

Charles Nolan — Corporal

Michael O'Donnell — Constable

Brian Sawyer — Inspector

Ronald Sondergaard — Staff-Sergeant

Frederick Tweed — Sergeant

POLITICIANS

Prime Minister John Diefenbaker

Health Minister Gordon Grant

Attorney General D.V. Heald

Prime Minister Brian Mulroney

Premier W. Ross Thatcher

PUBLISHERS

John T. Gorman

Pamela Donald-Gorman

OPERATIONS MANAGER

Edward Jensen

MARKETING MANAGER

Joan Jensen

RELIGIOUS

Canon Douglas Gregory

Pastor Edward Post

Reverend Gerald Spence

ROAD PATROL

Roy Lang

VICTIMS' RELATIVES

HOFFMAN FAMILY

Victor Dominick

Emma Hoffman

Reinhold Hoffman

PETERSON FAMILY

Martha Finlayson

Evie Helgeton (Lang)

Helmer Helgeton

Lee Hill

Norma Johnson

Cyril Mayo

Elsie Mayo

Fred Peterson

Martha Peterson

The Last Word

A LMOST 10 years later…Victor, perpetually plagued with paranoid schizophrenia, remained hospitalized at Penetanguishene, steeped in history, surrounded by exceptional beauty, home to what was once Canada's only asylum for the criminally insane.

"He's out there," the then-little girl who escaped his deadly rampage stated, days before yet another anniversary of the near total annihilation of her family. "He doesn't scare me."

S UMMER 2001, more than three decades since Colin, Dorothy, Evelyn, James, Jean, Larry, Mary, Pearl and William Peterson had their lives stolen. Thirty-four years to the day to be exact.

PT – Hi Victor. How are you doing?

Victor – Today I'm out of money. I sold my bicycle cable.

PT – I'm just calling to follow up last month's telephone chat to let you know I'll be out to see you in a couple of weeks.

Victor – What happened in the past has faded. I don't think about it much. I thought about it the other day when I went to the cafeteria.

Two days later a senior mental health centre official confirmed that despite longstanding concerns by authorities that the first printing of *Shell Lake Massacre* "caused a lot of reaction, a lot of hassles about Victor's community releases" the visit would be allowed.

"He's capable of making his own decisions," she said. "He does not want to talk about the crime in any way, shape or form. No tape recorder." Those were the rules. Hard, fast, clear, understood. In a mere 14 days, they would be put to the test.

S ETTING: Leask, village of the son gone terribly wrong, the community that welcomes you with its faded green and white entrance sign, *Our Youth Are The Future – Challenged*

To Be Our Best.

The dogs are gone, the gas pumps have vanished and the once shiny Shell Oil service station off the highway, with the motto *Service is our Business*, has been vacated. On Main Street, Ed Musich's still dilapidated two-storey hotel, with its four new-fangled, money-hungry slot machines, remains the focal point. His patrons and their non-imbibing neighbors don't talk much about what the local boy did at Shell Lake so very many years ago, or about his family, forced to live their remaining time on earth with the unshakeable memories of the dark past.

Robert died in the local hospital in 1995 at the age of 84. It was a fairly large funeral, about 175 paying their respects at the Legion Hall. "Everybody comes in smaller communities," said funeral director Irwin Hawryluk, who ironically, as a young man, started out in the burial business at the funeral home in charge of laying the nine Petersons to rest.

Allan has moved away from the family farm, his will to work the land gone. As for the homestead itself, it too has died. The house and outbuildings endure without life, deserted, where strangers are greeted with an ominous sign, warning about trespassing, located on the edge of an abandoned tree-lined road, overgrown with tall Prairie grass.

SETTING: Shell Lake. Alvin and Marjorie Simonar still live across the highway from the tiny place where madness struck. Around their farmhouse, most of the talk is about children, grandchildren and Alvin being confined to a straight-backed chair, barely able to move after falling off a roof and crushing several discs in his back. The Simonars can no longer see the Peterson home. Burned to the ground, its remnants hidden by thick bush, the little white house is no more.

In the late 1990s Phyllis moved back to Saskatchewan. Her marriage had ended and it was a chance for her to move closer to Kathy, near Spiritwood, up the highway from the killing field.

SETTING: Spiritwood. Phyllis cheerily answered my unexpected phone call from the Simonar residence and readily agreed to get together for a coffee to discuss updating *Shell*

Lake Massacre. It was graduation night and to help out, she had promised to work at the local coffee bar/service station so that one of the teenaged staff members could attend the special celebrations. Our meeting would have to be fast, she explained, but it would be nice to see each other and get caught up. She was right on all counts. About 20 minutes, quick, pleasant and newsy. We agreed to meet again, after the latest was learned about her family's deranged killer.

P ENETANGUISHENE is synonymous with fresh air, country living and founding cultures going back more than 1200 years. It proudly proclaims, *Your Destination, Our Heritage* and blissfully beckons, *Come And Make Your History A Part Of Ours.*

"It's hard to talk with my friends," Victor said when plans were first being formed in July for the late summer visit. "You can't socialize with the patients. They're paranoid. They're afraid of intimidation."

At the hazy beginning of a glorious Labour Day weekend, about a five-minute cab ride from the closest hotel, the time had arrived to spend several hours with Victor, see how he was doing, explore his psychotic disordered mindset, obtain the last word after his horrible wasting of so many human lives.

Up the concrete steps to the aged administration building and inside its well-seasoned entry, a short wait began on a hard, wooden bench, just around the corner from a cramped, central office. Busy Barb from dental, with three lost souls aimlessly wandering the surrounding hallways and morning tasks at hand, offered to call Victor.

Within a flash – far too rapid if Victor had to come from somewhere else on the grounds – a burly, powerful looking man with a crooked ball cap, an open, blue, sweat-stained work shirt, bulging pockets and the air of a maintenance worker efficiently going about his business, hurriedly came through a back door, brushed past and abruptly stopped a few feet away.

At first, we didn't recognize each other. Within seconds we were shaking hands. Victor was surprised. He later explained that he was expecting me the next day. For now, he was there to get some spending money out of his account for the weekend. And he stepped over and did that. And then he came back to me and asked, "Who are you here to see?"

From our confused start we headed out, chit-chatting along the way to his present day confines, past the former shop building, the tennis courts, and a streamlined bicycle that Victor reckoned was worth $300. He placed one of his giant hands on the lower bar, claimed the engineless bike had a motor and began to laugh.

Inside the Brebeuf building, Victor had to get to work. It was lunchtime and that meant helping around the cafeteria, cleaning tables, emptying trays, taking out the garbage. His father had always claimed that the son gone wrong was a good worker and he was proving him right. Lunch was quickly finished and Victor, once his duties were done, would join me.

Victor emerged from the cafeteria. The wide-ranging conversation would finally get underway. Bibles, bikes, money, marriage and much, much more. And even though his day of carnage was not on the agenda, it too would ultimately surface.

"Lunch was good," Victor started off. "We had hamburger. I had two pieces of lettuce and two pieces of tomato." Interspersed throughout with a mix of visitor nods, smiles, comments, questions, and a great deal of listening, his diverse thoughts poured out.

PT – I've been watching you work. I told you this before and I'll say it again. Your dad always said you were a good worker.

Victor – I get paid to work three hours a day. I get paid $1.25 an hour and make $26.25 a week. I don't get paid for it but sometimes I clean the floors. I do it in case someone slips and falls. I don't want anyone to get hurt.

PT – You used to work hard on the farm.

Victor – I love working. I almost went to buy a chainsaw before the crime. I was going to cut wood in the bush.

PT – The last time I was here you were talking about some of your fights. Do you still have the odd battle?

Victor – I wrecked my shoulder. My fighting days are over. Now it's just horseplay. Little jabs or making funny walking movements. When the staff see it they say, 'Quit that fighting or you'll go to Oak Ridge!' Before, it would have been a crisis. Now it is very comical.

PT – You told me when we were walking over here that you have your own room now.

Victor – I sleep in the room all by myself. Sometimes I'm afraid to go in there. Sometimes I scream. I make my bed and get out. Nobody's caught me. [laughs]…There's some kind of curse in that room. Someone died in that room. It's right next to my old one. I moved on October 26, 1994. I have to clean my room.

PT – When I called you to set up our visit you instantly knew the dates of the long weekend even though it was a couple of months away. You're pretty good with your dates and numbers.

Victor – You get dates if you read the Bible too many times. I'm afraid to read it. I consider it to be a big history book. An old diary. They don't want me reading the Bible. I sound like a Bible. I sound like a prophet.

PT – What have you been doing over the last few years to keep yourself busy?

Victor – I keep myself occupied. I don't like brand new bikes because all you can do is ride, ride, ride. Nothing needs fixing unless you get a flat tire. I buy used. I bought one for $60. It wouldn't shift gears. I fixed it. I'm thinking ahead. I keep bike parts because the new ones are plastic. They're not going to last. Sometimes I want to work on the bike but I can't do it. Something inside keeps me from doing it.

Escaping air from a pop bottle startled Victor. "What happened?" he asked. When told what it was he responded, "I thought it was a tire on my bike." Then he laughed.

PT – This doesn't seem to be a place where there's a lot of joy?

Victor – Some people don't laugh around here. But one guy calls me Johnny Appleseed. One time I knew it would rain if I watered an apple tree and it did. I told him we should play a trick on nature. When it's too dry we should wash our cars and watch it rain. It would make people buy cleaning supplies to wash windows, wash cars. It would rain like the dickens. We could become famous. [laughs]…I can really teach too. I learned myself. I went to Grade 9. I taught them more things than they taught me. I should have quit school long before I did. They could have made a nice movie for Penthouse or Playboy about a nice young man like myself.

Another patient arrived and began interrupting. He gave Victor a dollar and asked him to get him a coffee. "When I get a chance," Victor respectfully told him.

PT – It's nice that you're going to help out.

Victor – I get stuff from the canteen for people who lose their privileges. They make up for it by friendship or by doing a little task. Sometimes I'm short and sweet. They have their head space. I have mine. I have to get my head together. Sometimes it's clear as a crystal bell, then there is a foggy day.

PT – *How would you say your day is going today?*

Victor – *It's a wonderful day today. I thought about you in my prayers. I blessed you to whatever it is that is up there. I don't know if it's called God.*

PT – *You've been here a long time. How would you say you're doing?*

Victor – *There's an invisible feeling inside me. I might live to be 150 to 200 years. There's always someone trying to kill me – the phantoms. I fight them off. I speak to them. They want love too. I hug 'em. They're boys and girls. Once all the boys arrived at one time. It's my little inner world. It's part of my life. The females and males do a helluva job. They've matured more. They want to be more like me. I'm still trying to stay true to my spouse. I don't want to mess around. I told one that I was married. She's really interested. Marriage is not for my life.*

PT – *Why do you think marriage is not for your life?*

Victor – *I decided not to get married because of what they told me on the farm. One guy couldn't work. He couldn't milk the cows or feed the pigs. He was too weak from having sex with his wife. Maybe he did it too many times. It didn't take long and he was just reading books. She was a hot woman. I always sent a Valentine's card to one of her daughters who was beautiful – 'Will You Be My Chick?' I was going to marry her. Then I saw her playing around with boys and then I saw her in the backseat of a car getting screwed. She wore short skirts.*

PT – *What did your dad tell you about marriage?*

Victor – *My dad would whip me. All in the mind. He wanted me to get married and have grandchildren. I didn't want to have anything to do with them. I wanted to break every bone in his body when I turned 21. I'm sorry I didn't know then what I know of God.*

PT – *I guess God can do a lot of things.*

Victor – *If I was God I'd put a nice cunt up there in the sky and men would go like rockets [laughs]…He could put all kinds of cocks up there but the women wouldn't go. One time I looked at the stars and thought they were the keys to the bottomless pit.*

PT – *Some of those phantoms seem to be friends. Are there any others with them?*

Victor – *I wanted to get one pet back in my head. I never named it. It was a very nice friend. It played games with me. If I get rid of them all they get mad. I got my pet back. It's a friend, someone to talk to.*

PT – What does this pet look like?

Victor – It's impossible to tell any kind of face. It doesn't have an image. It's just there. The voice has no identity whatever. It's not male or female or animal. I ask questions he doesn't want to answer. He's not always in there now.

PT – Do you still see angels and the devil?

Victor – I don't imagine them anymore. Satan they say is the real devil. He was at one time the most perfect angel. He was a pure, loving, kind workable angel, according to the Bible. Man can be the worst devil. A good man can be the best angel.

PT – Do you still get headaches?

Victor – I very rarely get them. Maybe once or twice a month. Sometimes three a month. The brain damage I have is the loss of names.

PT – What's your life like in a place like this?

Victor – My life used to be routine. It's not like that here. We have time schedules. I like it better here than on my dad's farm, except that place up there – Oak Ridge – is hell. If I go to prison I'm a dead man. I thought I was up there but it never happened. Up there they told me to talk if I wanted to get out. I told them what I was thinking and it wasn't acceptable. It is a mind-eating world. Say something wrong and I'm medicated. Some doctors should be tarred and feathered. Devious things were going on at the farm too. Every place has things you can pick apart.

PT – How did you feel when your dad died?

Victor – My brother Richard sent me a letter about my dad's death. I was happy. He bawled me out so many times. Ever try to eat at the table with him? I told him about it but he never did anything about it. I got the letter in November. Dad was already buried. I wouldn't go to the funeral anyway. It would be too risky. Somebody would go after me. I don't even want to fire a gun now. The closest would be a starting pistol. The finger is as good as a gun. You can point it and go bang, bang, bang, bang. It feels good. When my dad died I was supposed to get a $2000 inheritance. I told them to put it in the bank and use it for oil and gas and send it later when they had a good crop. I haven't got it. I could use it to buy a truck. Make some money hauling furniture. It would be helpful. I could buy some extra Coke or a package of cigarettes.

PT – Ten years ago you started going into the community on supervised visits. Are you still doing that?

Victor – I go downtown, sometimes to garage sales. At one place there was a nice, sexy girl wearing a short skirt. Her skirt was way too short. I don't know if she was wearing panties. It looked that way. I was sexually disturbed that day but only slightly. Not disturbed, getting it on. Looking at any kind of woman could disturb a man. Sex is out the window. My sex is just verbal. The safest sex is no sex. Every girl has a disease. When you get close to girls they have a smell like a snake. I get close to it I have to quit. They look good. But doing it is something else. The same thing on the farm.

PT – How was it the same on the farm?

Victor – Animals smell differently. I never screwed any animal with my penis. I tried but never succeeded. Mom and Dad were in the yard one time and I got scared. Bernice caught me once. Cats are too small. A calf sucked me off once. I damn near died. I had to pull away. He came after me. I'll never do that again. Put a calf loose on someone and they would never rape or kill or steal. It's the worst punishment in the world. With a woman criminal I don't know what to do. Maybe put a goat on her. How come the government doesn't hang car thieves? They still hang horse thieves in some places. And a car can be worth $20 000. I almost killed a guy once when we were castrating a pig. He was an enemy of mine. I'm stumbling in my thoughts...

PT – That's OK. Sex seems to be on your mind quite a bit.

Victor – They don't trust me with the girls. I don't know why. I've never had sex. I'm better off I didn't. I always ran away. I could shower with a naked woman and there would be no trouble. I think I'm born that way.

PT – It's just about time for your supper but I want to ask you a couple of other things. When you were on the farm you had a friend as a sounding board. What do you do here?

Victor –I talk to myself or talk out loud. I have a fierce growl. Two or three days ago I used it just for the hell of it. Nobody wants to hear me or they'll lock me up.

PT – Do you ever lash out at anything?

Victor – I've hit walls. Last weekend I did that when I tried to kill a big queen bee. I have problems with my eyes. When I was a kid I ran into a barbed wire fence. I kept having hallucinations. I have a speech problem. I'm loaded with all kinds of problems. I'm unloading them here.

PT – Do you ever break anything?

Victor – In July the heat was too much for me. I was being too much like an angel. I had to do something wrong. But I never broke a window. On the farm I broke a window. Dad bawled me out. Why did it have to be that way? You can't go through life without breaking a window, otherwise the win-

dow man wouldn't eat.

PT – Have you ever lost your privileges?

Victor – It only happened twice. I couldn't go outside or to the canteen.

PT – Did you ever get any advice from anyone about what to do when strange things enter your brain?

Victor – The doctor told me to bang my head with a Coke bottle. It makes stuff go out of your head. It worked for me. I told a few patients and they laughed at me. But kids will do that with a rattle. I have my own control. But medication helps. They have medication for suicidal people. I could never be suicidal.

PT – You've known the inside of an asylum longer than you've known freedom and you've been constantly drugged up. How is your medication working?

Victor – My medication has changed over the years. At first it's like a high octane engine running rough. I take pills every day. I don't even notice the side effects. My reflexes are good. My aim is good when killing flies. My handwriting is OK. The only side effect is confusion. I know what to do, I don't know what to do. I can't think fast enough. There's a lot of confusion in the world. Nature is made up of confusion. My next goal is not to be confused by all of the confusion around me.

PT – I believe drug use has a bearing on weight, although naturally there are a lot of other factors. When you were 21 you weighed 165 pounds and 10 years ago you had ballooned to 230 pounds. How's your weight doing?

Victor – I was over 300 pounds. I cut back on the food. The staff helped me stop robbing the trays. I was eating eight or nine hamburgers and 12 wieners. My pockets were always full. I weigh 250 pounds now. I want to shed 50 to 55 pounds.

It was now late afternoon. Drug time, or as the sweet voice on the intercom politely intoned, "Please come for your medication." Victor and his fellow patients heeded the call. But before he joined the line-up, we agreed to meet at 10 the next morning.

"If I'm asleep wake me up," were among his parting words. "I might stay up late and watch TV."

CROSSROADS – *At the corner of Railway Avenue and Main Street, the ancient hometown hotel reminded Victor of one of the turning points of his long lost youth. "It looks different," he said of the hotel. "It's a nice little area. There's something spiritual. One time during my final school year, the police were looking for a rapist. I was so horny that day I had to take my clothes off. They wouldn't let the kids out of school. I laid down on a path. I was hugging the ground. The police came but they never saw me. It was my last day to get an essay done. I failed my Grade that day. I walked to town. I bought a ball glove for $12."*

SHATTERED – *Looking at this photo of his abandoned boyhood living room, Victor recalled the Shell Lake Massacre. "This is the old TV room. There used to be an oval mirror between the windows. It cracked and fell to the floor after the day I was arrested. My mother almost had a heart attack."*

FORTRESS-LIKE – *Shadowed by a modern activity centre, Oak Ridge has been home to the criminally insane since the Dirty 30s. Victor, who has been in custody for 34 years, was in the maximum security institution for more than 23 years before being transferred to his new surroundings, further inside the grounds to your left. To the right, not pictured, is Ontario's new multi-million dollar central north correctional centre. The controversial private-sector operated super jail was built to house 1200 offenders remanded in custody or serving terms of less than two years.*

CONSEQUENCES – *"I'll bet you I got 50 years," Victor said as he thought about how long he has been in captivity and what the future holds. He made the same half century bet to police shortly after his 1967 arrest, when he speculated how much time in custody he would get. As for the future, "I'll probably stay here forever," said Victor. "If I wanted to I could easily get out of here. Why leave a place like this? Any odd behavior and a policeman would run me in. I don't know how to live out there. I want to stay here. I'm good here. I'm not going to run away. You can stamp that on steel like a licence plate. My word is as good as gold. We got a good system here. These guys aren't too crazy. They're like people on the street. They've just got medication in them."*

SOARING seagulls, cawing crows, chirping chipmunks, acorns aplenty – sights and sounds that marked the start of another unremarkable mid-morning Saturday for those whose daily lives, with their imposed limits, revolve around No. 500, at the lonely end of Church Street.

Entering the manicured mental health centre property, now devoid of any sign of patient or staff activity, Victor's broken bike could soon be seen in the distance, resting safely at the base of a huge tree, exactly where he had left it the day before.

Inside, Victor was near the entrance. It was time for the second day of our visit, an occasion that would add to the public record about the worst recorded crime of its kind in Canada and its tormented perpetrator haunted by unwanted squatters in his head.

"Good morning, Peter!" Showered, shaved , shampooed hair combed forward, wearing a freshly laundered shirt and a change of slacks, Victor was in bright spirits. "Do you have an outline of what you want to talk about?" he asked. Then, in the midst of the answer, unexpectedly interjected in machine-gun rapid style – "Do you have AIDS? You're skinny. Are you faithful to your wife?"

Without waiting for a response, Victor turned and we were on our way outside where our conversation would soon get back on track.

PT – What did you do last night?

Victor – I went to sleep watching a movie with Loretta Lynn. She's damn good looking. She can sing like a bird. Maybe better than a bird.

At that moment a brown chipmunk scurried by, across the worn patch of grass, home to numberless discarded cigarette stubs.

Victor – That's a little chipper. There's a curse on me if I kill a flying squirrel. I killed two of them. I touched one when I was a kid. He jumped on my shoulder. He almost kissed me. I was sick afterwards. I could have shot 60 to 70 squirrels in a day. The most I averaged was 37.

Victor then talked about a variety of subjects ranging from Penetanguishene being "a nice little town," to broadcasting where "someday I'll probably work at the CBC," to helping a panel write healthy books "for young people to grow up right."

PT – You like to talk about books, writing and authors.

Victor – I met Ayn Rand from the dead. She's inside me and I'm inside her. I carried her book around in my back pocket and it wore out. I taped it together. It fell apart. It was worth more than millions of dollars to me, because that's my girl inside me. I had to rebuild her. She was dead. I went to her grave. I went to her tombstone. She was the best friend I ever had. Did the evil spirits ever get mad at me when I did that. We were like man and wife. They may make her book illegal.

A detached voice on the public address system interrupted. It was lunchtime. Victor said he didn't feel like eating, mentioned being unable to walk over to Oak Ridge or he'd lose his privileges, then decided to go for something to eat, but not before wondering aloud – "I don't remember these pants. I must have got them at the friendship centre."

He was back in the near blink of an eye with a turkey or chicken bun, he wasn't sure, nor is everyone all the time, a red mug of milk, and a great deal more to reveal.

Victor – They told me I was possessed. I have spirits in my head but I blow their brains out. I shouldn't say that. The devil's no match for me. He's in jail. He's right in my head. I'm the bottomless pit. He was in my belly, now he's in my head. He can't go anywhere. God doesn't give a damn what I do wrong. I got a job to do and I'm doing it. I'm not going to let the devil drive the world crazy. No way. It's hell. There's only a little bit of heaven now and then.

PT – I've got a couple of brochures here about some places in the area. One of them is Castle Village at Midland. It's a place where you can see Hickory Dickory Dock and have a visit with Little Red Riding Hood.

Victor – They're fancy pictures. I've heard of them. Alice in Wonderland, I refused to read that book. The pictures would move my imagination. The Mad Hatter is in there, so is Alice. It would drive me crazy. My teacher and my mother told me to read it. Then I threw the book in the stove and my mom pulled it out and burned her hand. I got heck from my dad. I told my dad I'll go to school and take some matches and gas and burn all the books. I didn't have to read it.

PT – But you read the Bible.

Victor – My dad forced the Bible on me. I just read it too many times. Going to church would make me sick. The glue, gas, tars in the car stunk. On a hot day I would come home and be sick. I ran away from home. Dad shook me up. I thought, 'Wait till I grow up. I'll shake you.' I shook him up with the crime. It was a real bad thing to do and I'm really sorry. But what's done is done. I still struggle on. My suffering and pain is for a whole lot of people who couldn't take it. It seems like I'm an instrument being used.

PT – Here's another brochure. It's about Santa's Village at Bracebridge.

Victor – I don't like Santa. I used to tell my dad I'd rather believe in Santa Claus than Jesus Christ because at least I'd get a present at Christmas time.

PT – At one point you were thinking of changing your name. Are you still planning to do that?

Victor – I was going to change my name to General Menstromoe. He was my spiritual armed forces. He was a great guy. He went bad too. He fought the devil. The devil was no match for him. I got him locked up too. The devil made a sucker out of him. It was a dangerous name. Don't write it in the book. But you could print it in the book. Might as well let the world go nuts. Or you could make up a name like Mike Hoffman. There's no such person in the world. They won't let you name a person Mike Hoffman, at least they wouldn't in my day. There's lots of names like that, that you can't name the kids. You have to check with the politicians.

PT – Speaking of politicians, what do you think of Prime Minister Chretien?

Victor – He's a great guy. I like him. As long as he can walk and talk he should do it. They should get rid of the Conservatives. People inside know that here. When they build a bank why do they build a police station two and a half miles away? Canada is a haven for criminals. They want to have them. They mean money. They let people speed. What would we do if we couldn't watch high-speed chases on TV? It would take the fun out of life [laughs]...You should have a clean slate to be prime minister. You should-n't do a crime like a psychotic. Part psychotic and part good should be prime minister. I don't want to be prime minister. There's lots of psychotics around here. If you can't find one take Jean Chretien and give him a needle. Then he'll do his job. Just so he can't remember everything, give him a pill. [laughs]

It was again time to clean the cafeteria tables, put away the trays, take out the garbage, but before he went inside Victor put the lid on his ever present Diet Coke. "If there's a bee in there he'll suffocate now," he said. When he returned he checked and determined, "He got out somehow. He must have been an intelligent one. [laughs]

PT – The sun's out.

Victor – It's not out. It's on. [laughs]...That's a good story for the kids. Kids who die come to me from all over the world. Their souls come. I feed them and clothe them. They're three or four years old. I don't take care of invisible babies. You can't see them. I can. You step on them. I get millions of them.

PT – I see your bike is still leaning up against the tree over there.

Victor – Girls' bikes don't have a crossbar. Why boys' bikes have a crossbar I don't know. A girl can wear a dress and get on easily. She can be standing if she's wearing a short skirt. But what are they going to do? You could see everything anyway. A man could hurt his balls. Then he's no good to a woman. If boys want to ride boys' bikes he's homosexual. I told the staff the reason I ride a girls bike is that I ride girls. [laughs]

The mind-crunching conversation continued with Victor being shown a copy of the Shellbrook Chronicle and recalling, "It's not too far down from Leask. It's been a long time since I've been there." Shown a newspaper article about a Grade 1 teacher from his old hometown who taped students to their seats to make them sit still in class, Victor commented, "They shouldn't charge her. Some kids are irritating. It's agitation to others. The most cruelest species in the world is man. Woman is more cruel. When a woman is cruel, she's cruel. A man is more sensitive. A woman can't control herself. She goes to the end of time. Even people eat themselves. I lost my train of thought…I gotta go in."

Soup crackers protruding from his pockets, Victor was quickly back outside after double-checking to make sure all of his noon-hour chores were completed and ensuring to follow the rules and sign out so that we could take a leisurely stroll over to the canteen for a drink and a couple of chocolate bars. A few pictures were snapped and developed along the way, including more dominant images from within the straitjacket of his mind.

PT – That's quite a headline in the paper – Harris Losing Voters' Trust. Looks like the premier is in trouble.

Victor – It's probably because of the Walkerton water scandal.

And it was. As the front page story confirmed, high on respondents' minds at the time of the survey was Premier Mike Harris' appearance before an inquiry that probed a tainted water scandal that left seven dead and 2300 sick in the central Ontario town billed as, "the perfect retirement community." The premier, the article recited, repeatedly denied that he was aware of public health risks when his government, in a cost-cutting move, dismantled policies protecting water.

PT – Back on the farm you used to trap weasels.

Victor – Two of them almost got me. I grabbed one by the head and stran-

gled him.

PT – *You also spent time with squirrels.*

Victor – *I used to farm a crop of squirrels. Bull squirrels eat little squirrels so they can screw again. There's thousands of them. They're known as a tree rat. They carry a plague. I was going to go wild one day. I tried to swallow a raw squirrel. But I couldn't do it. It tastes like spruce gum or bark. Porcupine is the same. They call it a tree pig, tree pork.*

PT – *What is something that you remember about your parents?*

Victor – *They taught me how to count money. My dad said, "You're going to be rich some day." I could count money for the Canada treasury but they won't hire me because I'm too honest.*

PT – *When your dad first took you to the mental hospital you were given shock treatments. Do you get those anymore?*

Victor – *No. The only time I might is if I fell off my bike and got brain damage. I used to wear a helmet.*

With the afternoon slipping by, our visit almost up, talk once again turned to books – the one that detailed the horror of the most ghastly, aimless mass killing in the annals of a nation.

PT – *Did you ever read the book about Shell Lake?*

Victor – *I read parts. I thumbed through, casting the wicked out of it. Not from you, from the devil. I injured the cover. I tore it off.*

PT – *What did you think about it?*

Victor – *I thought the rain barrel by the house was made out of wood, not metal. My dad had two horses for years and years. I rode one to death. The other was sold to a fox farm. Dad only got $50. My dad's horses were in that yard – they bolted.*

PT – *Anything else?*

Victor – *I don't know her (Phyllis). She knows something. She saw something that is not me. God is keeping her safe. A good person grows up good. Her family was slain and that's the most horrible thing that could happen to anybody. She's doing OK. I'm glad.*

PT – *I'm going to be seeing her. Do you want me to tell her anything? Can you say you're sorry?*

Victor – *I can't say anything like that. I'm not happy either. I don't think about it. I just don't think about it. Tell Phyllis that I was convicted of the crime in Shell Lake, Saskatchewan. I don't feel guilt. I feel shame. I gotta live with that shame for the rest of my life. There was a *tall man in my door*

---

* After his arrest 34 years earlier, as outlined on Page 149, Victor told police that he had fought with the devil and referred to his tormentor as being tall, black, and having no genitals.

that morning. I see him here. It seems like a dream or a nightmare.

Victor was shaken. His eyes watered, hands trembled, saliva dripped onto his shirt. "Life is a test," he concluded. "When you leave school that's when school begins."

CURELESS – *There is control but no known cure for paranoid schizophrenia. Victor, who said he once dreamed of being hanged nine times, remains a virtual prisoner of his own head. Filled with demons, his astonishingly complex, warped universe is wrenching to behold. As we walked the hospital grounds, perched at the entrance of Penetanguishene Harbour, with its commanding view of Severn Sound, he stopped to smell a beautiful bed of flowers bordering the historic, stone-walled administration building. "Some people say life is a lot like hell," he said. "I say they should look at the flowers. Look at the geese overhead. It's like heaven." Shortly after came the call for the regular 4 o'clock medication, time for our visit to end. We bid a quick goodbye. Then, swiftly, Victor pivoted – and in one fell swoop – with no looking back – headed in to continue his personal doomed existence of never-ending treatment.*

"If he ever feels the urge again, or whatever it's called, I hope God's with the people he's around because they're going to need Him."

– Phyllis, 2001

MORE than 2000 miles away from the repository for the desperate, at the end of a long, tree-shaded gravel road, rich with golden, autumn leaves, Phyllis was exactly where she wanted to be – in familiar surroundings, not far from her childhood home, in a big, cozy farmhouse, in the middle of the Prairies, close to family and friends.

She has James, named after the brave grandfather he will never meet; Kathy and Lee; a new beau, a friend from years gone by; three black horses, and Sarah, part Labrador, part German Shepherd, who affectionately shows unrequited love to strangers by jumping up and licking them in the face.

Phyllis, who teaches at a local pre-school and is having the time of her life, obligingly took time out of it to contribute to the last word.

PT – So how's life treating you?

Phyllis – I don't think I've been happier. Life is good back here. It's a different kind of life. But it's a good one. We're busy all the time.

PT – When you read the story about Shell Lake, how was that for you?

Phyllis – I read it together with my niece. Neither of us knew what was going to be in it.

PT – After you read it, did it jog any memories, did it play on your mind?

Phyllis – I wondered if all of us kids would have got up and done something, would it have made a difference? And then I remembered, I did remember actually, Dad hollering at us to tell us to stay in bed. So that's why we stayed. We were good kids. We listened for a change.

PT – Was there anything else you recalled?

Phyllis – That was pretty much it. I don't try to remember it. I guess there's always a way that you could find out and remember all of it. But there's that blockage there for a reason, I'm sure.

PT – Did your reading make you wonder about anything else?

Phyllis – I thought about Victor a bit. Not so much him, but the day pass, him being allowed to go out. It doesn't scare me, personally, because he's not ever going to come back and get me and hurt me again, I know that. But it scares me for the other people who are out there.

PT – I was able to speak to Victor and he's still highly medicated for a disease for which there's no cure. I asked him if he could say something to you, whether he would apologize and he said he couldn't do that because it wasn't him. He said he feels no guilt, but he feels shame. And so what do you think of that, when he is unable to say he's sorry, but explained it the way he did?

Phyllis – I don't know what to think of him as a person. It was him who went in the house. It was him who did it. But I guess if you believe in God, then there was something else there too.

Having lost her family to a madman, Phyllis has unshakeable views about law and order and holds well-founded concerns about the so-called justice system – opinions widely shared in the West. She questions the vast sums of money it is costing taxpayers, including herself, to house those involved in serious criminal acts; wonders why those in custody are not required to work as a form of payment for their atrocities; and is deeply frustrated that the person who single-handedly slaughtered her mother, father and seven siblings – after he was prematurely released from an insane asylum – is still allowed into the community.

PT – One of the things that Kathy mentioned was that there had never been an apology from the hospital or Saskatchewan Health for the release of Victor before that horrible time in Shell Lake. Have you since received an apology?

Phyllis – No. Do you ever think the government is going to accept blame for it? I don't think so. There never will be anything. It's not so much that they released him the first time, it's what they're doing now. He's basically been released again, on his day passes. And they can say whatever they want about the medication, that he's controlled by medication, but he's still out there and there's innocent people out there who he's in contact with. They did it once and now they're doing it again. I just think those people are crazy, the ones who are taking care of him. Why would you let him out? It's like they're playing Russian Roulette with all these people. It's not that I'm really angry, it's a frustrating feeling. Most people learn from their mistakes. But obviously our government and our system isn't learning from any of the mistakes that they're making, because they just keep doing it over and over and over again.

PT – Would it make you feel better if he never got out?

Phyllis – They've obviously said he's never going to be cured of it, so why are you taking your chances letting him go during the day? And there's lots of people who have done lesser things than he did who aren't let out on passes because people are concerned. There's child abusers that once they get out there's big notices put up and the whole city knows that they've moved in. But yet no one's telling people that this guy is out on the street. If you live anywhere out there you could be meeting him. I worry about the other people out there. I wouldn't want it to ever happen to anybody else. The government should do something about it. There should be steps taken to make sure that it never happens again. Even if it isn't a whole family, one is too many.

PRIDE & JOY – *"James knows who is grandparents are and he knows that he was named after his grandpa," said Phyllis. "We talked about what happened and I told him, 'It's not ever going to happen again.' And that's pretty much the end of it."*